ROBERT BURTON'S RHETORIC

RSA·STR

THE RSA SERIES IN TRANSDISCIPLINARY RHETORIC

The RSA Series in Transdisciplinary Rhetoric is a collaboration with the Rhetoric Society of America to publish innovative and rigorously argued scholarship on the tremendous disciplinary breadth of rhetoric. Books in the series take a variety of approaches, including theoretical, historical, interpretive, critical, or ethnographic, and examine rhetorical action in a way that appeals, first, to scholars in communication studies and English or writing, and, second, to at least one other discipline or subject area.

Other titles in this series:
Nathan Stormer, *Sign of Pathology: U.S. Medical Rhetoric on Abortion, 1800s–1960s*

Mark Longaker, *Rhetorical Style and Bourgeois Virtue: Capitalism and Civil Society in the British Enlightenment*

Robin E. Jensen, *Infertility: A Rhetorical History*

Steven Mailloux, *Rhetoric's Pragmatism: Essays in Rhetorical Hermeneutics*

M. Elizabeth Weiser, *Museum Rhetoric: Building Civic Identity in National Spaces*

Chris Mays, Nathaniel A. Rivers, and Kellie Sharp-Hoskins, eds., *Kenneth Burke + the Posthuman*

Amy Koerber, *From Hysteria to Hormones: A Rhetorical History*

Elizabeth C. Britt, *Reimagining Advocacy: Rhetorical Education in the Legal Clinic*

Ian E. J. Hill, *Advocating Weapons, War, and Terrorism: Technological and Rhetorical Paradox*

Kelly Pender, *Being at Genetic Risk: Toward a Rhetoric of Care*

James L. Cherney, *Ableist Rhetoric*

Susan Wells

ROBERT BURTON'S RHETORIC

An Anatomy of Early Modern Knowledge

THE PENNSYLVANIA STATE UNIVERSITY PRESS
UNIVERSITY PARK, PENNSYLVANIA

Library of Congress Cataloging-in-Publication Data

Names: Wells, Susan, 1947– author.
Title: Robert Burton's rhetoric : an anatomy of early modern
    knowledge / Susan Wells.
Description: University Park, Pennsylvania : The Pennsylvania
    State University Press, [2019] | Includes bibliographical
    references and index.
Summary: "Illustrates how Oxford scholar Robert Burton
    used the resources available to a seventeenth century
    academic: genres and languages, as well as academic
    disciplines such as medicine and rhetoric. Demonstrates
    how early modern practices of knowledge and persuasion
    can offer a model for transdisciplinary scholarship today"—
    Provided by publisher.
Identifiers: LCCN 2019021361 | ISBN 9780271084671 (cloth)
Subjects: LCSH: Burton, Robert, 1577–1640—Knowledge
    and learning. | Burton, Robert, 1577–1640. Anatomy of
    melancholy. | Rhetoric.
Classification: LCC PR2224 2019
LC record available at https://lccn.loc.gov/2019021361

The Pennsylvania State University Press is a member of the
Association of University Presses.

It is the policy of The Pennsylvania State University Press to
use acid-free paper. Publications on uncoated stock satisfy the
minimum requirements of American National Standard for
Information Sciences—Permanence of Paper for Printed
Library Material, ANSI Z39.48-1992.

For Abigail Rose Linn

Contents

Illustrations

Acknowledgments

My dissertation advisors, R. J. Kaufmann and Warwick Wadlington, asked me to read *The Anatomy of Melancholy*, and set me on the long road to this book. But it would never have been written without the help of many others. I am happy to have the chance to thank some of them here.

My colleagues at Temple University, Eli Goldblatt and Shannon Walters, have encouraged me in this project and patiently helped me unknot its problems; the chapter on translingualism especially benefited from conversations with Lawrence Venuti about language choice and translation. My years at Temple were enriched by the company of Rachel Blau DuPlessis, Kate Henry, Joyce Joyce, Michael Kaufmann, Sue-Im Lee, Peter Logan, and Steven Newman. Daniel Tompkins and Nichole Miller expertly helped with Latin texts but are not responsible for my errors. Temple University and the Temple College of Liberal Arts generously supported this project with sabbaticals, grants in aid, and travel funds.

Rhetoricians and scholars of writing, including Debra Hawhee, Ellen Barton, and Lisa Melançon, supported this project. Jeanne Fahnestock was a valuable guide to the mysteries of Melanchthon and generously shared her work in progress with me. The Rhetoric Society of America offered a buzzing, active, intellectual home. Seminars and workshops offered by the RSA and the International Society for the History of Rhetoric provided irreplaceable specific advice. I am particularly grateful for Carolyn Miller and Victoria Gallagher's 2011 RSA Summer Workshop on genre theory and Laurent Pernot's 2012 ISHR seminar on the epideictic. Many thanks to the Pittsburgh Rhetoric Colloquium and the working group on history and medical rhetoric at the 2017 Symposium on Rhetoric of Health and Medicine, T. Kenny Fountain, Barbara Heifferon, and Stephen Pender. The monthly meetings of the Working Group on Early Science and Medicine at the Philadelphia Consortium for History of Science, Technology, and Medicine shaped my understanding of early modern scientific and medical practices.

I am grateful to the librarians who answered my questions, found my sources, and put up with my irregular shelfmarks. No question was too obvious or too obscure for Kristina DeVoe at Temple's Paley library. Librarians at Christ Church, especially Janet McMullin and Alina Nachescu, guided my research from beginning to end; staff members Sophie McMinn and Cristina Neagu helped with copies and illustrations.

This book has been realized through the support of Kendra Boileau, Editor-in-Chief at Penn State University Press. The manuscript reviewers, Daniel M. Gross and Angus Gowland, offered generous expert help and collegial challenge in exactly the right balance. Leah Ceccarelli and Michael Bernard-Donals, editors of the series on Transdisciplinary Rhetorics, provided valuable suggestions at several stages of the project. I am grateful to Alex Ramos and Duncan Burns for expert copy editing.

My last and deepest thanks go to my family, Hugh Grady, my chief travelling companion, and Laura Rose Grady, Aaron Linn, Abigail Rose Linn, and Constance Grady. They have made this work worth doing and were my sovereign remedy against melancholy.

1

A Monstrous Anatomy

I ask you to imagine two different copies of Robert Burton's *The Anatomy of Melancholy*, a book that was published in five editions from 1621 to 1651. The *Anatomy* discusses melancholy in three compendious partitions, treating the causes and cures of this malady, a significant medical and social issue in early modern England. I first encountered the book in the compact three-volume Everyman edition (1961–64), modestly bound in black cloth.[1] Like the one-volume paperback version of the same edition recently published by the New York Review of Books Press, these books were intended to be read rather than studied.[2] The editors were faithful to the motto of the Everyman Library, "Everyman, I will go with thee and be thy guide, in thy most need to go by thy side." They italicized and parenthetically translated Burton's frequent Latin quotations; textual issues are firmly sidelined; the volumes themselves are compact and light. These are the books I read for my comprehensive exams in the mid-1970s, taking refuge from the Texas heat in the energetically air-conditioned university library. I was fascinated by the text, especially its long digressions interrupting the orderly divisions, and its expansive preface, "Democritus Junior to the Reader," which found melancholy, folly, and madness in every rank and condition of life. The author's pseudonym, "Democritus Junior," referenced the laughing philosopher, an intriguing identity for an Oxford professor. But I had nothing at all to say about the book. This sprawling, polyglot text did not fit any of the categories of my graduate program, and in my traditional department it was never taught and seldom referred to (although there were rumblings about Stanley Fish's chapter on it in *Self-Consuming Artifacts*, published in 1972).[3] I left those three meaty volumes behind—they seem to be in the Library Depository now—and thought of them as an unvisited location in the canon, suggesting a way of reading specific to its time and place, utterly at ease with its learning. Burton's amused voice rustled in my memory: thin, rhythmic, quizzical, the voice of an eccentric and intimate friend. Many years later, I encountered a face

2 ROBERT BURTON'S RHETORIC

that matched that voice in Hans Schäufelin's painting *Melancholiker*, the cover image for this book.[4]

And then there is a second version of *The Anatomy of Melancholy*, the six monumental volumes of the Clarendon edition published by Oxford University Press from 1989 to 2000.[5] Here, three volumes of meticulously edited text are supported by three volumes of commentary, indexes, and references. When, in recent years, I ventured back to the *Anatomy*, this edition had changed the scholarly landscape. Hundreds of Burton's ubiquitous quotes were verified and sourced; his odd words were defined; the marginal glosses were restored and translated; textual variants were catalogued. It was possible to work on the *Anatomy* in a responsible way without replicating Burton's lifetime of reading. Oxford University Press did not part with these books lightly. When I started, the pound was strong against the dollar; even today, it would cost nearly two thousand dollars to buy all six volumes from the publisher. So I hunted used book sites every June and July, when university libraries are known to deaccession surplus books, and slowly I acquired the three volumes of text. (The commentary came to market more quickly, priced to sell.) These volumes made my vague sense of Burton's erudition more specific and more daunting: who knew that Plutarch had written so much? Who was Crato of Krafftheim? I still heard the voice I'd imagined for Burton, quizzical and confidential. Now I had tools for discerning the multiple voices that spoke around and under it, the voices that Schäufelin's melancholic youth listens to so intently.

My book takes these voices as expressions of diverse early modern practices for constructing knowledge. It wrestles with such questions as what, for Burton and his contemporaries, counted as knowledge. How did they make their knowledge count? How did expert writing come to be organized in disciplinary frameworks, with specific genre norms and rhetorical constraints? How did knowledge move through the uneven fields of early modern learning, among traditional professional discourses such as theology or medicine, across respected disciplines such as philology, and around emerging knowledge practices, such as those of travel and the new sciences? How can we observe language moving through the porous membranes that separated these ways of knowing? My framework for approaching these questions is rhetorical, since questions of how knowledge is organized and made persuasive are central to rhetorical theory. With Burton, I hope to recreate for myself and my readers the fluid movement of ideas and tropes among medicine, divinity, and cosmology, and to reconstruct the rhetorics that sponsored such movement.

Burton's book marks a specific moment in the development of disciplines, a moment when fields of knowledge were distinct but not restrictive. The boundaries Burton encountered have alternately consolidated and softened in the three hundred years between the initial publication of the *Anatomy* and the Everyman edition I used. For Everyman, the *Anatomy* inhabited a loose discursive field; it was part of their series in Philosophy and Theology, and they needed no finer distinction for a publishing project directed toward popular self-education. In that context, Latin was an obstacle, as were expensive books, and the public-spirited press avoided them both.

The Clarendon edition speaks of a different disciplinary formation: a community of expert readers, scholars of literature or of early modern thought and culture, located in institutions that could sponsor their access to a bulky, expensive text. These readers would be undaunted by a little Latin, and curious to trace the odd Burton quotation, but not so deeply immersed in Latin and neo-Latin literature that they could identify it themselves. The change in the disciplinary locations of these two editions produces, in effect, two Burtons. I argue that disciplinary differentiation has become so central to our experiences of knowing and not knowing that we necessarily read the *Anatomy* through contemporary disciplinary frames, even as we acknowledge that those divisions were unknown to Burton. In the current literature, we can find arguments that the *Anatomy* is best read as a book of religious counsel, as a strictly literary text, or as a work of humanistic scholarship. Perhaps if we try to glance athwart our disciplinary lenses, we can discern the freedom and porosity of Burton's knowledge practices, even if our view is oblique and partial.

My book will not settle on any of the views of melancholy that Burton airs. Nor will it show that Burton was or was not a stoic, or a misogynist, or that he meant his utopia seriously or satirically—these, and other questions that better scholars than I have assayed, are not my interest here. Instead, I undertake the thought experiment of bracketing all these local issues, and especially those concerned with melancholy, its adjuncts and its treatment, and focusing instead on how Burton's text negotiates the competing and contradictory demands of disparate knowledge practices. It is in that rhetorical negotiation, shaped by his recognition of the exigency of care, that Burton invests textual energy, rather than in the resolution of any particular issue. Indeed, many of the most significant propositions in the text of the *Anatomy* are contradicted elsewhere in the book. (The only thing I myself am pretty sure about is that Burton disapproved of standing water, popery, and Paracelsians.) I take as my guide an inscription in one of Burton's books, the text of James Shirley's play *The Wedding*. There, Burton recorded an anecdote about the ubiquity of contradictions: "A certaine pastor of Conningberg in Prussia in a funeral sermon over one that lay solemly to be buried, after he had spoken much of his vertues and largely commended him to the Auditors told them, this is a testimony and relation I had from his kindred and friends, now I [cross out] ye shall here another cleane contrary [cross out] of mine who knew him as well, or better than they."[6] This doubled, contradictory sermon is a compressed model of the *Anatomy*, which offers clean contraries without resolution.

There are four possible scholarly and critical responses to Burton's exploration of contradiction, positions analogous to the four corners of the square of oppositions, a medieval graphic representation of the relationships among categorical or hypothetical statements. An assertion could be read as true and its denial false; the denial could be read as true and the assertion false; both assertion and denial could be true; both could be false. Or, in terms of the *Anatomy*:

> Burton's utopia is an ideal state, not a satire on utopias.
> Burton's utopia is not an ideal state, but a satire on utopias.
> Burton's utopia is both an ideal state and a satire on utopias.
> Burton's utopia is neither an ideal state nor a satire on utopias.

The square of oppositions was a staple of early modern arts teaching, and Burton would have danced students around it many times. It is not surprising that he generated this range of choices, variations on its traditional category statements. He was not alone in adapting this figure; since the four corners of the square suggested the four elements and the four humors, early modern physicians also used it as a generative device for proposing diagnoses.[7] Burton's text repurposed this shortcut to confirmation or refutation, torquing it into a way of multiplying possibilities.

But multiplied possibilities become problematic in the face of exigency. Since Burton was offering advice on the serious, painful condition of melancholy, he would not have expected readers to simply marvel at the skill of his negotiation. The melancholic must do something: take or refuse counsel, accommodate or resist feelings of fear and sorrow. What Burton's book offers is not a set of directions but a model for choosing among or combining alternatives. The *Anatomy* is not therapeutic because of the propositions it advances, but rather because it shows how a reader can contain the uncertainty of contradictory information.

Just as we can take the assertions of the text as grounds for experimenting with disparate forms of knowledge, we can read in its contradictory advice an experiment in deciding on a course of action in imperfectly known circumstances.

In summary, while we cannot know Burton's intentions about specific issues, we can be sure that he wanted to write a book that advanced contrary propositions to readers in need of reliable advice. Two things follow from this statement. First, whatever succor the *Anatomy* offers the melancholic reader is not to be found in the propositions about melancholy that Burton advances. Second, the *Anatomy* does not support a reading that "it is impossible to tell whether A is true or not true," since such a stance would abandon Burton's therapeutic exigency. His book, perhaps, is not only about melancholy but also about knowledge and action.

So, what could this monster be, this anatomy without melancholy? If we turn the text over and look at its seamy side, we can trace out a web of exchanges and borrowings among nascent differentiated discourses circulating in early modern academic and cultural sites, the places where melancholics were most likely to be found. The texts of Greek and Roman antiquity are relevant, and so are the humanist commentaries on them; so are the Scriptures, and the vast circulating farrago of reformation religious controversies. But the *Anatomy* also puts medical *consilia* and case histories in conversation with joke books, with stage plays in English and Latin, with cosmological speculation and travel narratives. If we bracket the theme of melancholy and instead consider the *Anatomy* as a vast meditation on early modern practices of knowledge, we encounter a text concerned with the tropes, genres, and languages that supported learned discourse. In the midst of this movement, where could stability be found? What sort of stability might the learned reader hope for? What might be the pleasures of renouncing stability? How can we cope with practices of knowledge that resolutely deny certainty but exigently require action? These are essentially rhetorical questions, and they will occupy us for almost all of this book. Only at the end, and very briefly, will I turn the text over, look at its surface again, and have a little to say about melancholy.

If, as twenty-first-century readers, we bracket the issues of melancholy, its causes, and its cures, we can use the *Anatomy* to think about the emergence of powerful disciplines whose discourses now shape our lives: discourses of political theory, science, and cultural history. They all emerge in Burton's text; their boundaries are so porous that arguments, tropes, and assumptions are traded freely among them. Propositions emerge to be aired and forgotten; a few pages later, their contraries are presented with equal authority. As readers who daily encounter the limits of sealed, immobile discourses, as scholars who work across disciplines, or as rhetoricians adopting transdisciplinary methods, what can we learn from this fluidity, this ease of exchange among discourses?[8]

Sorting through contradictory frames is only half the problem. Burton's readers faced the exigency of a disease that was treated through Galenic modifications of daily regimen. Every hour of the day presented questions that must be answered: Should I eat lettuce? How much should I sleep? Such questions suggest that we bracket the specific issue of melancholy and consider it instead as a powerful anchor for the demands of exigency. The *Anatomy* is then available as a model for acting on partial, imperfect, and contradictory information, under the pressure of time, on matters of urgency. In this framework, *The Anatomy of Melancholy* confronts the central issues of rhetorical theory: the presentation of provisional knowledge, the weighing of contradictory and plausible truth claims, the demands of uncertain situations. While the *Anatomy* is not a book of rhetorical theory, it is certainly a deeply rhetorical text.

To show why we need such a reading of *The Anatomy of Melancholy*, I will select and analyze four influential readings of the text, beginning in the 1960s, to discern the shared premises that support divergent critical opinions. I will then sketch out an account of the learned and popular discourses available to Robert Burton as a seventeenth-century academic and discuss how the *Anatomy* negotiated that field for its readers. Since I hope that my book will be of general interest to students of rhetorical theory and history, these sections will also orient readers who are not specialists in early modern academic cultures.

There are no useless readings of *The Anatomy of Melancholy*. Any scholar who works through the three partitions, situates the book in some kind of frame, and sidles out to say something sensible about it has done a service. This is especially true of the recent books by Angus Gowland, Mary Ann Lund, and Stephanie Shirilan, which are supported by substantial research into the context of Burton's writing.[9] But any scholar who comes to the *Anatomy* in search of positive statements about melancholy is likely to run afoul of the contradictory structure of the book and be forced to settle on some corner of our square of oppositions. We could designate those positions, crudely, as "A is true and not-A is false," "A is not true," "A is true and A is not true," and "It is not true that either A is true or that A is not true." Any of these positions would yield a less interesting book than the one Burton wrote.

Four Readers

Nobody could be bored with Rosalie Colie's discussion of the *Anatomy* in her *Paradoxia Epidemica*.[10] The impulse for writing this book, according to Colie's preface, was itself a contradiction worthy of Burton: she sought to reconcile the New Critical understanding of paradox, irony, and tension as expressions of personal vision with the early modern uses of these tropes to order discourse. *Paradoxia Epidemica* is an attempt to recover an early modern tradition; the book is also a romp through the touchstones of mid-twentieth-century criticism— Donne, Herbert, Spenser, and Shakespeare—with surprising detours through reformation theology and early modern science. No one has been more alive to the undecidability of *The Anatomy of Melancholy* than Colie:

> The climate of Burton's book is of opposites and oppositions, contradictions and paradoxes: we become so acclimated to these anomalies that we tend to overlook their meanings in the large. Burton never presents his readers with a choice between one explanation for melancholy and another different or contradictory explanation. He does not present us with either the Galenical or the homeopathic remedy for any symptom. He does not present us with the choice between being and not being melancholy. His is a pluralist world, accommodating all the alternatives, even some which in conventional logic close one another out.[11]

For Colie, Burton's world is one where the Galenic view of melancholy as a disease and the Aristotelian view of it as an incitement to genius can be presented *seriatim*: they are not posed as alternatives; one does not dispute with the other; two categorically opposed statements are simply laid into a text as if it were a zone where the principle of noncontradiction held no power. In the many decades since *Paradoxia Epidemica*, nobody has understood better how fully the *Anatomy* inhabits that zone: in its multiplication of genres, its self-reference, its mad layering of learned discourses. If a scholar has to pick a position on the square of oppositions that Burton constructed, there is none better than "A is both true and not true," and nobody has occupied that position better than Rosalie Colie.

I like to think of Colie, poring over the puzzles of the *Anatomy* with her students at Iowa, filtering sensibilities formed by the New Criticism through the problems posed by Eliot's "Tradition and the Individual Talent." Neither of these issues is alive for us in the same vivid way; our mandate is not that of the cold war literary scholarship. (Colie took up those broad cultural and political questions more explicitly in other contexts, particularly her correspondence with Hannah Arendt.[12]) But the action that concerns *Paradoxia Epidemica* is limited to the force of paradox itself, as it reaches from the frame of the text to grasp and immobilize the reader.

This is a cleaner world than that of the *Anatomy*, where the poor melancholic wonders if he could eat a fish that lived in muddy water, or if it would be safe to break a sweat. Burton's text combines a dizzyingly balanced play of contradictory propositions, frames, and genres with an iron exigency: we are all melancholy; everything in the world is a potential cause of melancholy; cures of melancholy are numberless; we must live in this world as the melancholy readers we all are. If the point of the *Anatomy* is the elegant balance of its paradoxes, then how can we do justice to the compassionate exigency of Burton's therapeutic purpose?

The issue of exigency is of even less concern to Stanley Fish in his chapter on *The Anatomy of Melancholy* in *Self-Consuming Artifacts*, "Thou Thyself Art the Subject of My Discourse." Fish's discussion of Burton was probably the most widely read scholarly discussion of Burton in the late twentieth century. A search of the databases shows roughly 250 citations, reviews, or discussions of this chapter between its publication in 1972 and 2000; it is likely that nearly every publication about Burton cited *Self-Consuming Artifacts*.

Readers who have followed Fish's work might expect this analysis to occupy the "A is neither true nor false" corner of our imaginary square of oppositions. That is not exactly what happens. For Fish the issues raised by Burton in the *Anatomy* were not of interest. Rather, Fish was interested in the structure of Burton's exposition, especially as it plays out for readers. Fish expands on Burton's proverb, "never a barrel better herring": "Every change of subject, every new topic, is another barrel, a container whose contents are, for the moment, unknown; and for that moment each barrel is the substance of a revived hope, the hope that when opened it will yield better herrings and that we will be among them."[13] Nobody would want to deny a writer named Fish the hope of being among the better herrings; that hope, sadly, is not fulfilled: "Every paragraph, every section shuts off another route of escape for the reader who resists the personal application of the general rule [that all are mad]. One by one the areas of an artificially segmented universe lose their distinctness, until the complete triumph of madness is not assertion, but an experienced fact."[14]

For Fish, every subdivision of the *Anatomy* renews the promise of definite knowledge about a specific aspect of melancholy or the world it dominates. He watches Burton make an assertion and then negate it by extending the topic at hand, perhaps by moving from one type of melancholy to another. Inevitably, the text encompasses all of lived experience and the original assertion is not only negated but meaningless: A is not true; it is really, really not true. Fish clearly finds this pattern frustrating, especially since Burton, unlike Bacon, Donne, Herbert, or Milton, does not point to an ineffable redemptory state outside language.

I wonder, though, about the invincible naiveté of the reader Fish constructs. Surely after the tenth barrel, readers realize that the game is not "find the better herring," but "what should we do with these barrels?" Fish's reading depends on taking each of Burton's local negations at face value: there is no end to madness, no cure for melancholy, no way of distinguishing one of its forms from another. In this reading, Burton's negation of his initial statement is final, to be taken as true. But Burton does not simply make assertions and then deny them: he asserts, denies, and returns to his initial premises as if nothing had gone wrong. It is an animating journey, deftly balanced between the rigors of its pattern and the possibilities of surprise. Stabilizing the text's motion at the point of denial drains it of energy. No wonder Fish is puzzled that so many readers have enjoyed the *Anatomy*: "What we have, then, is a total unity of unreliability, in the author, in his materials, in his readers, and in the structure, a total unreliability and a total subjectivity. In the face of such a depressing unity, why is the *Anatomy* not a more uncomfortable experience than most readers report it to be?"[15] Fish imagines readers who approach each new topic in hope that here, at last, Burton will make a clear assertion: such readers would be perfect partners in a game of three-card monte but have never yet been seen on land or sea.

Fish's chapter forcibly set a problem for subsequent criticism: how to crack the code of Burton's contradictory assertions and stabilize the text. That search drew upon two strong currents: the reaction against deconstructive readings, with their preference for *aporia*, and the turn toward historicism beginning in the mid-eighties. History, particularly the history of melancholy, seemed to offer a foundation for assertions about Burton's world, and thereby to offer clarity about what the text says. This faith is not misplaced. However dizzying Burton's whirlwind of assertions, no reader has come away from the *Anatomy* convinced that Burton did not support monarchy, or that he was an atheist, or that he hated learning. The pattern of the text, his social location, and the discourses available to Burton, allow us to place these positions outside the domain of the text.

But these assertions are not the point of the *Anatomy*. I argue that this is the case even when the proposition in question is more urgent for us than purging or bloodletting, as in the question of Burton's misogyny. What do we make of the awful things that Burton repeatedly says about women? That question became pressing with the emergence of feminist criticism, and it is the central issue in the third of the texts I will discuss, Mark Breitenberg's chapter on Burton in his *Anxious Masculinity in Early Modern England*.[16] Against my own political commitments, I propose that arguing either side of this question arrests Burton's wavering movement.

Breitenberg argues that masculine subjectivity, especially early modern masculine subjectivity, is necessarily anxious. Early modern anxiety is not a sentiment but a disposition of the cultural unconscious, generating the hierarchical structures intended to contain it. Patriarchy causes anxiety; anxiety supports patriarchy. Early modern humoral theories encoded masculine fragility: if everyone was made of the same four elements and the same four humors, then there was no essential difference between men and women. Breitenberg's book argues that *The Anatomy of Melancholy* understood male anxiety as embodied, operating simultaneously on the levels of the body, the state, and nature. Not surprisingly, his reading of the *Anatomy* focuses on the final partition's discussion of love melancholy. Breitenberg reads Burton as asserting, with Galen, that melancholy is a disturbance of bodily fluids, so that there is no difference between physiology and psychology. Both are related to the state of the body politic. Melancholy was experienced as an invasion of interiority by a feminine, unregulated Other and a symptom of political disorder. The sprawling text of the *Anatomy* is intended to purge this excess with repeated lessons in misogyny: satire on foolish lovers who worship women, warnings that marriage will shackle a man to a troublesome and disgusting wife, horrified accounts of women's allurements and deceptive wiles. The lover has lost his masculine dignity; Burton will cure him by arousing disgust for the beloved woman.

It is not hard to find support for all these assertions in Burton, whose castigation of women has all the ignorance and exuberance of middle school boys' talk. But nearly all the assertions in this chain, all the statements that "A is true," are balanced by contradictory statements that "A is not true" later in the text. The Galenic understanding of melancholy as a disease, for example, is undercut by assertions that reference the celebration of melancholy in *Problemata* 30.1, attributed to Aristotle, and in Marsilio Ficino's *Three Books on Life*.[17] Burton observes: "Why melancholy men are witty, which *Aristotle* hath long since maintained in his Problems: and that all learned men, famous Philosophers, and Law-givers, *ad unum ferè omnes Melancholici*, have still beene Melancholy; is a Probleme much controverted" (1:421). And Breitenberg himself writes of the "pleasure and satisfaction" that Burton seems to have taken in his own melancholy and his account of the condition.[18] While the *Anatomy* connects psychology and physiology, that connection is not seamless. In the long "Digression of Anatomy" that interrupts his preliminary exposition for thirty-eight pages (1:139–61), Burton works out how the body and mind affect each other, with many cunning mediations and a fair number of external interventions. The horror of melancholy as an invasion of the Other is offset by its universality—if all are melancholy, how can there be an Other? And the misogyny that is so prominent in the section on love melancholy is less interesting to Burton in other sections of the text. Stephanie Shirilan has painstakingly shown that diatribes against women in the *Anatomy* are regularly balanced with admissions that men are as bad as women, or that they give women good reason to act as they do.[19] In the endless whirligig of propositions that propels the *Anatomy* forward, every "A is true" is followed by an "A is not true." Fish, focusing on the gradual retraction or "self-consuming" of the assertion, holds that Burton really meant "A is not true." Breitenberg, relying on the energy and weight of Burton's many misogynistic statements, dismisses the retraction and holds that the text intends to say "A is true." I argue that these positions are equivalent, that there is no principle for deciding between them, and that they are both marginal to the work of the text and to the pleasure readers have taken in the *Anatomy*.

At this juncture, aligning with the position that Burton intends neither the propositions he advances in the *Anatomy* nor his contradictions of them is a tempting alternative. This position has been elaborated by R. Grant Williams in his essay "Disfiguring the Body of Knowledge: Anatomical Discourse and Robert Burton's *The Anatomy of Melancholy*."[20] Williams contrasts Burton's *Anatomy* with texts such as Helkiah Crooke's *Microcosmographia*, which for him exemplify a practice of dissection that relates parts to wholes, producing reliable knowledge. Williams sees anatomical texts developing lucid arguments through the logic of synecdoche; he contrasts these presentations with Burton's image of Democritus in his garden: "about him lay the carcasses of many severall beasts, newly by him cut up and anatomized . . . to finde out the seat of this *atra bilis* or Melancholy" (1:6). Burton observes that Democritus's research was "left unperfect, & it is now lost"; his own *Anatomy* will take its place (1:6). Nothing could be further from the anatomist's composed and layered disclosure of structures, their relations and their attachments, than this carnage of random animals, rifled over in a fruitless search for a point of origin of the ubiquitous humor of melancholy.

For Williams, the very structure of the *Anatomy* expresses Burton's refusal of any stable form of knowledge, or as he puts it, his practice of "disfiguration." Instead of the expressive figure of synecdoche, Burton employs the loose, open-ended list, or synathroesmus. A list offers no guidance about the importance of its members, particularly when, as is customary for Burton, it ends with a trailing "&c," or et cetera. On the level of arrangement, Burton's organization of the partitions of the *Anatomy* is inconsistent: the first discusses causes and the second, cures; they are organized as thesis and antithesis. But the third partition, on love melancholy, corresponds to an organization by species. The initial address, "Democritus to the Reader," does not introduce the text that follows, to say nothing of the wandering conclusion offered in the first edition. Within each partition, the orderly development of the *Anatomy* is disorganized by frequent, extensive digressions.

Williams connects the synecdochic logic of conventional anatomies with the Lacanian theory of the mirror stage, the moment when the young child integrates a diffuse experience of his or her body with their reflected image and thereby enters the world of knowledge, the domain of the imaginary. A refusal of this integration is therefore a profound renunciation, fragmenting both the knowing subject and the objects of knowledge. Williams's analysis of the depth of this refusal is especially telling because it places Burton's contradictions at multiple textual locations: however cleverly we reconcile the conceptual and structural contradictions in the assertions of the text, we are outwitted by contradictions on the level of the sentence, the arrangement of the book, and the development of its sections. There could be no more uncompromising statement that, in the *Anatomy*, both "A is true" and "A is false" are untrue.

Like Colie's celebration of the multiple assertions of the *Anatomy*, Williams's reading of it as a nihilistic text is entirely plausible unless we consider the question of exigency. And exigency is at the heart of Burton's statement of his purpose: "to anatomize this humour of Melancholy, through all his parts and species, as it is an habite or an ordinary disease, and that philosophically, medicinally, to shew the causes, symptomes, and severall cures of it, that it may be the better avoided" (1:110).

We could read the *Anatomy* as a disfiguration of its subject, a derangement of its "parts and species," in which the contradictions between medicine and philosophy are richly displayed and never resolved, but we cannot neglect the drive to avoid melancholy, to put this information to use, whether as good counsel or as an experience of radical indeterminacy. For Williams, this orientation of the *Anatomy*, central to its rhetorical purpose, is elided by Burton's foreclosure of the subject of knowledge. If there is no knower, how can there be an exigency of choice?

The four readers I have discussed represent four representative decades in Burton criticism: the 1960s, the 1970s, the 1990s, and the 2000s. Some of their readings are historicist; some are relatively presentist. All are historically informed, and all integrate their readings of Burton with more general discussions of seventeenth-century literature and culture. Although none of these scholars is blind to the movement and energy of the *Anatomy*, their interest is focused on the propositions advanced in Burton's book. How can a writer advance two contradictory ideas? If a writer advances an idea definitively, can we discount his offhand dismissal of it? What do we do with a writer who contradicts both his original assertion and his refutation of it? My work in this book will be to contextualize these questions as responses to early modern practices of knowledge, to emerging paradigms of study, explication, and observation. I will do my best to fight shy of Burton's tangled assertions and denials, to keep my eye firmly on the seamy side of his web.

Learning's Burton

Let us first consider Burton's relationship to early modern practices of knowledge. What disciplines would the sixteen-year-old Robert Burton have encountered as he began weaving his web in 1593, when he matriculated as an undergraduate, joining his brother William at Brasenose College, Oxford? (William would later publish the comprehensive *Description of Leicester Shire*, a landmark in British local history.[21])

We know very little about the specifics of Robert Burton's undergraduate life, and he vanished from university records between 1593 and 1599, when he entered Christ Church as a Student, at that time a junior undergraduate rank. Some biographers suggest that he might have left the university because his family ran short of money; others, that he may have suffered from illness.[22] Some identify him with the Robert Burton described in the notebooks of the astrological physician Simon Forman. That patient suffered from melancholy; Forman saw him five times in 1597, prescribed medicines, purges, and phlebotomy, but noted "he carieth death upon him."[23] There is some evidence for this identification: Forman's patient was twenty years old, Burton's age at the time, and a passage from an unpublished manuscript by Forman appears in Burton's astrological notebook.[24]

Burton received his bachelor's degree in 1602 and his master's in 1605. With his second degree, he assumed again the rank of Student, now roughly equivalent to "Fellow."[25] He continued at Christ Church until his death in 1640, serving for a time as Clerk of the Market, and after 1624 as the college librarian. He wrote Latin plays, provided Latin verse for university collections, participated in lectures and disputations, taught students, and obtained a living, a position that provided him income, in 1616. He oversaw the publication of five editions of *The Anatomy of Melancholy* in 1621, 1624, 1628, 1632, and 1638. He was known as a surveyor; he reported seeing the moons of Jupiter through a telescope (2:62). His astrological notebook included broad speculations as well as directions for finding lost objects and drawing up natal charts. He cast his own horoscope and insisted that it be included on his funeral monument in Christ Church cathedral.

Burton's Oxford was an active intellectual center, committed to both scriptural and humanistic scholarship, and open to the influences of the emerging new sciences.[26] Some of the disciplines of the university, like medicine, philosophy, and divinity, are familiar to us; we could find courses in them in any contemporary university. But we would be hard pressed to recognize modern scientific disciplines in their early modern predecessor, natural philosophy; in fact, as practices of knowledge, all of these subjects were quite distinct from their modern incarnations. The daily life of university students and teachers has also changed. Oxford University was populated by very young students, had no departments, and did not really give courses, let alone grades. The university took responsibility for students' religious formation and good conduct. What practices of knowledge did they sponsor? Which did Burton take up?

Burton's Learning

We have a number of accounts of the course of study at Christ Church in the sixteenth century; they give us some idea of the education Burton received and provided. The Carnsew brothers, studying in the 1570s, kept diaries of their work. In the course of their studies, the brothers wrote five definitions of *homo*; they read Sallust and *ad Herennium*; they made exercises; they wrote epistles and syllogisms *per impossibile*, proving that a proposition is true by showing that its opposite is impossible. They also studied mathematics, anatomy, Aristotle's ethics, and works in logic and rhetoric. Their reading included puritan tracts and the rhetoric of Rudolph Agricola, which they outlined in tables.[27] This course of reading coheres with what we know of the sixteenth-century arts curriculum, with its prescribed lectures and readings in grammar, rhetoric, and logic, and with the orientation of Oxford to producing able civil servants as well as well-trained divines.

The books that Burton owned and cited in the *Anatomy* are deeply rooted in this tradition, especially as it was interpreted by such northern humanists as Erasmus and Melanchthon. Burton quoted extensively from Seneca, Virgil, Horace, Juvenal, Pliny, and Cicero, as we might expect from a university scholar with humanistic training. But he also summons a crowd of other writers from Greek and Roman antiquity to his pages: Pausanias, Ausonius, Petronius Arbiter, Philo Judaeus, Pliny, Ptolemy, Gellius, Lucian, and Persius, among others. He cites no fewer than thirty-six works by Plutarch. He followed the humanist preference for the Greek and Latin fathers: Chrysostom, Cyprian, Eusebius, Jerome, Tertullian, and Augustine appear more often than the scholastic theologians Aquinas, Bonaventure, or Scotus. Since the canon of antiquity began with Homer and ended with Boethius, it included over a thousand years of writing, and Burton's explorations in it were wide-ranging. Burton was also versed in early modern humanist scholarship, including philology, philosophy, and political theory: the *Anatomy* quotes the Dutch poet Heinsius, the earlier rhetoricians and humanists Juan Vives and Julius Caesar Scaliger, both the NeoPlatonist Marsilio Ficino and the NeoStoic Justus Lipsius, and the Jesuit theologian Leonardus Lessius.

Burton was by vocation and profession a divine, but we know little about his specific religious beliefs. In the *Anatomy*, Burton wrote on sin as a cause of melancholy, on prayer as a source of healing, and on the treatment of religious melancholy. He satirized both Roman Catholicism and Puritanism. In the preface, as "Democritus Junior," he mocked both the "three-crowned Soveraigne Lord the Pope, poor *Peters* Successor, *Servus servorum Dei*," and "our Nice and curious Schismaticks" who "abhorre all ceremonies, and rather lose their lives and livings, than doe or admit any thing Papists have formerly used" (1:40, 41). But you will not find a clear elucidation of predestination in the book; nor does Burton wade into the nature of the Eucharist, the number of sacraments, or any of the other issues that vexed early modern theology. Democritus Junior dismissed such writing as useless contention (1:21), but Burton read his share of religious polemics. Nicolas Kiessling's inventory of his library, on which I lean heavily throughout this book, lists 462 titles on theology, the Bible, and liturgy.[28] Annotations in these books show us a man absorbed in the religious issues of his day, carefully annotating works of theological polemic such as Franciscus Collius's *De animabus paganorum libri quinque*, on whether virtuous pagans could have been saved, or Robertus Loeus's *Effigiatio veri sabbathismi*, on Sabbath observance, or Zacharias Ursinus and David Pareus's *Explicationum catecheticarum*, a catechism in which Burton wrote notes on salvation, the Holy Spirit, and other religious topics.[29] Since Christ Church cathedral was connected to the college, Burton's duties would have included preaching there. Burton observed that "I might have haply printed a Sermon at *Pauls-Crosse*, a Sermon in St *Maries Oxon.*, a Sermon in *Christ-Church*, or a Sermon before the right Honorable, right Reverend, a Sermon before the right Worshipfull, a Sermon in Latine, in English, a Sermon with a name, a Sermon without, a Sermon, a Sermon, &c." (1:20). Titles comparable to these found a home in Burton's extensive collection of sermons.

While Burton did not engage religious controversies in the *Anatomy*, religious issues shape the text's warp and woof. Discussing poverty as a cause of melancholy, Burton criticizes the rich who "may freely trespasse . . . they may securely doe it, live after their owne lawes, and for their mony get pardons, Indulgences, redeeme their soules from Purgatory and Hell it self" (1:347). In his subsection on the relation between physician and patient, Burton writes "Of those divers gifts which our Apostle *Paul* saith, God hath bestowed on man, this of Physicke is not the least, but the most necessary" (2:11). Such references are common throughout the *Anatomy*. Here again, discourses are mobile and the boundaries between them are porous: religion is a resource for criticizing the rapacity of the rich and praising the usefulness of medicine.

Given Burton's training and profession, it is not surprising that twentieth-century scholarship on *The Anatomy of Melancholy*, while acknowledging the breadth of his interests, presented him as primarily a humanist with deep commitments to Christianity. E. Patricia Vicari observed that "Next to Christianity, the strongest influence on Burton's mind was Renaissance humanism."[30] And her observation is borne out in Nicolas Kiessling's analysis of Burton's library: "As one might expect in the library of a member of an Oxford college in the early 1600s, the majority of books concern theology. . . . His holdings in history and literature . . . are very extensive and follow theology in number."[31]

The category "literature," however, did not exist for early modern scholars or readers; what Burton would have called "good letters" included poetry and other kinds of imaginative writing (but not necessarily prose fiction or vernacular plays), history, and treatises such as Hooker's *Reason of Church Government*.[32] Rhetoric held a special place in this domain: while the basic texts that everyone studied in childhood were often used but seldom cited, it is almost impossible to overestimate the importance of Erasmus, and the trained, skillful practice of persuasion was highly valued, both inside and out of the academy. As a central element of good letters, rhetoric shaped both traditional and emerging discourses of knowledge, supplying the means for making observations present to readers, the templates for organizing physicians' case histories, and the tropes, figures, and affective resources for popular writers. As we will see, it offered critical resources for Burton's project of investigating disciplinary movement and exchange.

Recent scholarship has demonstrated the breadth of Burton's interests, including his curiosity about natural sciences. Oriented to the work of his contemporaries, Burton had a lively interest in the kind of literature—plays, joke books, travel books—that would not have counted as "good letters." Often written by university trained writers, these texts abandoned the world of learning for the public theater, or were posted as broadsides. Burton also extended foundational university studies in letters and philosophy into cognate disciplines such as natural philosophy, disciplines that would themselves give rise to (and confront) emerging practices of observation. To follow these connections, and to understand what Burton did with his wide-ranging interests in the text of *The Anatomy of Melancholy*, will take a bit of unfolding, beginning with an account of how early modern scholars understood natural philosophy and its relation to medicine, astronomy, and the emerging sciences.

Natural philosophy occupied a liminal space in the program of study that early modern English universities inherited from their medieval predecessors. It was a science, a systematic deductive study that produced certain and permanent knowledge. But it dealt with material things, with bodies and their relationships—a constantly changing and endlessly variable congeries of objects. Medieval philosophers struggled with this tension, and it did not evaporate in early modern thought.[33] The curriculum in natural philosophy was based on Aristotle, and so this discipline focused on the four Aristotelian causes, especially the final cause, or purpose, of an object. That focus wobbled and blurred in the early modern period, although long after Burton's death Isaac Newton would still write of God, "We know him only by his most wise and excellent contrivances of things, and final causes."[34] Newton's statement coheres with the general belief of early modern natural philosophers that God was the final cause of the universe, but Aristotelians and corpuscular physicists, who studied particles and their movements, understood divine causality differently. They disagreed with each other about the nature of "substance," the material that constitutes all bodies, and about how change occurs.[35] These questions were not anterior to natural philosophy; they were an intrinsic part of the field, liable to emerge in treatises about the migrations of birds or the movement of objects. Such questions had implications for natural philosophers' understanding of the human mind and its vicissitudes. Daniel M. Gross has demonstrated their importance for reformation philosophers, especially Philipp Melanchthon. Writing about the end or purpose of physics, generally considered the primary division of natural philosophy, Melanchthon observed, "It treats the order, quality, and motion of all bodies and forms in nature, the causes of generation, corruption and other motions in elements and in other bodies generated in the mixture of elements, it investigates and reveals however much the darkness of the human mind yields. . . . Wondrously, souls are affected by all of nature."[36]

Resolving problems of causality and change required theories that operated simultaneously on different levels, or that rested on incompatible axioms; therefore, the early modern natural philosopher fell back on the secure foundations of his field, the Aristotelian texts and the rules of logic. But natural philosophers also drew upon a range of strategies to connect those foundations with uncertain natural events. This work was textually mediated; since no scholar assumed that science progressed, the Greek and Latin physicists and botanists enjoyed signal authority. Work in natural philosophy would often begin by citing the writings of antiquity, and for many writers a quotation from Aristotle was enough to resolve a difficult point.

It would be a mistake to call the writer of natural philosophy a "natural philosopher," as if this scholar unlocked the door to a Department of Natural Philosophy every morning and idly paged through an issue of *The Journal of Natural Philosophy* at night. It is true that "natural philosophy" designated a well-defined field of study, with a technical vocabulary, canon of theoretical texts, and traditions of communication and proof. But a work in natural philosophy could be produced by a divine, a philosopher, or a historian. Consider such writers (all quoted by Burton) as José de Acosta, a Spanish Jesuit historian who also wrote on the natural history of the Americas, *De natura novi orbis libri duo* (Salamanca, 1589); Jean Bodin, the political theorist who also wrote a comprehensive treatment of natural philosophy, *Universae naturae theatrum* (Hanau, 1605); and Girolamo Cardano, who wrote on game theory, produced works on music and consolation, and also wrote *De Subtilitate* (Basel, 1560), a wide-ranging account of natural phenomena. We could add other canonic early modern figures such as Scaliger and Melanchthon, and many other minor writers. While there were scholars whose main work was in natural philosophy, just as there were those who concentrated on theology or antiquities, it was not at all unusual for an individual to produce works in a variety of fields in the course of an intellectual life. Natural philosophy, with its close ties to the philosophical treatises every academic studied, was an available discourse rather than a specialized profession.

The three professional disciplines—divinity, medicine, and law—were linked to the branches of philosophy offered in the beginning arts course. Natural philosophy sponsored the profession of medicine; it was the source of the "*praecognita*" of medicine—theories of the elements and the humors, as well as such basic concepts as substance and accident or potency and act. But while natural philosophy was in principle an investigation of what was true in all of nature, medicine was necessarily occupied with specific individuals and their illnesses; it focused on what was emergent in a particular illness at the time of treatment. While natural philosophy proudly claimed the certainty of science, medicine claimed certainty only for its description of the common processes and vicissitudes of bodies, for its descriptions of what usually happens. But diagnosis, prognosis, and treatment, as everyone understood, were uncertain, chancy businesses. While natural philosophers investigated unchanging laws, physicians worked to rectify the constantly changing humors, consulting texts such as Hippocrates's *Airs, waters, places* to balance objects and forces that changed with the seasons, time of day, and weather. It was the work of the physician to search out what was *praeter naturam*, or outside nature, to remove obstructions, to reestablish humoral balance, or to correct excessive heat or cold. Facing so many variables, the physician could not guarantee certainty and his practice was therefore considered to be a conjectural art.[37]

Like natural philosophy, medicine could be either a lifelong profession or an occasional study. The physician could be a zoologist, a botanist, a mathematician, a natural philosopher. (There is an article to be written about the many rhetoricians who were also physicians, including Giorgio Valla, Giovanni Garzoni, Pierre-Jean-Georges Cabanis, Rudolph Agricola, Thomas Linacre, and that hardy perennial in any collection of early modern polymaths, Julius Caesar Scaliger.) Like natural philosophy, medicine valued the works of antiquity, and since important texts of Galen and Hippocrates were being discovered and translated into Latin, the medicine of Greek and Roman antiquity was in effect new learning. The ancient texts were joined by a rich current literature, both theoretical and practical. Physicians collected the letters they wrote to each other and to their patients, published their case notes, and generally joined the cacophony of shared knowledge that was early modern learning.

Conceptual ties between rhetoric and medicine were ancient and tangled. Both disciplines dealt with individual cases; both were conditioned and located in time, oriented to activity, and reliant on the uncertain evidence of signs. Neither worked by reasoning deductively from unchanging principles. Nancy Struever has characterized this shared orientation to *kairos* and deep contextualization as a "rhetorical-medical mindset," a term that is quite accurate, although it would have puzzled early modern practitioners of either art.[38] Since my book is a work of rhetorical history and analysis, and since the ostensible subject of *The Anatomy of Melancholy* is (by some lights) medical, I will discuss Burton's use of rhetoric and medicine at some length in coming chapters. The affinities between rhetoric and medicine—uncertainty, particularity, imbrication in time—the very qualities that made them suspect to early modern scholars in search of certainty—were supports to Burton's interest in exchange, in mobility, and in the deployment of tropes from one field to another.

But these were not the only texts that Burton loved, collected, and used. He was interested in the full range of disciplines associated with natural philosophy: natural history, cosmography, and the evolving "chymistry," which in his

lifetime included alchemy, astronomy, and optics.[39] In Burton's copy of Conrad
Gesner's alchemical text *Euonymus, sive de remediis secretis* he wrote definitions
of a list of alchemical terms such as *calcinatio, solutio,* and *sublimatio*.[40] He practiced surveying, which was considered a lowly "mechanical art," and he delighted
in the new maps. The borders between these practices were fluid, as were those
between the emerging sciences and practices of knowledge that modernity
would reject, including astrology. Early modern astrology integrated mathematics and astronomical observation well before Isaac Newton's *Principia*, and so it
had more in common with the new science of astronomy than did text-bound
academic astronomy.[41] Burton's "astrological notebook," written in the blank
pages in his copy of Cyprianus Leovitius's *Brevis et perspicua ratio judicandi geni-
turas, ex physicis causis extructa,* recorded his own horoscope and Queen Elizabeth's, as well as passages from a range of authors including Tycho Brahe,
Gerolamo Cardano, Simon Forman, and Ptolemy.[42] He noted the latitude and
longitude of cities, and Thomas Harriot's description of sunspots.

Not all of Burton's interests were so scholarly. Anthony Wood, in his brief
biography of Burton, reported that his close friends found him "very merry,
facete and juvenile."[43] Burton's youthful cheerfulness—or perhaps his desire to
counter melancholy with mirth and merry company, as he advised in the *Anatomy* (2:116–24)—led him to collect a wide range of amusing texts. His library
included plays from the London public and private theaters, books of travel, and
joke books, as well as romances and poetry. In the blank pages of one of his
books, he wrote three Latin epigrams, including this sober account of a joke:

> Cum Radamantheum stetit ante Tribunal Erasmus
> Ante joco scribens serio damnor ait?
> Cui Judex, libri dant seria damna jocosi,
> Si tibi culpa jocus, sit tibi poena jocus.

> [When Erasmus stood before a Radamanthean court
> He said, Is one writing in jest to be condemned in earnest?
> The judge replied, jest books do serious harm.
> If your guilt is a joke, let your punishment be a joke.][44]

Whatever the perils of fooling around, Burton still found jokes, merry tales,
and other entertainments irresistible; he recommended "*Jucunda confabulatio,
sales, joci,* pleasant discourse, jests, conceits, merry tales" (2:117). Since he also

warned against drinking too much, neglecting business, or falling in with bad companions, Burton had nothing to fear from Radamanthus's judgment.

Burton's will offered first choice of his books to the Bodleian Library; the librarian John Rouse inventoried his collection and found sixty-one "Comedies & Tragedies." These books, along with poetry and comic works in English, were remanded to Christ Church library; they were too numerous for the Bodleian, and Bodley had banned such "baggage books" from his library.[45] Kiessling's inventory of Burton's library includes sixty-four plays in English. Burton's taste in drama is surprising; the closest thing to it I can imagine would be finding out that Derrida's Netflix log alternated between *How I Met Your Mother* and *Battlestar Gallactica*. Burton had none of Marlowe's or Shakespeare's plays, although he owned some of their poems. He favored Beaumont and Fletcher (nine plays, separately and in collaboration), the scholarly Chapman (five plays), the farcical Heywood (nine plays), the sensational Middleton (five plays), and the copious Shirley (eight plays). His collection leaned toward comedy and included titles published in every decade from 1600 to 1640.

Burton's library included 109 unique books, editions that survive only in the copies he owned. These include the 1602 edition of Shakespeare's *Venus and Adonis*, a rather racy poem for a divine. Also among the unique copies are two versions of the highwayman ballad *Adam Bell*, dismissed as "Ridicularia" by the librarian Rouse, the poems in *Pasquils fooles-cap sent to such . . . as are not able to conceive aright of his mad-cap*; Thomas Deloney's *The Garland of Good Will*; and *A Booke of Merrie Riddles*.[46] Thomas Hearne, writing in 1735, correctly observed that the Bodleian bequest included "Pamphlets, now grown wonderful scarce, . . . [and] other little merry books."[47] Such "little merry books" mingled happily on his shelves with collections of sermons, works by Plutarch, travel books, and collections of medical cases. Burton's learning speaks of an elastic temporality, opening out from the texts of antiquity to the most ephemeral of nonsense books—although what could be more ancient than a riddle? Individual volumes include a range of knowledge practices: moral and religious reflections are found in medical books; an anatomy opens a commentary on Aristotle; merry tales dot a medical case book. With their scratchy bachelor markings in the margins, their Latin tags inscribed on the title pages, and their lists of authors and specialized terms written on the blank pages, Burton's books record a mobile mind at work among porous disciplines, rearranging information, texts, and scraps of narrative among them. His library speaks of a world of clear hierarchies, but also a world of fluid movement and exchange among disciplines, a world where knowledge responded to exigency by curing diseases, stirring up religious devotion, or resolving political problems.

My book is an investigation into the movement and exchange that Burton constructed in the *Anatomy*. To return to the discussion of the two editions of Burton's book with which I opened this chapter, I read the notes of the Clarendon edition into the compact Everyman edition, so that my discussion folds the commentary into the text and unfolds the text into the commentary. That process necessarily leads me to Burton's learning, to the investigation of his own very material books and his practices of reading, excerpting, and adapting, including his use of texts that he loved, used, but, as far as we know, did not own, such as the writings of Cicero, Melanchthon's *Liber de Anima*, and Erasmus's *Adages*. Taking together Burton's personal library and the other resources available to him, we have a map of the republic of letters in one of its early seventeenth-century iterations.

We cannot say that Burton was an active citizen of that imaginary state, a community based on exchange among scholars, transcending national and confessional boundaries, mediated by personal ties, correspondence and exchange of specimens, and eventually organized by learned journals.[48] We have only the thinnest records of any personal ties between Burton and colleagues anywhere outside Oxford, and learned journals did not begin publication until decades after his death. Yet his world of learning was international; his authorities, distributed in time and space; his reading, inclusive of Roman Catholics, reformers, physicians of all persuasions, and a full range of political theorists. Burton's demeanor as Democritus Junior is anything but the cosmopolitan polite tolerance that the republic of letters recommended to its citizens, but his reading was as voracious and varied as that of any collector of humanist manuscripts or rare plants.

I will investigate Burton's practices of knowledge and persuasion, focusing on two textual structures—genre and choice of language—and on two disciplines—medicine and rhetoric. While the recovery of the rich, mobile, and consequential world of Burton's learning is important, it is also my hope that this recovery supports readers in their adventures in the three compact volumes of the *Anatomy*, or the new readerly editions to come, books that will have much to teach us about the rhetorical power of the *Anatomy* for showing how knowledge and expertise could become more mobile and convivial.

In chapter 2, "Burton's *Anatomy*: Genres as Species and Spaces," I argue that while contemporary genres are closely associated with distinctive disciplines (the monograph with humanities; the scientific essay organized by Introduction, Methods, Results, Discussion, and Conclusion with sciences), such genre boundaries were anything but secure for early modern writers, who moved easily between historical examples and philosophical speculation and wrote "treatises" on history, philosophy, grammar, and geometry. The genre of *The Anatomy of Melancholy* has long been a subject of debate; this chapter argues that the *Anatomy* is productively read as an example of layered and sedimented early modern genre practices. I argue that our current understanding of genre is shaped by the powerful metaphor of Darwinian speciation and suggest that supplementing this understanding with more spatial metaphors allows us to see genres as facilitating movement among knowledge practices by constructing points of exchange among them.

Chapter 3, "*The Anatomy of Melancholy* and Early Modern Medicine," investigates Burton's avid study of medical literature. He owned and annotated many books by physicians, including many by medical humanists. As an academic discipline, medical humanism integrated textual investigations of the newly recovered works of Galen and Hippocrates with observations and medical letters collected and distributed among physicians and other interested scholars throughout Europe. The issue raised by these materials would become central to new observational sciences: how can individual cases generate secure knowledge? Medicine was a central point of exchange among emerging practices of observation and the textual disciplines of humanist scholarship. *The Anatomy of Melancholy* constructs specific nodal points that facilitate such exchanges, including conventions for reporting medical cases that supported the construction of general statements. Burton also used the narrative structures distinctive to the literature of regimen, a very popular form of medical advice, to form new kinds of narrative temporalities. In Burton's hands, the concept of *spirit*, a central idea in both natural and moral philosophy, connected bodily experiences, the external world, and the experiences of thought, affect, and will.

Just as Burton used medicine as a storehouse of shapes for thought, he found in rhetoric figures for constructing mobile, polyvalent texts about uncertain and changing objects. Chapter 4, "Burton, Rhetoric, and the Shapes of Thought," investigates how Burton used the resources of early modern rhetorical theory. He leaned heavily on the topics, as developed by Rudolph Agricola, especially definition. He delighted in the expansion and elaboration of *copia* demonstrated by Desiderius Erasmus, especially in the commentaries of the *Adages*. Both the topics and the techniques of amplification had been part of the armamentarium of rhetoric since Greek and Roman antiquity, but early modern rhetoricians shaped these devices into flexible ways of developing information and exchanging forms of knowledge. Definition developed from a static practice of demarcating the defined object by genus and species into an investigation of all its qualities, adjuncts, and associations. Agricola called this investigation a "perlustration," and Burton took full advantage of his invitation to wander. And while the polyvalence of Erasmus's use of *copia* is well known, we have yet to appreciate how productively the figure, engrafted into the comments on proverbs in his *Adages*, generated multilayered narratives. Both perlustrating definitions and polyvalent *copia* sustained the traditional role of rhetoric: to transform propositional knowledge into the grounds for affect and action, to make knowledge count. This chapter investigates Burton's use of the rhetorical theory advanced by Agricola and Erasmus to show that, while Burton was not at pains to give readers a stable account of the causes of melancholy, he wanted the *Anatomy* to form in them the habits of mind and body that would prevent or cure the illness.

Our understanding of the relations among learned languages and vernaculars in early modern culture, like our understanding of genres, is shaped by an evolutionary metaphor of speciation: learning used to be in Latin, and then it adapted to the modern vernacular languages. This narrative obscures the relations of mutual influence and exchange among learned languages, including Latin and modern vernaculars, especially as they played out in universities. I present an alternate narrative in chapter 5, "Translingualism: The Philologist as Language Broker." Throughout the sixteenth and most of the seventeenth centuries, Latin was preeminent in scholarly communications among physicians and natural philosophers; it has been called "the national language of the republic of letters" and it was an important literary language throughout Europe. Latin also offered other virtues: a Latin text was more stable than one in the changing vernacular, hence the custom of translating works from modern languages into Latin, even if they had already been rendered in English. Using the framework of translingual theory, which sees languages as suites of communicative practices rather than as self-contained systems, I consider the interactions among the multiple languages in use at Oxford in the seventeenth century.

Burton participated in a language community that was organized around Latin, that sought to use it as a communicative practice, and that valued other languages ancient and modern. I investigate his location in the polyglot culture of Oxford and discuss the language politics expressed in his Latin poetry. I consider the implication of his choice to publish the *Anatomy* in English but to include abundant Latin quotations. This diglossia establishes Burton as a language broker, an individual who facilitates exchanges among languages: a difficult and rewarding role. The early modern equivalent for "language broker" might be "philologist," a term sometimes applied to Burton, indicating a wandering, spontaneous movement among texts rather than technical scholarship in language.

Finally, I will consider what these investigations mean for rhetoric, both as a practice of persuasion and as a disciplinary study. In particular, what do they suggest about rhetorical practices that predate the development of contemporary disciplines? Burton's rhetoric was not, and could not have been, transdisciplinary, but it models possibilities of movement and exchange that might be useful to current transdisciplinary theorists. His model suggests possibilities for a transdisciplinary practice oriented to movement and exchange rather than to the identification of commonalities or differences; such a practice sponsors a productive approach to the exigencies of melancholy. Such a practice also values the transformation of disciplinary resources as they enter new contexts. It would join toleration of uncertainty with a desire to put knowledge to use, however provisionally.

2

Burton's *Anatomy* | Genres as Species and Spaces

When Robert Burton's *Anatomy of Melancholy* was first published in 1621, it seemed to inaugurate a new genre rather than participate in a recognized "kinde" of textual performance.[1] There were cognates, to be sure: the early modern literature of health, in prose and verse, was extensive, as were books of spiritual advice and consolation. The essay was an emerging genre, and medical literature for both professional and lay readers was widely available. For early modern readers, genre boundaries were porous. Health books included spiritual counsel, and books of consolation advised on diet and exercise. But *The Anatomy of Melancholy* cannot be contained in even these loose topical borders. Readers put the text to wildly variant uses: because of its abundant Latin quotations, some readers understood it to be a work of philology; others used it as a source of counsel for melancholy friends or as a psychological encyclopedia.[2]

Contemporary scholarship has had an even harder time with the genre of the *Anatomy*, although not for lack of trying. Northrop Frye considered it a Menippean satire; Eleanor Vicari characterized it as a sermon; Douglas Trevor held that it is best characterized as a printed commonplace book; no less a genre theorist than Rosalie Colie declared that she had worn herself out working on it. Angus Gowland, in his essay "Rhetorical Structure and Function in *The Anatomy of Melancholy*," argued that the *Anatomy* is an epideictic text. In *The Worlds of Renaissance Melancholy* he identified the genre of the book as the cento—a text composed, like a patchwork, of quotations from other works, a position he has elaborated in a recent essay. Mary Ann Lund argued that it is impossible and fruitless to assign it to any genre.[3] Daunted though I am by this list, I will discuss the genre of the *Anatomy*: for early modern readers as for us, assigning a text to a genre means deciding what kind of knowledge it offers. This is not to say that genre assignments are stable or univocal, but rather that signaling the genre of a text in a subtitle or introduction provokes reader's expectations— expectations that could be confirmed, frustrated, or transformed.

For any stable understanding of genre, *The Anatomy of Melancholy* was a scandalous mixture. Early modern writing is rich in genre scandals: the tragicomedy, the romance, the verse epistle, none of which could be securely placed in any of the received genre hierarchies. Later scholarship identified other genres that resisted categorization, such as the domestic tragedy or the epyllion. These genres seem problematic because they transgress accepted boundaries: tragedy must end with the fall of the hero; the epic must be extensive and heroic. But a work as radically mixed as the *Anatomy* was simply anomalous. I argue that such genre scandals spring from our contemporary understanding of genres as evolutionary species. As species, we see genres as bound by what Alastair Fowler, adapting Wittgenstein's term, calls "family resemblances," so that genres are seen as signs of a remote common origin.[4]

Evolutionary metaphors underlie genre analyses in both rhetorical and literary genre theory; everywhere, the controlling metaphor is biological speciation, particularly Darwinian natural selection. Although these metaphors, for obvious reasons, were absent from genre scholarship until the nineteenth century, they now limit genre study to sequential temporal relationships, rendering invisible the layering and interpenetration that connect both rhetorical and literary genres. In such a sophisticated iteration as the work of Franco Moretti, genre theory draws explicitly on speciation as a way of investigating the relationship between form and history. Drawing on Darwin's famous diagram of the "tree of life," Moretti sketches out a theory of "natural selection and extinction" for genres.[5] Moretti's theory has been influential in fields far from literary criticism, as demonstrated in Nicolas Pethes's evolutionary account of the relations between fictional and clinical case histories.[6] I propose an alternate framework more hospitable to multigenre texts such as the *Anatomy*: the use of spatial metaphors. Burton's fluid movement among genres and the deftness with which he uses them as vehicles for textual exchange call for such alternative metaphors.

The need becomes more pressing if we also consider the relationship between literary and rhetorical genres. Literary genres are an unlimited suite of forms, often referenced in the title of a text: *The Tragedy of Hamlet, Prince of Denmark*; *Pride and Prejudice: A Novel*. Rhetorical genres are generally limited to the three outlined in Aristotle's *Rhetoric*: the deliberative, which deals with future actions; the forensic, which deals with past facts; and the epideictic, which deals with praise and blame. The rhetorical genres are rooted in situations: the need to decide on a course of action, to apportion rewards and punishments; to recognize exemplars of community values or to castigate the unworthy. Both literary and rhetorical genre schemes originated with Aristotle, who used the same term for both rhetorical and poetic genres, *eidos*: the deliberative, forensic, and epideictic were rhetorical *eide*, just as the epic and tragedy were poetic *eide*: "The species [*eide*] of rhetoric are three in number; for such is the number [of classes] to which the hearers of speeches belong."[7] These genres were distinguished by situation and exigency rather than form. Literary genres, on the other hand, were considered to be stable "kinds" of texts, usually determined by such formal features as meter, but sometimes by the ethos of the writer: Aristotle held that serious writers would produce tragedies.[8] According to critics in Greek and Latin antiquity, literary genres were never indeterminate: poems belonged to genres, each poem to one genre, whatever the ambiguities of actual poetic genre performances.[9] Poetic genres were defined in opposition to one another: what was comic was not tragic; the lyric was the not-epic.

The limits of Aristotle's genre systems indicate their purposes. Since they cannot account for texts such as the *Rhetoric* or the *Poetics*, this genre theory is not intended categorize all possible discourses. Since literary genres and rhetorical genres respond to different criteria, neither theory can exclude the other, so that we could have (and have had) deliberative comedies. But current literary genre theory and rhetorical genre theory, seen as distinct, independent systems, express different orientations toward knowledge. In rhetorical genre theory, knowledge is located in time and space, related to an audience, demonstrated through the everchanging demands of *logos*, and made effective through the cultivation of *pathos*. Rhetorical genre theory offers transdisciplinary rhetoric a fluid understanding of how knowledge claims can be organized, communicated, and transformed. For literary genre theory, knowledge is located within texts, which offer affective experiences distinctive to each genre; formal qualities of the text are seen as simultaneously directing readers to a particular genre experience and producing that experience. Since Philip Sidney's *Defence of Poetry*, literary genres have been charged with this reorientation of affect rather than with providing verifiable information; literary genre theory offers transdisciplinary rhetoric a way of thinking about affect.

Aristotle's *eidos* was rendered into Latin as *genus*, establishing the link between genres and the kinds of living things. So we read in *Rhetorica ad Herennium*: "Tria genera sunt causarum, quae recipere debet orator: demonstratiuum, deliberatiuum, iudiciale," or "There are three kinds of causes which the speaker must treat: Epideictic, Deliberative, and Judicial."[10] The term "*causarum genera*" was commonly used by Roman writers; for example, in Cicero's *De partitione oratoria* we read of "*causarum genera*," or "kinds of causes or occasions for speaking." Quintilian followed Cicero in designating the epideictic, the judicial, and the deliberative as "kinds of cases," alternately using the words *parte* and *genus* to identify them.[11]

Literary genre theory stabilized in Roman hands, but rhetorical theory became more fluid: Horace, that inveterate mixer of poetic genres, rejected the idea of mixed genres entirely, asserting a "law of genres" in the *Ars Poetica*, but Quintilian wondered whether the three canonic rhetorical genres could cover all the available speech situations.[12] He asked how, if the conventional Aristotelian genres were "parts" of oratory, they differed from other "parts" like invention, expression, arrangement, memory, and delivery. If the "parts" were distinguished according to the speech act of the rhetor, then there might be an unlimited number of genres: apologizing, warning, explaining, begging, and so on. If they were distinguished by the venue of the speech, there might be only two: public or private. Quintilian recorded these controversies and then accepted the traditional three genres, noting that they refer to ways of speaking rather than to categories of speeches.

Quintilian originated a lively tradition within rhetorical theory of treating the Aristotelian genres as provisional and of questioning the three traditional forms, which, however, remained quite durable. Instead of adding genre categories, rhetorical theorists followed Aristotle, holding that rhetorical genres could be nested or incorporated into one another: an epideictic speech could deliberatively persuade an audience to imitate the virtues that were being praised; a forensic speech might include policy arguments about, for example, the advisability of showing or withholding mercy. By late antiquity, genre frameworks had become richly confused for both rhetoricians and writers about literature. The apparatus of pedagogy articulated the rhetorical genres with other systems for staging students' progress, especially the progymnasmata: a student would write a fable, a literary form, in order to offer counsel, a deliberative rhetorical genre. At the same time, theoretical scholarship in rhetoric took into account profound changes in the functions of the genres, particularly the epideictic. Theories of poetic genre independently developed ways of accounting for the genre diversity of late antiquity while maintaining an essentialist understanding of each genre as a unique category.

The Anatomy of Melancholy, then, entered a complex and changing genre field—or rather, two overlapping genre fields. How did these two genres of genres combine or overlay one another for Burton? These questions are hard to answer if we think of genres as species with their own natural histories; they are easier to think through if we imagine genres as territories with multiple points of contact and nodes of exchange. The *Anatomy* is a crash course in that kind of reading.

Species and Spaces

Metaphors of natural selection offer a powerful framework for understanding how species emerge, change, and die. These evolutionary schemes and tropes are sometimes used explicitly as explanatory devices in rhetorical scholarship. In a typical essay, Michael Shepherd and Carolyn Watters observe that cybergenres demonstrate how "the new functionality afforded by the new medium drives the evolution . . . of replicated genres . . . through variations on those genres until novel genres emerge that are significantly different from the original genres."[13] Scholars discussing hybrid genres come close to imagining that two genres can get together and make genre babies. Evolutionary tropes are also powerful in literary genre theory. Franco Moretti, as we have seen, has advanced a theory of literary history based on the cultural selection of randomly generated textual devices.[14] Evolutionary frameworks can function implicitly, as in this formulation by Alastair Fowler: "The Renaissance was not always characterized by new forms; often it worked by adapting old forms or imparting to them a new spirit. The majority of the principal kinds had already been available in the Middle Ages. . . . But in the new historical or external context, these medieval kinds changed profoundly."[15] Here, genres, like biological species, adapt to their environment, working with the available (genetic?) material.

Whenever it is invoked, the evolutionary framework orients us to seeing genres temporally, as objects that move through time, that have their own histories. Texts are marked by genealogical ties to their genre ancestors; influential texts have genre descendants. The powerful evolutionary orientation of genre theory, like all terministic screens, occludes some questions while illuminating others. It is very useful for thinking about diachronic change and for showing relations among texts. It assumes that texts, like organisms, struggle for finite resources. It obscures genre relations that are complex or contradictory, or the possibility of a text generating readers and practices of reading.[16] The work of identifying the genre of a particular text demonstrates those problems. Texts are located in multiple temporalities: they respond to plural traditions, including those that shaped a writer's education; they were read or neglected in particular ways; as we analyze them, we reanimate them in the present. Unlike biological species, texts do not struggle for finite resources: the attention of readers expands as attractive texts become available. Texts generate both their readers and their successors, but the relations of readers and writers that support inter-textuality are not easily understood through genetic metaphors. These relation-ships can slip through the metaphors of speciation. Most of all, spatial metaphors obscure the possibility of rupture, of radical textual innovation.[17]

If we supplement temporal genre metaphors with spatial ones, we can move more easily between literary and rhetorical genres. For early modern readers, these borders were quite permeable. In his *Defence of Poetry*, Philip Sidney admitted that he had "strayed" from poetry to oratory in explaining poetry's affective power but insisted that poetry and oratory have "such an affinity in this wordish consideration" that he could not help wandering.[18] Wordish affini-ties, salient for Burton and his readers, emerge most clearly in a spatial frame-work, where alternate terministic screens of location, extension, contiguity, and enclosure could become as generative as the familiar evolutionary frames. We could speak of adjacency, overlapping, sedimentation, nesting, embedding; of separation, isolation, invagination; of pocket genres and genre fields. In dis-cussing genre change, we could consider such operations as assemblage, divi-sion, and budding. In such a context, we would not use genre membership to think about the text's offspring, but about its partners in exchange. With these metaphors, we can trace the intersections and layerings of genre in the *Anatomy* more precisely. Such an approach will allow us to take seriously Derrida's claim that "A text cannot belong to no genre, it cannot be without or less a genre. Every text participates in one or several genres, . . . yet such participation never amounts to belonging."[19]

In spite of their distinct conceptual frameworks, rhetorical genre theory and literary genre theory overlaid and enclosed each other in the early modern period, as demonstrated by two exemplary points of exchange: the expanded definition of the epideictic and the associated figure of amplification. Both are salient to *The Anatomy of Melancholy*, which is associated with the epideictic as a teaching genre, and which celebrates a festival of amplification. Rather than attempting a comprehensive history of the epideictic or amplification, I will thumb some tattered snapshots that trace their fortunes. Reflecting on these moments of exchange, we can begin to speculate about the rhetorical resources available to Burton and his readers.

The Epideictic: Hiding in Plain Sight

Nowhere was the flexibility of Aristotelian rhetorical genres more evident than in the epideictic, which would be adapted to such diverse forms as the homily and the blazon. Aristotle linked the epideictic to situations of display, but the genre was also adapted to deliberation and counsel in late antiquity, and to both the emerging poetic genres and the exigencies of explanation and teaching in the early modern period.

In the second half of the third century, Menander Rhetor produced two treatises on the epideictic: they were included, with Aristotle's *Poetics*, in Aldus's 1508 collection of *Rhetores Graeci* and translated into Latin by Natale Conti as *De genere demonstrativo libri duo* (1558), entering the early modern storehouse of rhetorical theory.[20] Menander dismissed the question of whether the epideictic was "species" or a "part" of rhetoric; it was, he wrote, one of the "parts, as it were, or kinds, or whatever one should call them" of rhetoric.[21] Then he moved on to the question of how to best praise a harbor. Julius Caesar Scaliger (1484–1558) referred to Menander's treatises in *Poetices libri septem*, but unlike Menander, he did not casually dismiss the question of genre distinction.[22] Although Scaliger adopted the three Aristotelian genres, he held that "*causa*," exigencies or reasons for speaking, could not be grouped into "*aut species, aut genera*," precisely because so many speech situations required a scandalous folding and layering of genres.[23] We might note that while Scaliger imagined species and genres spatially, he modified Aristotle's principle of genre definition. While Aristotle understood rhetorical genres as determined by situations rather than features of texts, Scaliger organized rhetorical performances by topic. Although he is generally considered an Aristotelian, Scaliger departed from Aristotle by reinventing the rhetorical genres as ways of classifying speeches rather than analyzing situations.[24] He also imported central elements of rhetorical genre theory into poetics—figures as means of exciting affect, the epideictic as a sponsoring genre for praise and invective—and insisted that poetry, oratory, and philosophy shared common ends and common means.

Early modern rhetoricians in England did not follow Scaliger; they saw the epideictic in Aristotelian terms, as a genre determined by situations. In Thomas Wilson's *The Arte of Rhetorique* (1560), the three "kyndes" of speech included "praise, or dispraise of a thing, or els in consulting, whether the cause be profitable, or unprofitable, or lastly, whether the matter be right, or wrong."[25] Wilson also recognized the possibility of genre nesting—passages of praise, profit, and fact could emerge in a text of any kind. But in poetic theory, the fortunes of the epideictic were quite different. George Puttenham's *Arte of English Poesie* (1589) never mentioned the epideictic, or the demonstrative, or any of their English synonyms, even though praise and blame are at the heart of his genre system.[26] The epideictic silently supplied a framework for Puttenham's poetic genres: praise of gods, praise of a monarch, praise of a woman, and so on. The epideictic is everywhere in his book; it is mentioned nowhere. This hiding in plain sight is typical of early modern literary genre theory: the epideictic is a territory too familiar to require mapping.

The epideictic was submerged into early modern poetic genre theory; in rhetorical genre theory, it was pressed into new shapes to accommodate textual forms that did not fit comfortably into the Aristotelian genres. Many of these forms were associated with new fields or methods of study. In his *De rhetorica libri tres* (1525), Philipp Melanchthon observed that the epideictic is a fundamental genre, the source of both the topics of invention and the entire method of judgment (*iudicandi ratio tota nascitur*).[27] He therefore included in this genre scientific texts—a class that conventionally included any texts that produced certain knowledge, such as works in theology, metaphysics, or natural philosophy. Such writing offered neither advice, legal evidence, praise nor blame. But for an educational theorist, these texts were significant, worthy of rhetorical analysis. The reach of Melanchthon's epideictic would broaden. Later, in *Elementorum rhetorices libri duo*, he renovated the epideictic into a related fourth genre, the didascalic, which he saw as a capacious teaching genre. "Est autem didascalicon genus, methodus illa docendi, quae traditur in dialectica, cuius particularem retinuerunt rhetores in statu finitivo. Est et demonstrativum genus, affine didascalico generi," or "This then is the didascalic genre, a method of teaching based in dialectics, which rhetoricians use to define a particular case. The demonstrative genre is closely connected to the didascalic genre."[28] Melanchthon locates the power of demonstration, first of all, in dialectics; there, a syllogistic argument that commanded immediate, intuitive assent was considered to be a demonstration. But Melanchthon grafts this sense of "demonstration" onto the traditional Latin term for the epideictic, which emphasizes the importance of making something present to an audience by presenting it with vivid sensory detail and affective power. Teaching was, for Melanchthon, a central cultural activity, and the didascalic/epideictic was its vehicle. The didascalic therefore formed both individual Christians and an emerging national culture. Teaching included both senses of demonstration, the logical presentation of reliable truths and the rhetorical persuasion to understand and apply them. Melanchthon even refunctioned the etymology of epideictic. Since Aristotle, the word *epideictic*, etymologically *pointing out*, had been understood as a reference to the genre's function of indicating the object of praise or blame to the audience; Melanchthon associated pointing with the epideictic power to teach by drawing the audience's attention to things they would not have otherwise known.

For early modern writers, then, the epideictic could be extended in many directions. For almost all theorists, it could serve a deliberative purpose; for some, it could also present a scientific demonstration, whether the demonstration was performed with a syllogism or a telescope. The epideictic as a "kind" of writing coexisted with literary genres that praised or blamed, such as the encomium or vituperation, and no less an authority than Cicero would have sanctioned such an overlap. We have known since the earliest work by Rosalie Colie (1973) and Alastair Fowler (1982) that early modern writers took genres, and genre decorum, seriously.[29] Rhetorical genres, however, could be taken for granted. While there were debates about sonnets, I have not found any disputes about the boundaries of deliberative speech; there were laws against satires, but not against forensic discourses. Every educated person learned the rhetorical genres in school and could use them as a way of understanding texts and purposes, but they were not terms of art in the emerging discourse of poetics.[30] The epideictic, then, was a ghostly presence in the early modern textual world. Most readers would have known what the term, or some equivalent, meant; they could have identified a funeral speech or a speech welcoming a visitor to the university as epideictic. Many readers, especially academic readers, would have understood the epideictic as a capacious genre that included all kinds of informative discourse. But it does not seem that anyone set out to *write* an epideictic text, except in the formal situations that required it, or that readers were dissatisfied with texts that did not display all the earmarks of the genre.

Affect was the nodal point where rhetorical and poetic genre theories intersected. Rhetoric's rich resources for describing the emotional power of tropes and figures could justify the power of poetry to arouse the will to action. Scaliger held that poets borrowed from rhetoricians the devices for exciting pathos as a means of persuasion and used them to arouse passions.[31] Such exchange between orators and poets was essential, implicit in Horace's injunction in the *Ars poetica* that poetry should mix the useful and the sweet.[32] It is not surprising, then, that for Scaliger poetic genres, like rhetorical genres, could be nested. Indeed, the intersecting criteria for genre attributions—by form (iambic or hexameter) or by matter (tragedy, epic)—offered him many niches for minor generic performances. For Scaliger and for other early modern theorists, the Homeric poems, rising above the restrictions of poetic genre theory, could be seen as the roots from which all genres sprung: these poems included the elegy, the lyric, the tragedy, and so on.[33] Early modern genre theorists expanded this possibility, advocating texts that included inset performances, understood as interior genres, moments in which the text escapes and moves into another poetic mode with its own distinct affect.

For both early modern poetic and rhetorical theory, affect was a disputed territory. As Richard Meek and Erin Sullivan observe, "emotion in this period did not follow a single template or social script, but rather was made up of multiple intellectual traditions and literary practices."[34] Early modern sermons were designed to arouse love of God and sorrow for sin, emotions valued in both reformation and counter-reformation theology.[35] But natural sorrows were accepted only provisionally and in moderation. Immoderate sorrow was held to strengthen the imagination, enabling it to overwhelm reason. Therefore, the mourner was urged to attend to counsel and pursue distraction to temper grief.[36] Sorrow was not the only emotion that was both praised and blamed. Greek and Roman philosophers rejected pity as pernicious to statecraft, but humanist writers such as Erasmus and Vives saw it as the foundation of political harmony.[37] When affect was valued, it was prized for its power to provoke action: Philip Sidney drew upon both southern humanist and reformed sources in defining an affective office as the mission of poetry: only through poetry could we "be moved to do that which we know, or to be moved with desire to know, *hoc opus, hic labor est*."[38] For Sidney, poetry, like the epideictic, fostered readers' admiration for virtue and hatred of vice.[39]

Attributes of the epideictic—the rhetorical genre most concerned with pleasure, most oriented to the emotions—circulated between the discourses of poetics and rhetoric. The early modern ideal of eloquence became a point of exchange between the territories of poetics and rhetoric, encouraging the development of verbal ornament appropriate to the decorum of poetic genres. According to Sidney, "the bitter but wholesome iambic . . . rubs the galled mind," while the satiric writer "never leaveth till he make a man laugh at folly."[40] Sidney's remark on the "affinity in this wordish consideration" between rhetoric and poetry spatializes these genre exchanges: the writer stands at the border, *ad finem*, between two "wordish considerations" and observes what moves between them, what is shared, and what is silently taken over. The epideictic was the site of exchanges between rhetorical genre theory and literary genre theory that enriched both these disciplines—although, as a rhetorician, I have been most attentive to how rhetoric has enriched poetics. Even when exchanges were bungled or misunderstood, something was communicated, and something was gained. If genres are seen as species, this traffic is obscured.

Since early modern rhetoric and poetics were not institutionally separated, one might claim that early modern rhetoric is early modern poetics, that the two discourses were more or less the same. The position, most magisterially developed by Brian Vickers, neglects the work of such writers as Scaliger and Sidney to construct a boundary between the two discursive arts. Rather than imagining a genetic prelapsarian unity between rhetorical genres and poetic genres, it is more productive to study the longstanding intersections and discontinuities between them.[41] From that perspective, the *Anatomy* is not simply an epideictic text, but a text that mobilizes the resources of the epideictic, especially to intensify affect.

Topics, Figures, and Genres: Amplification

Aristotle observed that "in general, among the classes of things common to all speeches, amplification is most at home in those that are epideictic," reserving enthymemes for forensic speeches.[42] In late antiquity, amplification sponsored the migration of epideictic topics for praise and blame. Menander Rhetor's second treatise on the epideictic, for example, included advice on writing the epithalamium, a speech in praise of the newly married couple and their families. Menander suggested praising marriage itself, and the marriages of rivers, of beasts of land and sea, of trees, and of gods. The speech could celebrate the virtues of the bride and groom, or the bridal chamber, or Hymen, or Eros.[43] These topics became the themes of the poetic epithalamion. Rhetorical devices for extending and varying praise would become markers of a poetic genre.

Rhetoricians used amplification to entrain affect within the temporal structure of the oration. For Rudolph Agricola (1444–1485), amplification allowed the orator to build emotion slowly; it operated both on the level of argument, as the orator multiplied reasons, and on the level of style, as the orator embellished and expanded them.[44] In *De copia*, Desiderius Erasmus (1469?–1536) established an intimate connection between amplification of words and ideas, observing that "The abundant style quite obviously has two aspects. Quintilian, for example,

among other virtues which he attributes to Pindar, especially admires his mag-
nificently rich style, manifested both in subject matter and expression. Richness
of expression involves synonyms, heterosis or enallage, metaphor, variation in
word form, equivalence and other methods of diversifying diction. Richness of
subject-matter involves the assembling, explaining, and amplifying of arguments
by the use of examples, comparisons, similarities, dissimilarities, opposites, and
other like procedures."[45]

Copious ornament moves from praise to blame and back again, as Erasmus
demonstrated in his discussion of the commonplaces related to changeableness,
a theme to which we will return in chapter 4. After collecting examples from
mythology—shape-shifting Mercury, the many forms of Jove, the wily Ulysses—
Erasmus moved to natural philosophy, which offered the changing moon, the
variable sky, the sea, and animals that can change color. All this material, conventionally used to augment speeches of blame, could be reversed to generate
praise: "If you were praising a man for all seasons, endowed with a versatile and
dexterous mind, you could dip into your 'inconstancy' cupboard and bring out
the polyp that changes color . . . you could bring out the flame which cannot
stand still, the sky which constantly presents a different face."[46]

Plato might have condemned this shuttling between praise and blame as
rhetorical corruption of language: the rhetorician is ready to turn phrases, to use
all of the available means of persuasion to prove whatever his judgment or the
interest of his patron recommends to him. Rhetoricians were not disturbed by
these possibilities: amplification laid the paradigmatic structures of variation
and expansion over the syntagmatic unfolding of the discourse in time. It connected the materials from which the speech is constructed—repeated sounds,
varied tempos, images of the world and all it contains—to persuasion, that
mysterious process in which a listener consents to be changed by a speaker.

For poetic theorists, as for Erasmus, amplification was both a multiplication
of words and an intensification of affect. Puttenham observed: "This ornament
then is of two sortes, one to satisfie and delight th' eare onely by a goodly outward shew set upon the matter with words and speaches smoothly and tunably
running, another by certain intendments or sence of such words and speaches
inwardly working a stirre to the mind."[47] Amplification also connected to early
modern anxieties about literary texts: their troubled veracity, their power to
arouse dangerous emotions. As Terence Cave has shown, amplification promised to represent the richness, indeed the inexhaustibility, of natural creation,

but it was also haunted by the possibilities of empty repetition and meaningless proliferation.[48]

If genres are seen as species, the relationship between amplification in early modern rhetoric and poetics is obscured. Figures such as amplification become species identifiers, like the square stems of mints. In this framework, early modern poetic amplification is a genetic inheritance from rhetorical amplification, something taken over, or even a debt owed by poetics to rhetoric. Although early modern poetics and rhetorical theory strove to differentiate their relations to affect and action, they did not become self-contained discourse practices. Both poetry and rhetoric claimed the power to move readers, but rhetoric was rooted in specific audiences and exigencies, while poetry sought a less focused, potentially broader, efficacy. Both claimed a signal power to form the will, but it was not the same will they sought to form. Hence the perennial early modern story of the orator or the poet as founders of civilization: poets or orators bring people together in groups and persuade them into civil life. How these labors are divided depends on the interests of the theorists, but often the poet gathered people together and the orator proposed good laws.[49] For a rhetorician, the temporal qualities of amplification were paramount, since they gave room for the development of affect. Poetic amplification, on the other hand, could exploit possibilities of self-reference and formal display. Amplification was a resource exchanged between rhetoric and poetics, but it changed in its travels.

Metaphors of spatiality can help us understand these relationships. The epideictic appears as an expansive territory, shadowy at its borders, straddling the domains of rhetoric and poetics, with frequent incursions into the deliberative and the forensic, and subterranean connections with the panegyric. We need not think of the epideictic as the same thing in all these manifestations, or as a one-and-done genre marker; we do not go looking for its DNA. Instead, we examine the layers and territorial inflections that mark such associated figures as amplification, seeing them as sites of exchange where resources for cultivating affect can move between rhetoric and poetry.

The Spaces of *The Anatomy of Melancholy*

This discussion of genre theory has led me far afield from the perennial genre puzzle of Robert Burton's *Anatomy*; it is high time I returned to it, even though identifying a genre can be an old-fashioned project. Identifying the genre of a text has never been interesting to rhetoricians. It has become less interesting for literary critics; contemporary literary genre scholars are more occupied with issues of genre history and theory. In 2011, for example, the editors of the academic journal *Genre* assured readers that they would maintain the journal's "long-standing interest in the conventions and discursive histories of generic forms" but announced a new emphasis on "the intricate relations between genre and its social, institutional, cultural, and political contexts."[50] But Claudio Guillén wrote long ago that the relation between genres and individual texts reminds us of "the virtues, and even the necessity, of studious puzzlement."[51] Perhaps studious puzzling over the *Anatomy* will demonstrate the generative power of a spatial framework for understanding genre.

Is it possible to do a genre analysis of the *Anatomy* by seeing genre as a site of exchange rather than a tool for classification? Burton offers an image of this overlay in the figure of Democritus Junior, whose address to the reader opens the text. Positioning himself as the heir of the laughing philosopher, Democritus Junior organizes the preface as a series of statements about himself, "the Anticke or Personate Actor" (1:1), and about the universal power of melancholy. This section of the book is usually read satirically. The satire ends with Burton's terse announcement, "I will beginne" (1:113). The main text of the book opens, organized in partitions and their subdivisions, offering information about melancholy in the traditions of the treatise or compendium, the book of counsel, and a host of other genres. With a simple performative, the voice of Democritus Junior both initiates the text and vanishes from it. His name does not appear for over a hundred pages, and then only in third person, as one of many ancient authorities. "I will beginne" is the fault line that separates the territory of satire from that of the treatise. Burton has constructed a genre space where the text moved on a tight pivot between genres, where we are invited to consider the relationship between these two forms, to imagine the treatise as spoken by the satirist. And this is not the only place where Burton multiplies genres; in the introduction to his treatment of love melancholy, he promises "boldly to shew myselfe in this common Stage, and in this Trage-comedy of Love, to Act severall parts, some Satyrically, some Comically, some in a mixt Tone" (3:8).

The text Burton produced moves through a range of forms rather than combining them: he identifies the *Anatomy* as satire, as a treatise, as a cento, as a *consolatio*, or as drama, satire, and comedy, but not as a satiricocento or a dramatic treatise. Each genre identification occupies its own space in the text, although the borders of that space are always indefinite and porous. Different possibilities emerge if we read the *Anatomy* in this way, as a multiplied or laminated genre, occupying different positions on the overlaid genre maps of early modern rhetoric and poetics. Or we might see it as a nomadic text that traveled into and out of the territory of the literary, across domains of discourse whose boundaries were, for mid-seventeenth-century writers, blurred and uncertain.

The Anatomy of Melancholy as Epideictic

The Anatomy of Melancholy participates in the rhetorical genre of the epideictic, particularly as it had been expanded by Philipp Melanchthon, a writer frequently quoted by Burton, to include texts intended to teach or inform. The epideictic was also closely associated with medicine through such rituals as the academic orations given regularly to medical faculties. Burton calls on one such "learned Lecture" to support his claim that the minister and the physician "differ but in object, the one of the Body, the other of the Soule, and use divers medicines to cure" (1:22). The academic oration enacted the humanistic affiliations of medical study, confirmed membership in the university, and demonstrated medicine's cohesion and expertise to visitors; orators spoke on epideictic topics such as "In praise of medicine," or "Of the antiquity and dignity of the medical school of Paris."[52] Like other expansions of the epideictic into the deliberative, these speeches also made tacit arguments for particular methods of study. Just as Menander Rhetor's epideictic orator could use a speech welcoming an imperial legate to recommend lenient taxation, the medical orator could engage debates between Galenic and Hippocratic medicine or argue against Paracelsan innovations.[53] Both physicians and scholars from other fields of study gave medical orations. As Nancy Siraisi observed: "Humanists outside the medical profession interested themselves in medicine and controlled a stock of rhetorical commonplaces on the subject."[54]

In an early essay, Angus Gowland argued that the loose definition of the epideictic in early modern rhetoric, its conversational and demonstrative quality, and its concern with ethics, all made it a hospitable genre for Burton.[55] Gowland pointed to the book's subtitle, which speaks of melancholy being "opened and cut up," as evidence of Burton's demonstrative project. But Gowland had little to say about the relationship between the text as epideictic and its other genre identifications, such as encyclopedia, medical treatise, cento, and satire. In his essay, rhetorical and literary genre identifications run on separate tracks, even though Gowland intended to show their relationships. The figure of amplification helps us to connect these two ways of looking at genre.

The text of the *Anatomy* is both ornamented and structured by amplification, the characteristic figure of the epideictic. On every page, Burton multiplies examples, supplies illustrations, and warns of possible exceptions. He delights in piling up synonyms: "many men are as much gauled with a calumny, a scurrill and bitter jest, a libell, a pasquill, Satrye, Apologe, Epigramme, Stage-playes, or the like, as with any mis-fortune whatsoever" (1:337). Here, Burton moved from speech acts (jest) to genres (satyre) to other literary forms (plays), establishing a dizzying route through the textual territories of abuse. Layers of *copia* deepened in successive editions of the *Anatomy*, as Burton added synonyms, qualifiers, and parenthetical examples.

Amplification also functions structurally in the *Anatomy*.[56] Amplification organizes its sentences and paragraphs, develops its arguments, and grounds its affective structure. The divisions of the book evoke partition, amplification's inseparable twin. Again, Erasmus is relevant. In Book 2 of *De copia*, "On Copia of Thought," he suggested that the writer take "something that could be expressed in brief and general terms" and "expand it" by dividing it into parts.[57] Partition was, for Erasmus, a form of display, like the slow uncovering of a precious object. Opening out, gradually displaying what has been hidden, and dividing something into discrete parts are all, as Jonathan Sawday has observed, the central actions of dissection, of anatomizing.[58] Readers first encounter Burton's use of partition in the ramified tables that summarize the book's structure, leading the reader from Partitions to Sections, and then on to Members and Subsections. This pattern promises order: we can always locate a particular theme in the general structure of the book. For some scholars, such as Stanley Fish and Ruth Fox, Burton's repeated divisions are not particularly logical: they found the separate treatment of love melancholy and religious melancholy in the third partition to be arbitrary, and they questioned distinctions such as that between general and particular symptoms of melancholy.[59] Whether or not this argument holds, Burton sometimes treated division as a way of classifying knowledge, and sometimes as a means of amplification, producing discourse that grew itself. The rigorously subdivided headings of partitions, sections, members, and subsections of the *Anatomy* offer both an organizational scheme and a device for generating text, a structural counterpart to the text's wandering prose. It is not wrong to note, with Terence Cave, that the quest for *copia* prompted writing that escaped "limits which formal treatises of rhetoric and dialectic attempt to impose on it," including presumably the limits of genre.[60] But the genre or "kinde" of the epideictic is itself structured as a practice of amplification; it is a genre that will continually exceed its own formal boundaries, searching for a new way to praise or blame, to leverage the confirmation of commonplaces into a new experience, a new sense of communal participation, a new idea.

The connection between amplification and the epideictic is supported by the mobility of *copia*, shifting from praise to blame and back again, as in Erasmus's discussion of changeableness. Following Erasmus's example of ambivalent *copia*, Burton offered contrary views of poverty. In the first partition, he showed that "Poverty and want are generally corsives to all kind of men," and that the poor are generally contemptible and slavish (1:351), but in the Consolatory Digression of the second partition, he observed that "considered aright, [poverty] is a great blessing in it selfe, an happy estate, & yeelds no such cause of discontent" (2:144).

If we see genres as species, then the question of whether the *Anatomy* "is" epideictic, like the other questions raised by the propositions of the text, will yield no stable answer. A spatial approach can take into account the engrossment of the text by the figure of amplification, moving the resources of language between the two domains of rhetoric and poetics, transforming verbal ornament into rhetorical invention and vice versa. Erasmus's tool of invention, the commonplace book, becomes an engine for producing ornamentation. The venerable rhetorical exercise of argument *in utramque partem* becomes a way of cycling through arguments, moving readers from one to the other, harvesting each of them for a distinctive affect without committing to any of them. Rhetorical resources move into the *Anatomy* from academic orations, as if through an underground passage constructed by Melanchthon's pressure on the epideictic as a teaching genre.

Genre Exchange in *The Anatomy of Melancholy*

Each of the proposals for a literary genre identification of the *Anatomy*—cento, satire, anatomy, and so on—can find support in Burton's text or in the practices of his early readers. Since discussing all of them would be exhausting, I will limit this chapter to the cento or collection of quotations, and the medical and scientific treatise, ending with a brief discussion of Menippean satire as a kind of antispecies.

From the perspective of a genre theory based on species, the cento and the treatise could not be more different. The early modern treatise was loosely defined by residual conventions of scholastic disputation and encyclopedic aggregation; the cento was a text assembled from short quotations. As locations for textual exchange, however, the two genres had a great deal in common. Both sponsored textual practices of aggregation and assemblage; in both, a combined text generated new meanings from a series of juxtaposed quotations. Both genres supported jokes, displays of virtuosity, and eruptions of vituperative energy.[61] Burton called the *Anatomy* both "this my treatise" (1:18) and "this cento" (1:11), but he never securely placed his text within either genre. The *Anatomy*, taken as a whole, is neither a treatise, although its affiliation to Melanchthon's didascalic suggests proximity to the genre, nor a cento, although it enacts a poetics of textual adaptation. Burton himself describes the migratory textuality of the *Anatomy*; bits of discourse move from one form to another:

> I neglect phrases, and labour wholly to informe my Readers understanding, not to please his eare; 'tis not my study or intent to compose neatly, which an Orator requires, but to expresse my selfe readily & plainely as it happens. So that as a River runnes sometimes precipitate and swift, then dull and slow; now direct, then *per ambages*; now deepe, then shallow; now muddy, then cleare; now broad, then narrow; doth my stile flow, now serious, then light; now Comicall, then Satyricall; now more elaborate, then remisse, as the present subject required. (1:18)

Like an orator embedding a deliberative passage in an epideictic speech, Burton embedded genres within his text and moved readers in and out of genre frames, mimetically correcting the constantly changing melancholic humor, teasing the sufferer into health. Such a genre structure participates in both rhetorical genres based on situation (the exigency of healing melancholy) and literary genre definitions based on imitation (like melancholy, the text wanders). The *Anatomy* does not mix genres to produce a new hybrid; instead, Burton assembles them to produce a dynamic experience of reading.

The Anatomy of Melancholy as Treatise

When the *Anatomy* was first published in 1621, the treatise was a central academic genre.[62] The *Anatomy* demonstrates the expansion of this form under the pressure of new practices of publication. English treatises from the middle of the sixteenth century took on a variety of topics. Some were encyclopedic: Thomas Smith's *The Common-wealth of England and manner of government thereof. . . . Also, a table added thereto, of all the principall matters contained in this treatise* (1601) described the social and governmental structure of England, including the court system.[63] A treatise could present a doctrinal argument, as did Henry Ainsworth's *The communion of saincts, A treatise of the fellowship that the faithful have with God, and his angels, and one with another, in this present life* (1615).[64] Or it could simply supply information, like Laurence Du Terme's charming *The flovver de luce planted in England. Or a short treatise wherein is contained the true and lively pronuntiation and understanding of the French tongue* (1619).[65] The term *treatise* denoted both slender mathematical texts and rambling encyclopedias. It marked scattered locations in the evolving territory of published texts rather than a lineage of textual descent. Burton knew the related genres for compiling medical information and quoted liberally from them, consulting *consilia, consultationes,* and *observationes.*[66] He followed the practices of university lectures and disputations, organized as commentaries upon texts, and also quoted from natural histories, which combined literary and textual commentary with direct observation; both these forms are near neighbors of the treatise.[67]

Although Burton accepted the constraint of showing melancholy "through all his parts and species" (1:110), he took on that task at the moment when it had become impossible. Whether for this reason, or because he refused the treatise's generic constraint of academic decorum (1:6), he would not securely locate the *Anatomy* as a treatise. The days of the comprehensive treatise were numbered: the publication of printed books was rapidly accelerating, and Burton despaired of keeping up. Some 1500 authors are quoted, with reasonable accuracy, in the text of the *Anatomy.*[68] Such a multiplication of writers, as Elizabeth Eisenstein has noted, leads to contradictory lines of argument: so many authors, Christian and secular, from the ancient and modern worlds, writing on the topic of the melancholy as a disease, state of mind, or affliction of the soul, could not be brought into harmony.[69] For Burton, the multiplication of texts also forecloses the possibility of generic regularity: he will write a treatise; he will "weave the same Web still, twist the same Rope againe and againe" (1:10), but without conviction in anything but the uncontainable multiplication of knowledge. The *Anatomy* did not achieve, or even aspire to, the generic closure proper to the "sober Treatise" (1:6).

During the second half of the seventeenth century, the territory occupied by the natural philosophic treatise would be ceded to the scientific essay, with its relative impersonality, its reliance on witnesses and testimony rather than quotation and compilation, and its focus on experiment and observation.[70] The scientific essay was a genre rooted in collaborative practices of material collection, exchange, and observation rather than in the contentious textuality of the treatise.[71] If we were guided by an evolutionary account of genre history, we might search the *Anatomy* for precursors of the scientific essay. Such a search would be fruitless: the observation-based essay in the *Proceedings of the Royal Society*, whatever its affinities with an earlier wonders-and-marvels practice of scientific writing, still followed a program deeply at odds with the textual interests of the *Anatomy*. We would be better off searching for cognates among the academic oration described above, epideictic speeches in Latin given at academic ceremonies, especially associated with the study of medicine. Both Melanchthon and Erasmus wrote such orations, expressions of the humanistic and textual investments of early modern medicine.[72]

To read Burton's *Anatomy* as a treatise is to encounter the limits of the compendium: the range of sources and the positions they advocate cannot be contained. The logic of comprehensive expansion blurs the observational clarity of the case studies that Burton includes as examples of symptoms or treatments. The book resembles the academic oration in its epideictic force, textual focus, and strategies of tacit argument but extravagantly exceeds the boundaries of that form. An evolutionary diagram that began with the compendium and ended with the scientific essay would have no place for the *Anatomy* to rest its head.

If we read the genre relations of the *Anatomy* spatially rather than seeing them as a struggle for the survival among species, the text emerges as a cunningly woven web rather than an evolutionary dead end: it laminates the practices of knowledge developed in the treatise with the practices of membership characteristic of the academic epideictic oration—practices that would soon be discarded in favor of personal relationships among trusted correspondents. It also integrates conventions for reporting observations and making arguments based on them that would characterize the new sciences. The *Anatomy* is not a flawed anticipation of the scientific essay, but a brilliant renovation of textual practices of comprehensive collection and commentary. It is all the more brilliant in the face of Burton's struggle with the flood of new books brought out by "*Franc-furt* Marts, [and] Domesticke Marts. . . . We are oppressed with them, our eyes ake with reading, our fingers with turning" (1:10–11).

The Anatomy of Melancholy as Cento

The Anatomy of Melancholy can also be read as a cento. Burton's assignment of the *Anatomy* to this genre is offhand, even defensive. After complaining against the flood of new books—the very issue that forecloses the possibility of a comprehensive treatise—he protests that he has not added to the glut, since "I have laboriously collected this *Cento* out of divers Writers, and that *sine injuriâ*, I have wronged no Authors, but given every man his owne. . . . I cite & quote mine authors" (1:11).

Cento can denote both a poem created from cleverly joined fragments of a classic text and a method of composition based on the compilation of authoritative quotations.[73] In antiquity, the cento brought together lines or half lines from a central author, typically Homer or Virgil, that generated a new poem.[74] Cento poetry—mythological, secular, or religious—remained popular during the middle ages, and its production was revived in humanist circles.[75] Late in the sixteenth century, Justus Lipsius characterized his *Politica* (1589) as a prose cento, claiming to have invented the genre.[76] The *Politica*, a neo-Stoic treatise that advocated absolute monarchy in a text composed of quotations from the ancients, was a possible, if infrequently quoted, source for Burton and suggested a model for the prose cento that combined play and serious purpose. All these authors would have been pleased to know that the cento form has flourished in the twentieth century, both in John Ashbery's "The Dong with the Luminous Nose" and as a classroom exercise to ease reluctant students into writing poetry.[77]

The hardy cento has occupied varied positions in the genre hierarchy. In the fourth century, Ausonius's preface to his *Nuptial Cento* consigned it to the realm of amusements, but it also offered a careful account of the difficulties of joining half lines.[78] These two valuations of the cento—as minor amusement and as virtuoso demonstration of skill—emerge and reemerge, and both are evident in Burton.

The cento, as Hugo Tucker has pointed out, is necessarily a multivoiced text, including both the original force of the quotations and their sense in the writer's compilation.[79] For Burton, the cento was a response to the flood of books—it was not writing at all, but the quite different labor of collection. At the same time, Burton's insistence that he will "cite & quote mine authors" locates his text at the intersection of the territories of the treatise, a technical scholarly production, and the "serious" cento, with its own virtuoso practices of quotation. We can see the cento and the treatise, then, as overlaid territories: the *Anatomy* participates in both the cento's play of references and the treatise's attempt to include all relevant authors.

Burton's purpose was not to join together quotations seamlessly, or to borrow their authority, but to animate multiple voices in the text. In reply to critics who might consider the *Anatomy* too satirical for a minister, he says, "I will presume to answer with *Erasmus*, in like case, 'tis not I, but *Democritus, Democritus dixit*: you must consider what it is to speak in ones owne or anothers person, an assumed habit and name . . . it is a *Cento* collected from others, not I, but they say it" (1:110). Like the mask of Democritus in the introduction to the *Anatomy*, the conventions of the cento provide Burton with a displaced speaking voice, as well as a safe-conduct into the territory of satire. Burton's method of handling genre issues is more significant than any of the genre identifications he advanced. *Because* his book is a cento, it is also a drama and a satire (and later, perhaps a consolation and a comedy, too). Burton did not maintain that his text has no genre: he demonstrated that it participated in many genres. He was not at all restricted by identifying the genres that he used: he referred explicitly to conventions of the cento, the treatise, the drama, the satire; he drew on the capacities of the epideictic; he wanted to mobilize the resources of genre assignment to direct readers to different capacities of the text. These genre assignments can be read as intersecting layers: the liberty of the satire opens out the technical restrictions of the cento; the scholarly rigor of the treatise tempers the affective power of epideictic amplification. If we were to define the literary genre of *The Anatomy of Melancholy* using the terministic screen of species, we might arrive at the useless conclusion that it is a "prose cento," and therefore a member of a genre that includes, as far as I can determine, only two texts, Burton's and Lipsius's. If we see it as mapping out multiple genres, the *Anatomy* then becomes a broad and layered territory that draws upon readers' expectations, prompting a range of rhetorical responses.

The Anatomy of Melancholy and Menippean Satire

Menippean satire is a limit case for the understanding of genres. Emerging and reemerging in quite different forms (prose, mixed prose and verse, drama), the Menippean satire cannot be stabilized within the metaphoric framework of genres as species.[80] Its identifying marks—scurrilous language, learned references, formal discontinuity, abuse—can be found embedded in other genres, just as the deliberative can be embedded in the epideictic. These earmarks of the Menippean shift into attributes of characters; they structure individual speeches in comedies or tragedies.[81] Frye, therefore, spoke of Burton integrating Menippean elements into the *Anatomy* rather than of the *Anatomy* as a Menippean satire.[82] And Edward Milowicki and Rawdon Wilson, theorists of the Menippean, follow Bakhtin in referring to it as a discourse rather than a genre.[83] Such a migration is a scandal if traits and genres are bound together in a tight Darwinian package: then, the Menippean becomes a kind of genre kryptonite, annulling the concept's power to categorize and group. In a spatial conception of genre, the Menippean is far less anomalous; it marks a point of exchange between prose and verse, between learned and popular writing; between textual structures and local features. The Menippean, in this view, becomes one of the many genre exchanges that the *Anatomy* effects, and no more the answer to the genre riddles set by the *Anatomy* than the cento or the treatise; it is one resource at the reader's disposal, one layer in the sedimented and pocketed structure of Burton's book.

The Genre Travels of *The Anatomy of Melancholy*

If genre were a matter of species classification, then identifying the literary genre of *The Anatomy of Melancholy* would be an absurd exercise. But remembering Carolyn Miller's definition of genres as "typified rhetorical actions based in recurring situations," or Anis Bawarshi's remark that genres are "forms of cultural knowledge that conceptually frame and mediate how we understand and typically act within various situations," we can see genres as supporting the exchange of discursive resources among fields of study.[84] The *Anatomy* then becomes a layered territory that draws upon and shapes readers' expectations. It is not a text without genre; it is a text of multiple overlaid genres, a text about genres.

Some might read the *Anatomy* as a hybrid genre, a concept ubiquitous in avant-garde poetry, film theory, and studies of popular culture. (See, for example, Christine Hume's playful card game.[85]) In fact, the idea of a hybrid genre is striking evidence of the strength of species models of genre: a hybrid text is seen as a descendent of two "parent" genres: the prose poem, the horror comedy. The genre hybrid, like the horticultural hybrid, is expected to be showy and vigorous. Although the term "hybrid genre" is associated with innovation and experimentation, it quite conservatively assumes that genres are essentially tools for classification. (The notion of the genre hybrid seldom appears in rhetorical genre theory, which has always assumed that genres can be nested or embedded.) The *Anatomy* is epideictic in organization and purpose; it recalls Melanchthon's expansion of the epideictic into a pedagogical genre. In its intertextual relationships and in its institutional setting, the *Anatomy* is a treatise; in its reflexive acknowledgement that comprehensive compilation is impossible, it becomes satiric. Readers are invited to place the *Anatomy* in other genres—the cento, comedy—when their features are foregrounded. These are not relations of hybridity, but of intrusion, expulsion, or layering. Jacques Derrida's "The Law of Genre" reads like a sober account of the *Anatomy*: "It is precisely a principle of contamination, a law of impurity, a parasitical economy . . . [,] a sort of participation without belonging—a taking part in without being part of, without having membership in a set. The trait that marks membership inevitably divides, the boundary of the set comes to form, by invagination, an internal pocket larger than the whole; and the outcome of this division and of this abounding remains as singular as it is limitless."[86]

By participating in a genre, the text marks itself as a made object occupying a position—quite possibly a temporary position—rather than exemplifying a class. The performance of genre membership opens space for reflection on genres as practices of knowledge, on textuality, on words as written marks rather than frictionless highways, a readerly reflection that potentially overwrites the overt content of the text.

The *Anatomy* is littered with multiple and contradictory marks of genre. Some, such as the epideictic commitment to amplification, are tacit and structural. Others are overt and local, as Burton invokes such genres as the cento, the satire, the treatise. Each of these marks moves the reader from the world of melancholy—a world of humors and affects—to a world of words and forms. Burton's multiple genres are sometimes nested, sometimes congruent to each other (a utopia is also a satire) or budded off from each other (deliberative advice to choose healthy air prompts an epideictic digression on the beauty and power of air). The genre markings of the *Anatomy* move us from books to bodies and then back to books. Like Democritus moving between his anatomy books and anatomized carcasses (1:6), each shift invites us to immerse ourselves in a different experience of textuality. Nothing in our work with either texts or bodies will bring us to that "seat" of melancholy that Democritus was after, or to a stable genre designation for the text; the amusement of chasing those nubs of the real will drive us through the many partitions and subdivisions of the *Anatomy*.

The *Anatomy* also constructs exchanges between rhetorical and literary genres. If rhetorical genre theories begin with audiences, exigencies, and arguments, they very quickly move to issues of form: we see the epideictic, and we look for amplification. To read the *Anatomy* as epideictic brings us into conversation with early modern genre theorists struggling to account for new discursive practices within the Aristotelian canon; it leads us to amplification as *topos*, figure, and structural principle; it raises questions of affect and will. Issues native to literary genre theory become salient to rhetorical analysis and vice versa. My investigation of the literary genre of the *Anatomy* began with definitions of formal qualities of the text, but that issue gave way to reflection about the intention of its genre experiments and variations. And with the issue of purpose, the whole conceptual apparatus of rhetoric re-emerges into our reading, creating an "invagination . . . larger than the whole."[87] Or it would be larger if anything could be bigger than the *Anatomy*, which so sprawlingly contains both itself and all its possible speculative readings.

3

The Anatomy of Melancholy and Early Modern Medicine

Among the books Robert Burton bequeathed to the Christ Church library was a modest medical volume, Prosperus Calanius's *Paraphrasis in librum Galeni de inaequali intemperie*, published in London in 1538.[1] This slender octavo offers a version of book 3 of Galen's *On the Temperaments*; it was not an important book for Burton, who left scattered pencil lines and checkmarks in its margins and referred to it a handful of times in the *Anatomy*. But on the title page Burton carefully wrote in ink, "Antidotum vitae sapientia: odi, nec possu[m], cupiens, non esse, quod odi sapientia odi, nec possu[m], cupiens, non esse, quodi odi."[2] Burton had adapted a line from Ovid's *Amores*: *odi, nec possum, cupiens, non esse quod odi*, or in Showerman's serviceable translation, "I hate what I am, and yet, for all my desiring, I cannot be but what I hate."[3] The first part of Burton's inscription translates as "The antidote of life is knowledge"; this proverb is usually given as "*antidotum vitae, patientia est*." The second part, the line from Ovid, echoes Paul's lament in Romans 7:15: "For what I will to do, that I do not practice; but what I hate, that I do."[4] Burton was fond of Ovid's tag, inscribing it again in his copy of Quintus Rufus Curtius's *De rebus gestis Alexandri Magni* and quoting it in the *Anatomy* (1:161).[5] The quotation from Ovid is at odds with the first part of his inscription in Calanius, which asserts that wisdom, including knowledge of specific subjects, is the antidote to the cares of life: Burton might have been lamenting his inability to use the remedy of knowledge, or he might have been complaining of the tedium of these undistinguished texts. Even though the meaning of Burton's inscription is obscure, its distribution is eloquent. For Burton, Ovid was a perfectly appropriate response to either a medical text or a book of history. The capacious web of *sapientiae* included medicine, the good letters of antiquity, and the doctrines of natural philosophy. In Burton's world, Calanius's discussion of windy melancholy sat easily beside Ovid's neat dactylic hexameter. What ecology of knowledge supported this commerce? What niche in that ecology did *The Anatomy of Melancholy* occupy? In particular, what role did medicine play in Burton's practices of knowledge?

The *Anatomy* is balanced among traditional scholastic forms of learning, early modern humanist practices of knowledge, and the scientific ways of knowing that would emerge a few decades after Burton's death in 1640. These discourses informed a range of disciplines, from divinity to medicine. The *Anatomy* speaks of a world that knew disciplines and professions, that saw battles among them for position and hierarchy. It also speaks of a world where disciplines were not fully differentiated and professional boundaries could be transgressed.[6] In this world, science meant a stable, reliable form of knowledge, proceeding deductively, in good Aristotelian fashion, to study universal phenomena. But while there were natural philosophers, and astronomers, and certainly physicians, the boundaries among them, as we have seen in previous chapters, were quite porous. Medical texts were open books to a humanist scholar, and Robert Burton made full use of them in the *Anatomy*.

Burton's interest in medicine is well documented, but critics have generally seen his use of medicine as a means to some more general end—moral instruction, perhaps, or religious counsel. Angus Gowland, in his careful analysis of medicine in the *Anatomy*, characterizes it as "a treatise that absorbed medical learning into a humanist philosophical enterprise."[7] More recently, Mary Ann Lund, after systematically describing Burton's use of medical authorities, concludes that the medical sections of the *Anatomy* are finally subordinated to a practice of "literary therapeutics," a curative practice based on reading.[8] I do not argue that Burton was really writing medicine, or that medicine was more important to him than divinity; I do claim that in Burton's world of unstable disciplinary boundaries, to identify the *Anatomy* with a central area of study is to read a text less mobile and less interesting than the one Burton wrote. As discussed in chapter 1, it is difficult to think past contemporary divisions among disciplines that condition our own practices of reading. But the *Anatomy* invites us to dismantle some of those practices, to find in its pages potential analogs to transdisciplinary practices that could be useful; these are gifts of the text.[9] We can read the *Anatomy* as a negotiation of knowledge practices that had not differentiated, exploiting their mobility in its content, structure, and organization. Burton moved the many forms of knowledge available to him into relationships that open lines of reciprocal influence. He quoted, cheek by jowl, theologians, physicians, and writers of antiquity. Burton's use of medicine demonstrates how he negotiated the particular practices of one kind of early modern specialized knowledge; similar studies could surely be done on his use of history or divinity.

After offering a general background to early modern medicine, I will organize this chapter in four parts, beginning with the medical case histories that stud the *Anatomy*. These narratives raise questions about the relative values of experience and deductive knowledge. Burton collected and presented them to heighten their probative force, using narrative forms distinct from those he favored for historical or literary narratives. The second part of this investigation concerns regimen, the multiplied and contradictory advice for daily conduct that was the stock-in-trade of Galenic physicians. Like the case history, the regimen raises questions about the reliability of knowledge practices based on experience; these questions are related to the central rhetorical concept of exigency. How should the reader make decisions on uncertain questions, based on partial knowledge? Then, yielding to the contagion of the *Anatomy*, I digress to consider the narrative construction of time in the regimen and suggest that it was a model for the complex temporal structure of Burton's text. Finally, I consider the concept of *spirit*, central to both early modern medicine and Reformation theology; spirit mediated the relations among parts of the body, between the body and the external world, and between body and mind. It was an important topic in both medicine and divinity, and Burton made use of both these literatures to construct spirit as a way of moving among disparate objects and methods. These four movements will perhaps give us a firmer grasp on what Burton meant when he set himself the task of anatomizing melancholy "and that philosophically, medicinally" (1:110), as if the connection between these two practices of knowledge could be negotiated with a bare comma.

Early Modern Medicine

The medical workforce in sixteenth- and seventeenth-century England was large and diverse, ranging from academic physicians steeped in medical humanism through regular practitioners, physicians touting the new Paracelsan or Helmontian medicines, to surgeons, bonesetters, apothecaries, midwives, and wise women. All of these characters populate the pages of the *Anatomy*, but in this chapter, I will pay particular attention to academic physicians and the texts they produced.

As a university subject, medicine was logically subordinate to natural philosophy, which studied things in themselves, using demonstrative logic to derive conclusions that were necessarily and universally true. But the medical degree, like those in divinity and law, was an advanced, prestigious credential. As we saw in chapter 1, natural philosophy dealt with issues such as form, matter, and sub- stance, and generated the *praecognita*, or foundational principles, of medicine: the elements, the temperaments, the humors. Since nature was seen as a direct expression of, and gift from, God, the natural philosopher dealt with ideas far removed from the everyday exigencies of illness, care, and cure. The physician, on the other hand, was deeply immersed in temporality: he deployed his knowl- edge of nature to address the issues of a particular suffering body, located in time and space, rather than considering an abstracted universalized body. His conclusions were notoriously uncertain, and what worked in one case might not in another. Despite this uncertainty, physicians' knowledge was deeply neces- sary. Early modern physicians lived with the dissonance between intellectual uncertainty and social necessity.[10]

Early modern medicine included a wide range of knowledges and practices: central among them, for Burton, was medical humanism, which relied on medical texts from Greek and Roman antiquity, commentary on those texts by scholars of the Arab world and European scholastics, the writing of "neo- teric" early modern physicians, and on a dense record of observations compiled from skilled contemporary medical practitioners. Medical humanist literature included works we might classify as philosophy, like Aristotle's *De anima* and the rich line of commentaries on that text, medieval and renaissance, European and Arabic, Catholic and Protestant.[11] It included the orations in praise of medi- cine written and delivered by Philipp Melanchthon, the many works attributed to Galen, the thirteenth-century Salerno *Breviary on the Kinds, Causes, and Cures of Diseases*, Avicenna's *Canon of Medicine*, Vesalius's *De humani corporis fabrica*, and the pseudo-Aristotelian *Problemata*. Medical texts became widely available by the end of the sixteenth century; they came in all shapes and sizes, from sumptuous folios to tiny handbooks intended for practicing physicians. Ancient writers jostled against moderns; observations were textualized and texts mined for cases that could be written up as observations. Reading ancient texts was not, in the seventeenth century, a pious exercise. Both of the central practices of early modern medicine, textual commentary and observation, originated in antiquity, with the physicians of Greece and Rome and the commentaries on them, and in the models of observation and case history they afforded. An early modern physician found models of observation in the Hippocratic *Epidemics* and the commentary on that text attributed to Galen. New editions of Hippocrates,

Dioscorides, and Galen were published, translated directly from Greek texts and making the ancient writers newly available. Important texts were recovered, including works attributed to Galen. Aulus Cornelius Celsus's *De medicina*, the only surviving volume of a much larger encyclopedia, was discovered in the Vatican Library in 1480 and widely published throughout Europe. Because of humanism's philological investments, textual commentary became a transformative practice; it fostered observational reports that networks of collectors and savants developed and disseminated. Translations and commentaries on the works of antiquity circulated among literate medical practitioners and laymen, as did works on surgery, pharmacy, and anatomy.[12]

The formation of early modern physicians reflected the importance of textual production and commentary to medical education. University-trained physicians, a small but prestigious minority, began with the arts course, and specific medical disciplines were rooted in the conceptual framework of natural philosophy.[13] While medicine was certainly recognized as a distinct domain of knowledge—catalogues of the Frankfurt Book Fair placed medical books in a separate section—it was not unusual for a medical text to veer into such topics as physiognomy, astrology, natural history, and travel literature. Since the body was seen as a metaphor for the state, writing on medicine also had potential political implications. Few publishing physicians confined themselves to medicine: most also wrote on other topics, including religious controversy, history, poetry, and philology.[14]

Medicine, then, like other early modern disciplines, was both a distinctive territory and a busy point of exchange. As one of the three recognized professions, it trained practitioners in a discrete body of knowledge about bodies and their vicissitudes. But the physician was also expected to know some astrology, a field that was still undifferentiated from astronomy, to identify and prepare simples, and to offer prudential advice. Many physicians were therefore active in the emerging science of botany and acted as moral or religious counselors. A physician had a relatively stable social identity but was not limited to a single field of knowledge.

Robert Burton's own library included a range of medical texts, from the works of the philologist and physician Hieronymus Mercurialis, nicely printed in Frankfurt and Basel, to a cheap handbook of simples, Ingolstadt's *Synonyma plantarum, seu simplicium ut vocant*, described as being bound in "dated waste paper."[15] Most of the physicians that Burton read and quoted, either from his own books or from other sources, are firmly located within the academic traditions of medical humanism—Giovanni Battista Da Monte, Jean Fernel, Antonio Brassavola, Prosper Calanius, Joannes Crato, Nicholas Piso, Gianbattista della Porta, and Andreas Laurentius. Burton would have been trained in the textual disciplines of the arts curriculum; as librarian of Christ Church, he was responsible for collecting books for all fields of study, including natural philosophy. An ordained minister, he was aware of the intense doctrinal debates of the early seventeenth century, and of their focus on the analysis of scriptural texts. An avid practicing astrologer, Burton often quoted from Marsilio Ficino's *De vita libri tres*, a treatise that connected Neoplatonist astrology with occult remedies. His own astrological practice, judging from his notes, was focused on the more mundane practices of judicial astrology, including casting horoscopes.[16] He treasured his surveying instruments, expressions of the impetus to put mathematical and astronomical observations to practical use.[17] Burton was therefore well versed in the practices of textual analysis and commentary that medical humanism shared with the arts curriculum, and also conversant with the revived disciplines of observation.

Nonetheless, Burton felt that his forays into medicine required some defense. In the introductory chapter of the *Anatomy*, "Democritus to the Reader," Burton takes up the question of why he, as a student of divinity, wrote on the "Medicinall subject" of melancholy (1:21). He offers several reasons: the urgency of his own melancholic condition, which had diverted him from divinity to this "by-streame, which as a Rillet is deducted from the maine Channell of my studies" (1:20); the folly of adding another treatise to the flood of religious discourses; and finally, the imbrication of body and soul in melancholy, a "compound mixt Malady" (1:23) that left the melancholic in "as much need of Spirituall as Corporall cure" (1:22). Melancholy was therefore not an "unbeseeming" topic for Burton, who declared himself "by my profession a Divine, and by mine inclination a Physitian" (1:23).

The *Anatomy* investigates melancholy as profoundly "mixt." In the opening of the *Anatomy* proper, Burton held that the first cause of melancholy is sin: sin leads us to "degenerate into beasts, transforme our selves, overthrowe our constitutions, provoke God to Anger, and heap upon us this of *Melancholy*, and all kindes of incurable diseases" (1:128). Melancholy can also be caused by fear and sorrow, which overtake the wisest. It is experienced as a material darkness of the brain that makes everything appear terrible, so that "the *minde* it selfe, by those darke obscure, grosse fumes, ascending from black humours, is in continuall darknesse, feare & sorrow" (1:418–19). This movement from interior to exterior and from body to mind, as we shall see, is mediated by the concept of spirit. The "naturall and inward causes" of melancholy, the darkness of burnt humors, work on the mind (1:418), but the vectors could also be reversed, since the melancholic's "avoiding of light" darkens his own humors (1:420). What is material becomes metaphorical without losing its material efficacy; fear, sorrow, and darkness all interact with each other.

Even this reciprocal movement is simpler than the relationships that Burton usually constructed, which moved from bodily humors to the passions of the mind, and from philosophical to political treatments of the passions. In his discussion of sorrow as a cause of melancholy, Burton began by quoting Hippocrates—but as the source of a metaphor naming sorrow as both the mother and daughter of melancholy, since "they beget one another and tread in a ring" (1:256). Burton's other authorities include the neo-Galenic physician Felix Platter and the church father John Chrysostom; the text swerves to the eagle that gnawed Prometheus, leading to quotations from the Bible and the customs of republican Rome. Fernel's account of the physiology of sorrow leads to a lament from the Psalms. And so it goes, through medical case studies and the monitory figures of Hecuba and Niobe, to a final quotation from Melanchthon on the relation between melancholy blood and the spirits. It is not as if Burton found a variety of distinct ways of thinking about sorrow and combined them, pulling them from their proper pigeonholes. The disciplines were already mixed: physicians offered metaphors; theologians discussed anatomy. Burton nests and embeds disciplines that were already nested and embedded. Explaining how melancholy encourages poetry, Burton finds a niche for humane letters in medicine; showing how the melancholy humor can become the "devil's bath," Burton embeds medicine in religion (4:191; 1:193). Such a plastic and malleable relationship among disciplines is entirely coherent with the structure of early modern "sciences of the soul," which were usually staged as commentaries or expansions of Aristotle's *De anima*; for Burton, the most significant of these was by Philipp Melanchthon, who will be discussed more fully below.[18] Since, in Aristotelian terms, the informing soul was intimately connected to the substance of the body, the *scientiae de anima* included elements of both metaphysics and natural philosophy, moving from anatomy to studies of perception and affect. Burton demonstrates how fluid that movement could be in his use of medical cases. He showed that a distinctive practice of quotation could connect rhetorical uses of *exempla* to the emerging practices of observation in medicine.

Cases, *Consilia, Observationes,* and Observation

Early modern medical writing was rich in narrative, in stories of individual patients, of illnesses and their treatments. Learned physicians and many of their practicing counterparts produced hundreds of these case studies in various genres. (Here, it is useful to keep the spatial metaphors for genre proposed in chapter 2 in mind.) *Consilia* were produced as advice to individual patients, who commonly consulted their physicians by letter; physicians replied, often at length. Physicians would exchange and forward these letters, and the *consilia* of well-known physicians were collected and published. Physicians also wrote accounts of their cases for both medical readers and the general public. Such *observationes* were especially common after the fifteenth-century publication of the Hippocratic *Epidemics.* (Hippocrates's title refers not to a mass outbreak of disease but to an illness "of the people," or perhaps "visitations" of the patient by the disease or the physician.) These accounts, emerging from the earlier *consilia* tradition late in the Renaissance, treated the details of the individual case as primary and the textual history surrounding it as secondary. In Gianna Pomata's account, *observationes* developed from an earlier medieval genre, the collection of cures, which joined recipes for medicines to very brief histories of the illnesses for which they had been used.[19] Collections of cures advertised the successes of prominent physicians; *observationes* focused instead on the natural history of the disease. The *observatio* foregrounds the history of a case that may or may not have ended in a cure, and it varies in length from a few lines to an extended account of an illness.

Both the *consilium* and the *observatio* drew on the conventions of early modern natural history, which combined anatomic and ethological information about animals and plants with myths, fables, proverbs, and etymology.[20] All these forms are examples of what Gianna Pomata has called *epistemic genres,* that is, genres that develop along with scientific practices and are oriented to the production of knowledge—for example, the essay, the recipe, the textbook, the encyclopedia. (We might think of these topics and forms as adjacent or connected territories in the vast geography of genre.) Pomata defines the particular exigency of the case: cases emerge when the decision-making rules of a practice of knowledge are no longer inadequate to address changing situations.[21] We might think of how Jesuit casuistry developed to support Roman Catholic confessors during the Reformation. Cases can excite popular interest: Jesuit sermons on casuistry drew large crowds.[22] They are closely connected to two other forms: the recipe, which in medical cases often appears in the description of the cure, and the commentary, which elaborates or adapts a received code. We could see this genre as a sprawling territory, connected to other textual forms oriented to exigency, adjacent to still other forms that organized broad practices of knowledge.

Cases are well represented in the medical books Burton owned. Many of the 131 identified by Kiessling included medical stories, either as freestanding collections or as inset examples in more discursive texts about illness.[23] These stories could be incorporated into the text of the *Anatomy* along with narratives drawn from the literature of Greek and Roman antiquity, from ancient or modern history, or from common report. Here are a few examples from Burton's discussion of the cures of melancholy, the first drawn from Franciscus Valleriola's *Observationum medicinalium lib. VI* (1588); the second from Salustius Salvianus's *Variarum lectionum de re medica libri tres* (1588); the third from Johannes Schenck's *Paratēr-ēseōn sive observationum medicarum, rararum, novarum, admirabilium et monstrosarum* (1609). Burton owned the first two books.

> I remember in *Valleriolas* observations, a story of one *John Baptist* a *Nea-politan*, that finding by chance a pamphlet in *Italian*, written in Praise of Hellebor, would needs adventure on himselfe, and tooke one dram for one scruple: and had not he beene sent for, the poore fellowe had poysoned himself. (2:17)

> *Salust. Salvianus de re med. lib. 2.cap.1. I saw . . . a melancholy man at Rome, that by no remedies could be healed, but when by chance he was wounded in the head, and the scull broken, he was excellently cured.* (2:245–46)

> *Schenkius observat. med. lib.1.* speaks of a waiting Gentlewoman in the Duke of *Savoyes* Court, that was so much offended with it [unwanted blushing], that she kneeled downe to him and offered *Bayrus* a Physitian, all that she had to be cured of it. (2:257)

These cases are typical of Burton's medical stories: they are assigned to a specific author, text, and setting; whether they are vivid or schematic, they present compressed narratives, generally but not always featuring an unnamed patient. Two things happen in these stories: the onset of an infirmity, and some kind of cure event: the search for a cure, the impossibility of a cure, the ingenious cure, or the accidental cure, to name a few variations.

As medicine changed during the seventeenth century, so did the issues presented in the individual case. Some of these changes challenged the hegemonic neo-Galenic paradigm on behalf of Helmontians and other chemically oriented physicians; others expressed a renewed interest in Hippocrates.[24] Other changes resulted from a new distribution of medical knowledge. For Galenic medicine, each illness expressed an imbalance in the individual, and so, ideally, would be treated in a distinctive way, with due attention not only to the patient's temperament, but to the season, location, and weather. Widely distributed medical books delegated such adaptations to the reader, who might be a physician or a patient. As direct observation became more important to medical learning by the beginning of the seventeenth century, collections of *observationes* became collaborative documents: Johann Schenck's *Paratēreseōn* collected cases from hundreds of writers, including Schenck's seventy-one correspondents.[25] Seventeenth-century *observationes* organized collective practices of observing and sharing clinical data; practices similar to the reading and writing of *observationes* were central to the development of disciplines of observation that would become cornerstones of the new sciences.[26] *Observationes* are not simply evolutionary descendants of *consilia*, since a text could move easily from one form to another. Rather, the early modern case is a territory occupied by both genres, holding ground adjacent to astronomical and geographical observations.

For Burton, the Galenic model was still in force, complicated, as Mary Ann Lund has demonstrated, by his situation as a writer for publication: he was not addressing an individual patient, but many unknown readers.[27] As an academic writer, he faced a quandary: how could medicine, which dealt with so many variables in patients and their circumstances, rise to the certainty that was the hallmark of an Aristotelian science? While practicing physicians implemented the rules of their art with confidence, academic writers who worked with medical materials, including Burton, sought to negotiate the status of medical observations closer to that of a settled fact.[28] The medical case, a typified story of an individual patient, raised a basic question about the creation of knowledge: how could such an individual experience support a universal claim?[29] Or, in another version, how could the observational practices of physicians generate knowledge as secure as that of natural philosophy? This issue led Aristotle to categorize medicine as an art rather than a science. Burton himself sometimes held that it was "no art at all" (2:209). Along with most early modern academic physicians, Burton did not accept Francis Bacon's argument that *experientia literata*, or learned experience, the comparison and collating of individual cases, could rise to the level of a science. But for academic physicians and for Burton, Aristotle offered a path connecting observation to knowledge.[30]

That path was long. As Lorraine Daston has shown, observation was never a simple, passive activity; scientific observation is a practice of communities and requires long training in attention and pattern recognition. Burton had access to botanical collections and anatomies that deployed detailed observation, but given his own training in traditional Aristotelian epistemologies, he probably understood the practice in terms quite different from those that would emerge in the new sciences.[31] In the world of academic study that Burton inhabited, sciences were sources of stable and certain knowledge; they worked by drawing conclusions from initial propositions that were, in the best case, intuitively self-evident. Natural philosophy, as we have seen, was such a science; medicine was not. But Aristotle also held that when such propositions are unavailable, science works with principles "determined as occurring either always or for the most part"; illustrating his point with a medical example: "honey-water is useful for a patient in a fever is true for the most part."[32] In medicine, where axiomatic transparency could not be achieved, the best course was to reason from what everyone observed to happen most of the time, which is to say from perceptions that moved into memory and constituted experience, as Aristotle had demonstrated in the *Posterior Analytics*. Peter Dear has shown that textual representations of what occurs "always or for the most part" were generally thin and unspecific: they did not include dates, names of observers, specific descriptions of the apparatus, or precise measurements. Galileo, for example, described his experiments loosely as having been repeated "often," or "hundreds of times."[33] While later scientific experiments would be confirmed by the presence of named, respectable witnesses and recounted in great detail, other strategies rendered these earlier cases credible.[34]

Burton's Cases

How did the cases that Burton included in the *Anatomy* negotiate these issues? Burton seems to have adapted the abstract rhetorical scheme that Dear describes for his accounts of medical cases, writing as if those illnesses typified the general course of things, so that there was no need to give elaborate details. Normally a prolix and very concrete writer, Burton, as we have seen, omitted striking details from his medical cases, compressing and combining them.[35] For example, Burton referred to a case from the *Practica* of Antonius Guainerius (fl. 1412–45) in discussing the dangers of long watching. Guainerius writes of two Germans who drank a lot of wine and within a month became melancholy. One German sang hymns, and the other sighed. After prayers were said to St. Bernard for their cure, the statue of the saint shamed the melancholics by pointing its finger at them.[36] This is a good story, one that Guainerius tells at length. But here is how Burton uses it: "*Guianerius Tract. 15 cap.* 2 tells a story of two Duchmen, to whom he gave entertainement in his house, *that in one months space were both melancholy by drinking of wine,* one did naught but sing, the other sighe" (1:218; Burton's spelling). No prayers, no shaming, no statue, no pointing.

Even more striking is Burton's use of a case from the *Discours de la mélancholie* of André Du Laurens (1558–1609, cited as Laurentius), a story he could have read in the English translation by Richard Surphlet.[37] Here is Laurens's story of a Sienese melancholic:

> The pleasantest dotage that ever I read, was of one Sienois a Gentleman, who had resolved with himself not to pisse, but to dye rather, and that because he imagined, that when he first pissed, all his towne would be drowned. The Phisitions shewing him, that all his bodie, and ten thousand more such as his, were not able to containe so much as might drowne the least house in the towne, could not change his minde from this foolish imagination. In the end they seeing his obstinacie, and in what danger he put his life, found out a pleasant invention. They caused the next house to be set on fire, & all the bells in the town to ring, they perswaded diverse servants to crie, to the fire, to the fire, & therewithall send of those of the best account in the town, to crave helpe, and shew the Gentleman that there is but one way to save the towne, and that it was, that he should pisse quickelie and quench the fire. Then this sillie melancholike man which abstained from pissing for feare of loosing his towne, taking it for graunted, that it was now in great hazard, pissed and emptied his bladder of all that was in it, and was himselfe by that meanes preserved.[38]

This story, worthy of Rabelais, was the fifteenth and last in Laurens's collection of melancholy cases; here is how Burton used it:

> The pleasantest dotage that ever I read, saith *Laurentius*, was of a Gentle-
> man at *Senes* in *Italy*, who was afraid to pisse, least all the towne should be
> drowned, the Physitians caused the bells to be rung backward, and told
> him the towne was on fire, whereupon he made water, and was immedi-
> atly cured. (2:112; see an even briefer reference at 1:399)

Burton clearly wrote with Surphlet's translation of Laurens in front of him and
followed him exactly for a few words, but the vivid, amusing details of Laurens's
account are radically compressed: we read only of the onset of the delusional
illness and the cure event of the feigned fire, with no arguments, no shouting
servants, no begging gentlemen.

At times, Burton briefly referenced or indexed cases rather than narrating
them: "*Mercurialis consil. 110.* gives instance in a young man his patient, sanguine
melancholy, *of a great wit, and excellently learned*" (1:400) or "*Laurentius cap. 7.*
hath many stories of such as have thought themselves bewitched by their enemies;
and some that would eate no meat as being dead" (1:401). Often, Burton offered
medical cases in batches, multiplying short examples and salting them down with
brief quotations from antiquity.

Although *consilia* often expressed the physician's care for the patient, Burton
abstracts them from this relationship. In his discussion of regimen, he quoted
extensively from Crato of Krafftheim's letter to a melancholy patient, but he
always framed the quotations as general guidance, rather than as personal advice.
Crato's *Consilium 21*, written to a melancholic nobleman, is full of personal
concern, invoking both the body and the mind of the afflicted nobleman at every
turn.[39] Crato reassures his patient that a cure is possible, that his illness was
caused by his conscientious labors, that he has the physician's full attention.
Burton repeatedly quotes Crato's advice about diet, exercise, and the like but
omits his personal comments except for one reassuring statement that a good
diet will lead to a cure (2:19).[40] For example, Burton paraphrases Crato's advice
on the effects of the passions, writing that they "overwhelme reason, judgement,
and pervert the temperature of the body" (1:248). This passage is a loose summary of an observation by Crato that Burton had marked in his copy of the
Consilia, "Moestitia vero universum infrigidat corpus, calorem innatum extinguit, appetitum destruit, concoctionem impedit, intellectum pervertit, et corpus
exiccat," or "Sorrow certainly weakens the whole body, extinguishes the native
warmth, destroys the appetite, hinders digestion, corrupts the understanding,
and dries up the body" (fig. 1). But Burton did not follow his account of the dire
effects of passion with Crato's advice to live a calm, happy life.

LIBER I.I. 145

cuit, eamque in diuerſas corporis partes
penetrare facit, id quod non parum ſan-
guinem ipſum, & vitales accendit ſpiritus. Mœſtitia verò vniuerſum infrigidat
corpus, calorem innatum extinguit, appetitum deſtruit, concoctionē impedit,
intellectum peruertit, & corpus exiccat.
Timor autem diſſoluit ſpiritus, cor infi-
cit,& animum attenuat. Quamobrē hæc
omnia prorſus vitanda ſunt, & pro virili
fugienda. Vita autem inſtituenda eſt hi-
laris,læta, ac trāquilla,&,vt Celſus inquit,
quærenda eſt delectatio ex muſicis can-
tilenis, iocis & fabellis. Hæc itaque ſunt
reuerende Domine,quæ ad victus regimen ſpectant. Ea ſi rectè Dominatio tua
ſeruabit, nihil mihi verendum eſt, quin
plurimum proficiant,cùm omnium tam
antiquorū, quàm recentium autorū te-
ſtimonio, nihil ſit quod magis cōferat ad
huiuſmodi affectionis curationē, quàm
recta & competens victus ratio,& preſer-
tim vbi morbus nō fuerit diuturnus,plu-
ribusq; annis inueteratus. Siquidem fa-
tetur Galen.lib.3.de locis affec. ſe quam-
plurimos curaſſe melancholicos tantùm

K

1 | Robert Burton's copy of Johannes Crato, *Consiliorum & epistolarum medicinalium*, vol. 1 (Frankfurt: Wecheli, 1592), Consilium 21:145. This copy was owned by Robert Burton, who marked passages that describe the effects of sorrow—cooling and drying the body, extinguishing its natural heat, destroying appetite, corrupting the intellect—and those that recommend that "your life should be merry, quiet, and happy." Photo: Christ Church Library, courtesy of the Governing Body of Christ Church, Oxford.

Burton was anything but a minimalist writer. In most of the inset narratives of the *Anatomy*, we find dense detail and narrative energy. Consider the contrast between his schematic medical cases and these historical and literary examples (sadly abbreviated) from the discussion of love melancholy:

> In this case [suffering from concealed love] was the faire *Lady Elizabeth*, *Edward* the fourth his daughter, when she was enamored on *Henry* the seventh, that noble young Prince, and new saluted King, when she broke forth into that passionate speech, "*O that I were worthy of that comely Prince. . . .*" (3:244)

> An honest country fellow (as *Fulgosus* relates it) in the kingdome of *Naples*, at plough by the Sea side, saw his wife carried away by *Mauritanean* pirats, hee ranne after in all hast, up to the chin first, and when he could wade no longer, swam, calling to the governour of the ship to deliver his wife, or if he must not have her restored, to let him follow as prisoner, for he was resolved to be a gallislave, his drudge, willing to endure any misery, so that he might but enjoy his deare wife. (3:264–65)

Both these stories are more sharply developed and expressive than any of the medical narratives. Both stories are extended and elaborated beyond my quotations: Elizabeth complains eloquently; the devoted husband and wife are reunited and rewarded. Even Burton's compressed nonmedical stories are presented in lively accounts, often with a named protagonist: "*Philopaemen* the Oratour was set to cut wood, because he was so homely attired: *Terentius* was placed at lower end of *Cecilius* table, because of his homely outside. *Dantes* that famous *Italian* Poet, by reason his cloathes were but meane, could not bee admitted to sit downe at a feaste" (1:355). The contrast between medical narratives and more fully developed historical or literary examples suggests that, for Burton, these two kinds of stories did different kinds of work. One of the epistemic projects of the *Anatomy* was the development of multiple narrative forms that could contain varied temporally situated evidence—multiplied and pared down or dense and extended—adapted to different practices of knowledge. In Burton's use of medicine, we can discern the difference between literary narratives and medical narratives, and understand why, for Burton, medical narratives might have required a flattening of character and incident.

As we have seen, early modern medicine, like all studies related to natural philosophy, rejected the probative force of the individual example; since medicine could only offer collections of such examples, it was not a science. Burton was certainly concerned about the uncertainty of medicine and the rocky status of the individual case; he discusses this issue in "Democritus to the Reader" (1:21) and again in the subsections "Physitian, Patient, Physicke" (2:11–13) and "Of Physicke which cureth with Medicines," where he excoriates medicine as "no art at all," although he also praises it as "a most noble and divine science" (2:208–13, 209, 212). While he was avid to collect the observations of others, Burton's own experience of direct observation was limited. We do know that surveying was a favorite hobby, that he had at least one experience with a telescope, and, of course, that there was also introspection. The question facing him was how to move the observation of a single patient from the category of story into the category of fact. In massing *observationes* and pruning their details, Burton combined the conventions of the treatise, with its comprehensive presentation of the authorities, with the emerging cultures of observation and compilation. His cases are the equivalents of Galileo's "many times" or "hundreds of times"; they also recall Aristotle's "what occurs always or for the most part." The textual authority of the treatise, based on the writer's comprehensive grasp of the available literature, merges with a collaborative authority based on the observations of many physicians in writing at different times and places. Not all Burton's collections of cases build to a pleasant unanimity; often Burton combined and compressed citations of cases, assembling patients' experiences until their variations gave way to consensus, or at least to defined alternatives: given enough *exempla*, patterns emerged.

In treating medical stories differently from those that were historical or literary, Burton could have drawn on a rhetorical distinction between two different uses of narration. Aristotle, Cicero, and Quintilian all recognized the persuasive force of examples, or *paradigmata*; they were a part of *logos*, concerned with relationships of similarity or difference rather than with striking details. Quintilian cites the practice of Cicero, who bundled examples much as Burton bundled cases, referring to his use of the *paradigma* in *Pro Milone*: "For neither the famous Servilius Ahala, or Publius Nasica, nor Lucius Opimius, nor the Senate during my consulship could be cleared of serious guilt, if it were a crime to put wicked men to death."[41] The streamlined *paradigma* was a way of turning individual instances into a form of knowledge that counted. The use of narrative to excite *pathos*, on the other hand, required ornament and detail to engage the emotions and make the speech more persuasive. Quintilian speaks of *enargia*, which sets forth ideas so that they "may as it were be seen; for our language is not sufficiently effective, and has not that absolute power which it ought to have, if it impresses only with the ears, and if the judge feels that the particulars, on which he has to give a decision, are merely stated to him, and not described graphically, or displayed to the eyes of the mind."[42] Burton used narratives both to confirm *logos* and to excite *pathos*: to confirm *logos*, he relied on *observationes* that he had abstracted, abbreviated, and collected; to excite *pathos*, he used historical and literary examples, rendered moving and present with details, named characters, and direct quotations.

Regimen

If *consilia* and *observationes* raised questions about the reliability of knowledge based on observations, books of advice for daily living or regimens, added another complication—exigency. The reader who consulted a regimen needed to make a decision about what to eat, how much to sleep, and whether her east-facing windows should be left open. Regimen was one of the most common discursive forms of early modern medicine, featured in both texts directed to physicians and popular health manuals. It regulated everything taken into the body or removed from it, everything that the body did or suffered: air, food, seed (whether masculine or feminine), blood, water, frenzy, night watches, morning walks. In a Galenic framework, regimen was the regulation of the six nonnatural things: airs, waters, places; motion and rest; sleeping and waking; food and drink; evacuation and retention; and the passions of the mind. (Modern readers are puzzled by the term *nonnatural*, since for us the environment and food are natural, but for early modern readers *nonnatural* meant "things in the world that affect the body rather than those born with it.") For Galenists, regimen was the sovereign method of preserving health and curing illness. Manipulating what entered and left the body made it hotter or colder, wetter or dryer, and therefore altered the balance of the humors. Distinct regimens were appropriate for different times of life, seasons of the year, prevailing winds, illnesses, constitutions, occupations, and genders. Regimen therefore offered a framework through which the long story of a human life was modulated, in which daily routines varied with the stately cycle of the seasons, but which could also accommodate crises and climacterics. While the story always ended in death, regimen offered a complex but predictable pattern of events randomly punctuated by the accidents of life. The recommendations of regimen were exacting; they dealt with every area of everyday practice; the patient who followed his physician's directions had enough to do, but one who supplemented this advice with printed texts on regimen would be hard put indeed. Regimen offered a model for narrative that was full of incident and that went, essentially, nowhere—a model that, I argue, Burton put to good use.

Medical texts on regimen were numerous and popular, including works from the Hippocratic canon such as *On Regimen in Health* and *On Regimen in Acute Illness*; Galen's commentary on the Hippocratic *On Regimen* and his many remarks on regimen in other works; the medieval *Regimen sanitatis Salernitanum*, a rhymed compendium of health advice; the Neoplatonic *De vita libri tres* of Marsilio Ficino (1489); books of medical cases and medical advice, such as Crato of Krafftheim's *Consiliorum et epistularum medicinalium* (1611); miscellaneous periodicals distributed by learned academies; and vernacular works, including the seventeen editions of Sir Thomas Elyot's *The Castell of Health* (1534) and its imitators. All of these texts are quoted freely and frequently in the *Anatomy*.[43]

Like Burton, the writers of regimen did not recognize clear boundaries between medical advice and other kinds of counsel, freely quoting biblical warnings against excess or the sin of drunkenness.[44] The writings on regimen varied in tone. The author could be bracing, like Socrates's stern physician in the *Gorgias*, ordering the chaos of bodily appetites rather than pandering to them like an indulgent cook. Regimens could be cut-and-dried lists of recommendations—eat less of this and more of that, sleep more in winter, purge periodically—or they could offer solemn counsel that the good Christian should not be gluttonous or slothful and should contain the passions of the soul to demonstrate prudent care for the body. Some vernacular regimens offered readers handy tables that showed both their temperaments and the proper diet to restore balance.[45] For Burton, there was no real boundary between regimen as a medical concept and as a moral imperative. In discussing how even reason and judgment, put to bad use, can do us harm, Burton suggests that "These excellent meanes [reason, art, and judgment], God hath bestowed on us well imployed, cannot but much availe us, but if otherwise perverted, they ruine and confound us. . . . If you will particularly knowe how, and by what meanes, consult Physitians, and they will tell you, that it is in offending in some of those six non-natural things, of which I shal after dilate more at large; they are the causes of our infirmities, our surfetting, and drunkenesse, our immoderate insatiable lust, and prodigious riot" (1:127–28). Excess produced disease: a seamless line connected sinful abuse of the nonnaturals to the permissive will of God, who allowed abuse to be punished by distemperature leading to disease.

There is no better example of Burton's use of the neo-Galenic advice on regimen than his mining of *Consilium 21* by Johannes Crato of Krafftheim, a text we have already met in this chapter. Crato (1519–1585) was a companion of Luther and close friend of Philipp Melanchthon; he corresponded with the chief physicians of his age, both Catholic and Protestant, including Conrad Gesner, Thomas Erastus, Girolamo Mercuriale, and Peter Monau.[46] Burton owned two of the five volumes of Crato's collected letters and *consilia*—a lovely set of octavos, printed in a beautiful italic and still bearing the marks of his restless, searching pen. No section is more heavily marked than *Consilium 21*. While Burton trimmed away nearly all of Crato's personal engagement with his patient, he was an enthusiastic retailer of Crato's advice on regimen: he quotes from it extensively in two long subsections of the *Anatomy* on causes (1:171–371) and cures (2:19–207), referring to this text as "that excellent counsel" (1:218) and "that oft-cited counsel" (1:221). Crato had provided his patient with an elaborate regimen ordering every aspect of life. Burton marked many of Crato's recommendations for each of the six nonnaturals, as well as his general remarks on the causes of his patient's melancholy: "causatur a cruditatibus, qui continuo in eius ventriculo gignuntur, & tam fortasse propter nimias curas continua studia & vigilias."[47] The nobleman's melancholy was caused "by undigested food, which continues to grow in the stomach, perhaps because of excess of cares, continual study, and watching," and so would be cured by "recta et competens victus ratio," a "correct and suitable dietary regimen."[48] But these were not the passages that Burton used in the *Anatomy*, which depersonalizes the very individualized advice of the *consilium*.

Burton instead drew on Crato's letter for extensive advice on "rectifying" the nonnaturals. While Crato is moderate and encouraging, Burton is consistently negative. Crato recommends a certain golden apple and allows that while unripe or acid fruits should be avoided, ripe or cooked fruit can be healthful. Burton flattens out these nuances and unpacks Crato's counsel into a list of prohibitions: "*Crato consil. 21.lib. 2* utterly forbids all manner of fruits, as Peares, Apples, Plummes, Cherries, Strawberries, Nuts, Medlers, Serves, &c." (1:216). This example could be multiplied endlessly; in all of the chapters on food and drink,

Burton grudgingly recommends only three items: whey, oatmeal and dark beer. He presents a regimen for melancholics that is both restrictive and maddeningly complex: "*Crato* will admit of no hearbs but borage, buglosse, endive, fennel, anni-seed, bawme. *Calenus* and *Arnoldus* tolerate lettuce, spinage, beets, &c. The same *Crato* will allow no roots at all to be eaten. Some approve of potatoes, parsnips, but all corrected for winde. No raw sallets; but as *Laurentius* prescribes, in brothes; and so *Crato* commends many of them, or to use borage, hoppes, bawme, steeped in their ordinary drinks" (2:23).

Jennifer Richards has identified a pattern of similar contradictory advice in vernacular regimen books such as Thomas Elyot's *Castel of Health* (1534) and Thomas Moulton's *Myrour or Glasse of Health* (1533). She traces this pattern to the commonplace book, where a variety of opinions are collected without being adjudicated.[49] Burton's reader might have been amused by the range of opinion, but perplexed about exactly what to eat. Are all roots forbidden, or are some permitted? Will correcting for wind render them healthful? How would you go about correcting for wind?

Sometimes Burton simply compiled all the advice that he could find and directed the reader to make his own choice. Sometimes he offered decision rules, as in his general advice on exercise: "This which I aime at, is for such as are *fracti animis*, troubled in minde, to ease them, over-toiled on the one part to refresh: over idle on the other, to keepe themselves busied" (2:83). There is no general rule here, but guidance for shaping individual regimens. Burton advised his reader to follow custom and appetite—counsel that might have been frustrating for a reader after many pages of contradictory medical advice: "*Cardans* rule is best, to keepe that wee are accustomed unto, though it be naught, and to follow our disposition and appetite in some things is not amisse, to eat sometimes of a dish which is hurtfull, if we have an extraordinary liking to it" (2:27).

In his adaptation of Crato and other neo-Galenists, Burton has torqued their serious and sensible counsel in two directions: first, he has rendered it impossible to follow their recommendations. What was general advice is presented as an iron law; what was a clear recommendation is riddled with a score of exceptions and caveats. Second, as we have seen, the dyadic relation between the patient and the physician who calibrates his recommendations to the patient's situation and temperament is lost; instead, advice is adapted to a distributed relationship between the author and his unknown readers, who can only be helped to negotiate the maze of recommendations and prohibitions.[50] This expansion is not unusual for early modern medical books, which offered themselves as ways for patients to self-treat. Appetite—the very faculty that, according to Crato, caused melancholy—is as good a guide as any to treating it.[51] In sorting out regimen, both reader and writer negotiated, again and again, the blurred boundary between the management of the body and the care of the soul, between expert scientific advice and individual prudence. Both were balanced between, on the one hand, the fascinating array of temperaments and the many ways distemperature could be caused or cured, and on the other the intractable need to identify and cure one's own imbalance.

For Burton, as we have seen, this dilemma was an extension of the problem of reasoning from particulars to universals, and by extension the problem of the scientific status of medicine. In the introduction to the *Anatomy*, Burton declared that "The whole must needs followe by a *Sorites* or induction" (1:65), placing induction and deduction as a complementary pair, moving indifferently from part to whole or from whole to part. The text can be developed equally well by a deductive sorites—a chain of linked syllogisms—or by assembling evidence of what happens "always or for the most part" to support an induction. Many of the physicians Burton quoted most often, for example, Cardan and Da Monte, actively debated the relation between concrete, observable instances and more philosophically privileged categories, such as universals and final causes.[52] These questions are also the bread and butter of rhetoric, which deals with what is likely or probable in a situation, rather than with what is definitely known and needs no debate. For physicians such as the medical humanist Hieronymus Mercurialis in his lecture *De modo studendi*, they were resolved in a practice of reading that recalls Aristotle's attention to repeated experience. Mercurialis counsels beginning students not to be content with one or two readings: instead, "you should turn your mind to it [your text] time and time again, and consult your friends and teachers, examine, and debate."[53] Mercurialis counseled students to prepare themselves for the exigency of medical practice with a discipline of textual reflection that was protracted, plural, and deeply social.

The *Anatomy* sponsors just such a reading practice, speaking in turn to the melancholic and his or her counselors, presenting multiple authorities, prompting comparisons between the textual body of medical literature and the living body located in a particular time and space. Aristotelian definitions of science were remolded under the pressure of new ways of observing nature and of producing and distributing texts. Collections of letters that had circulated in manuscript from one physician to another now became collections of *epistolae* and *consilia* that anyone could buy and read, premediating the circulating philosophic journal. Just as large audiences flocked to sermons on casuistry, lay readers, especially the well-off readers who could afford them, bought medical books in vernaculars or in Latin.[54] (I will discuss the relation between Latin and vernacular medical texts more fully in chapter 5.) Just as a university graduate who practiced law might own a book of natural history for its accounts of wonderful beasts, he might own a medical book for its illustrations, amusing cases, or tales of wonder.[55] Readers could also find the issues of regimen weighed and debated and review them "time and time again."

It was one thing for a physician to write a letter to an individual, responding to the patient's written description of disease. It was another to copy that physician's letter and circulate it to other physicians, and still another to combine it with similar letters. In the collections of *consilia*, the letter served as a model of good practice in a specific set of circumstances, rather than as advice to a specific patient. Here, the case is an individual instance, an indicator or sign that was read within a professional framework as evidence of what worked "always or for the most part." When the letters or counsels were printed and distributed in large editions, the system of signs that connected individual events to relatively stable medical knowledge was disrupted; the instance or *exemplum* was now being read by an ordinary reader, evaluating the *consilia* from whatever framework was available. Each reader was left to compose a regimen from a part of the whole storehouse of medical knowledge.

Burton offered no resolution to this quandary, a paradigm of the ways that traditional practices of knowledge were becoming both essential and impossible in the seventeenth century. He was expert in those practices, including compilation, collation, and commentary. His grasp of the literatures of Greek and Roman antiquity was comprehensive; his understanding of the contemporaneous neo-Galenic medical literature and its chief rivals was exemplary. None of this wisdom is discounted in the *Anatomy*, but none of it does much good, either. Authorities are arranged to highlight their contradictions; citations are multiplied; footnotes, glosses, and quotations obscure the contours of the argument. A little later in the century, spectacles of experimentation would be performed before assemblies of sober, respectable witnesses; such communal performances were not available to Burton.[56] Instead, he constructed *ethos* by deploying textual authorities in all their complexity, crossing the boundaries of disciplines that had not yet consolidated, combining Seneca with Fernel in the best tradition of medical humanism. Burton's authorities frequently disagree, and the time that pulses through his marginal glosses moves irregularly from antiquity to "our

Neotericks." Nothing holds together this jumpy account of various texts about various mental processes—nothing, that is, except for the author, quoting and citing so that his work "showes a Schollar" (1:19), and for the reader, consulting the text repeatedly, discussing it with friends, and comparing it to her experience.

But Burton does not allow us to throw our hands in the air, declare that it is impossible to sort things out, and collapse into skepticism. We cannot live without the nonnaturals, and so we must sort through the authorities that Burton has assembled but not reconciled. We must weigh the balance between appetite and advice and make a choice among probabilities without the security of a deductive science. We are in the territory of exigency, the uncomfortable rhetorical domain where we make judgments on the basis of incomplete information. In this domain Burton tentatively moved among the difficulties and contradictions of the central practices of knowledge of his time: religion, humane letters, and natural philosophy.[57] He compiled authorities, suggested ways of choosing among them, explained their recommendations, and urged the cultivation of prudence. He offered ways to understand contradictory advice. On the question of natural baths, for example, Burton noted that his authorities had different opinions about them, but that they might be useful depending on the type of melancholy or the heat and composition of the bath water (2:10). He advised that rules for building a house (a favorite topic of regimens) that worked in Italy might not work so well in England (2:62). He urged that melancholics "never bee left alone or idle" (2:106); the advice of friends was critical to the proper ordering of regimen. None of these practices offered any promise of certainty, but as they are repeated over the many pages of Burton's advice, they offer ways for readers to discipline themselves to the work of making contingent choices.

Regimented Time

Just as regimen served as a model for negotiating exigency under conditions of uncertainty, it also provided Burton with a way of representing temporality, of structuring narratives without climax or resolution. Discussions of the nonnaturals by Hippocrates and Galen offered Burton narrative tempos and devices for connecting events that would shape the distinctive frame of the *Anatomy*, with its energetic forward movement and its refusal of conceptual resolution.

For Hippocrates, regimen was organized in intersecting cycles of long and short time, of development and crisis. *On Regimen* insisted that the physician's knowledge must take into account the multiple temporalities of the patient's stage of life, the time of year, the changes of winds, the movements of the stars and of "the whole universe, from which diseases exist among men."[58] These temporalities are further punctuated by the uneven tempo of the illness itself. In his system of critical days, those when an illness moved toward resolution, Hippocrates articulated complex, interrelated cycles of time: "The fourth day is indicative of the seventh; the eighth is the beginning of another week; the eleventh is to be watched, as being the fourth day of the second week; again the seventeenth is to be watched, being the fourth from the fourteenth and the seventh from the eleventh."[59]

Galenic texts complicated these structures even further, projecting multiple crises that repeated during the course of an illness. The Galenic *On Critical Days* warned physicians against improvements that came without a crisis—without vomiting, diarrhea, anxiety, or other evacuations of body or mind, cures were not to be trusted.[60] Not all crises were equal: those on the seventh day were both common and benign; those that fell on the sixth day of an illness were rare and deceptive. In the literature on regimen, the crises formed a series of rhyming days, each reflected by and forecasting those to come, telling the sufferer what to expect in the course of the illness. The days of crisis formed their own epicycles; they recursively revealed what had already happened in the body and suggested a prognosis. Since the patient in crisis is anxious, restless, and plagued with a variety of distressing symptoms, Galen declares that "the condition of the patient is likened to that of a man who has been brought before a judge who condemns him to death. On this meaning the name 'crisis' is placed, that is to say, the verdict or the judgment."[61]

These representations of time differ from those of other narrative structures available to Burton such as exempla, dramas, histories, or travelers' tales. Regimen orders time in interlocking cycles: the long cycles of the lifespan, as individuals slowly exhaust their supply of heat and moisture, and of the year, as each season brings a new range of challenges and dangers. These cycles change abruptly in response to puberty, childbirth, the seasons of the year, shifting winds or extreme weathers. They are open to endless variation: to drink a glass of water is to take in the occult and subtle influences of the stars that shone on its source. The physician's work is to place a malady within these temporal cycles and to articulate its future course, attending to the critical days and shifting the patient's regimen as required. There are long stretches when nothing much happens, which give way to crises with their own rhythms, closing with death or cure. The temporality of regimen is not a vast wash of indistinguishable days; it is highly rationalized and structured. The four elements wax and wane, lose and reestablish balance in ways that are intelligible to the both physician and the skilled layman. Regimen is syncopated; its tempos shift according to their own laws, as Hippocrates warns in his first Aphorism: "Life is short, the art long, opportunity fleeting, experiment treacherous, judgment [*krisis*] difficult."[62] These are not the temporalities of literary or historical writing, which move readers from conflict to resolution. Nor does regimen follow the temporal structure of emerging scientific practices, in which repeated observations give evidence of a universal truth. Rather, regimented time is the temporality of rhetoric, constrained by exigency, responsive to long durations, searching after judgment, and punctuated by *kairos*, the opening that allows for persuasion. It is not accidental that in Aristotle's *Rhetoric* "crisis" denoted the audience's judgment of an argument.

This is also the temporality of *The Anatomy of Melancholy*, which moves pell-mell but develops its themes at a glacial pace, which refuses resolution but presents readers with the need to judge among impossible choices. Like the Hippocratic regimen, the *Anatomy* is clearly structured: its divisions are laid out in the ramified diagrams presented in the initial synopsis and referenced in the heading of each book, chapter, section, and subsection, just as they were in medical books that Burton owned (4:170). But just as the Hippocratic march through the seasons can be complicated by a shifting wind, Burton's movement through his divisions is waylaid by digressions large and small, by repetitions of examples and advice, and by contradictory conclusions. The first digression, "Digression of Anatomy," emerges a mere eighteen pages into the body of the text and continues for twenty-two pages. While Burton proposes to cure, or at least prevent, melancholy, he periodically assures us that this task is futile: all of his readers, without exception, will come under the sway of this humor; all we can hope for is that universal risk might engender universal compassion: "*Quae sua sors hodie est, cras forè vestra potest* [His fate today may be yours tomorrow]; wee ought not to bee so rash and rigorous in our censures, as some are, charity will judge and hope the best; God be mercifull unto us all" (1:438). Regimen shared this pessimism: the physician did not cure so much as offer a prognosis that told the ongoing story of the illness, and struggle to reestablish humoral balance, restoring the ever-diminishing supplies of moisture and heat—a losing game if there ever was one.

The narrative of the *Anatomy* has no central crisis, no resolution, no clear distinction between the main line of argument and subsidiary questions. In contemporary narrative theory, such a structure is seen as foregrounding the act of narration rather than the events of the story. Gerard Genette distinguishes the narrative utterance (the act of telling) from the narrative statement (the events as they are told) and from the object of the narrative (the events that were recorded in the narrative).[63] In the *Anatomy*, the narrative utterance orders the events of the text. Rather than following a narrative structure that orders recommendations by the cycles of the year, the lifespan, or the day, the text insists on the perplexed and none-too-helpful narrator caught in those intersecting cycles, carefully compiling contradictory views, doubling back on himself, and refusing to deliver an authoritative judgment. In this narration, events can always reverse themselves, but they seldom resolve.

Burton's adaptation of the narrative structure of regimen is evident in the subsection "Love of Learning, or overmuch Study. With a Digression of the Misery of Schollers, and why the Muses are Melancholy" (1:302–27). This complaint against the woes of the scholarly life begins with the familiar massed references to medical writers, all of whom emphasized the importance of regimen: Leonard Fuchs, Felix Platter, Ercole di Sassonia, Jean Fernel, Giovanni Arcolani, Rhasis (Abū Bakr Muhammad ibn Zakariyya al-Razi), and Levinus Lemnius. Most of these writers were Galenists, although Fernel is generally considered a Neoplatonist and Lemnius was more closely identified with Hippocrates; all were included in the broad canon of medical humanism. According to these authorities, since the life of the scholar lacked exercise and variety, their untiring labor left them especially vulnerable to melancholy. Burton augmented these physicians' warnings with examples of the course of scholarly life that replicated the long cycles of the regimen: "how much time did *Thebet Benchorat* employ, to finde out the motion of the eight spheare, 40 yeares and more, some write, how many poor schollers have lost their wits, or become dizards, neglecting all worldly affaires, and their owne health, wealth, *esse* and *benè esse*, to gaine knowledge?" (1:304). Into these expansive epochs of labor, analogous to the life stages of regimen, Burton inserted protracted but bounded stints of intense searching for patronage, usually futile: "after some seaven years service" (1:308), "after twenty yeares study" (1:314), "he shall serve 7 years" (1:323), "at length after ten years sute" (1:324). In both the long cycle of the scholar's life and the shorter cycles of the scholar's career, the same thing happens: labor toward a goal that it almost never reached. Burton's stories of scholars have nothing in common with the well-structured narrative temporalities available in early modern fiction or drama, but they are analogous to the long periods of regimen, which shifts its prescriptions during the protracted movement from infancy to youth, from adulthood to age.

These periods extend indefinitely until they are closed by a crisis, and they are almost always closed by a crisis. Just as an individual constitution can be distempered by a bitter wind or a hot day, a scholar may fall from favor: "if he offend his good Patron, or displease his Lady Mistris . . . [,] he shall be dragged forth of doores by the heeles, away with him" (1:308–9). He is tempted to enter the *"Simoniacall* gate" (1:323) by purchasing an ecclesiastical living; if he finally obtains a benefice, he enters a life of obscurity: "he must turne rusticke, rude, melancholise alone, learne to forget" (1:324). The framework of the medical regimen assumes that the same customs of sleep, diet, exercise, study, and recreation will be repeated day after day, modified slowly with the seasons and the weather, modulated over the years of the life cycle, but altered radically when the patient is threatened by disease. Burton's picture of the scholar's life draws upon these tempos, creating a kind of antiregimen: repeated, relentless labor, continuing over years, modulating into new, more exacting labor, occasionally interrupted by self-destructive behavior or the end of an intellectual career.

Such wavering and syncopated tempos mark Burton's unconsoling adaptation of the gospel story of the Bethesda. In John's gospel, Bethesda is a pool stirred periodically by a healing angel (John 5:1–8). Burton's Bethesda offers patronage to the poor scholar rather than healing to the sick. Burton, as the poor scholar, waits for the "good houre" when a position might become available, just as the sick waited for an angel by the pool of Bethesda. But when an office opens, corrupt clerks "step betweene, and beguile us of our preferment" (1:323). For Burton as a melancholy scholar, waiting at Bethesda was pointless but compulsory: there would be no "good houre" for him; no redeemer will tell him to take up his bed and walk; the longer he stays, the more he is pushed aside. His long wait; the irregular opening of possibilities; the healing crises frustrated by greedy rivals: all of these import the narrative structures of regimen into the registers of satire and social criticism. Regimen allowed Burton to tell a story that other narratives had not yet learned to represent. The narrative temporality that Burton adopted in the *Anatomy* was available to later writers who sought to derail the forward traction of narrative while maintaining its energy. Laurence Sterne and Samuel Taylor Coleridge were both devoted readers of the *Anatomy*;

each, in a different way, eluded narrative closure. Later, Herman Melville, William Gaddis, and Samuel Beckett, all disturbers of the well-ordered plot, would turn to the *Anatomy*.[64]

I offer this analysis of Burton's use of the narrative structure of regimen as an alternative to thematic approaches to the study of his use of medicine, and indeed to such studies in medical rhetoric more generally. Sometimes, Burton mined medicine for its way of understanding the body or of advising the sick; at other times, the medical literature offered him a way of structuring knowledge. Among the practices of knowledge that move and change in the *Anatomy*, few are as mobile as medicine, or as generative on multiple levels. Burton's relation to medicine was not limited to a series of dietary recommendations; medicine organized time in a way that allowed him to simultaneously display multiple levels of embodied experience in a text, to advance multiple hypotheses without closure. The temporality of the *Anatomy* would not structure the emerging literature of experiment, but it would remain available as a way of rendering the openness and multiplicity of lived experience.

Moving Spirits

For Burton, one of the most useful concepts in the armamentarium of early modern regimen was that of *spirit*, variously understood as a gaseous substance inside the body, as the substance connecting body and soul, as the soul itself, and as a semi-material substance connecting the universe as a whole with each individual person. The concept of *spirit* is among the most mobile in all of early modern medicine. It could be used to name both the quite material vapors formed from liquid humors (a medical concept), the *anima*, or rational soul (a concept central to both early modern theology and humanities), and the neo-Platonic *pneuma*. We can understand some of the complexity of spirit by tracing its journeys through various early modern practices of knowledge; following this path locates Burton at the borders of disciplinary differentiation, taking advantage of the porous boundaries among early modern fields of study.

Let us begin with the neo-Galenic medical spirits. Galen saw the body as governed by its principal organs: the heart, the brain, and the liver. These organs produced the spirits described by Galen in *On the Doctrines of Hippocrates and Plato*: the natural, the vital, and the animal.[65] The natural spirits promoted growth; the vital supported life and could be detected in the heartbeat, pulse, and breath. The animal spirits (think *anima*, or soul, rather than beast) enabled movement, thought, action, and sensation; they were associated with the brain and were thought to work through the dense vascular network of the *rete mirabile*, an organ described by Galen and disproved by Vesalius. In the Galenic scheme, the spirits circulated through the arteries, while blood moved through the veins. Since spirits were formed in the organs from humors, the quality and quantity of a humor affected the spirits that were made from it.[66]

At the same time, Reformation religious thinkers understood *spirit* as a divine essence, the soul, or perhaps the subtle substance that communicated between body and mind. Ideas that emerged as metaphors in religion—spirit as light, ascending spirits—read out as anatomical information in physiology, so that the airy, vaporous spirit of physiology could become the upward-tending spirit of religion, and vice versa. The field is complicated by neo-Platonist and Paracelsan theories of spirit as a vehicle connecting the body and mind to vital universal forces.

For early seventeenth-century readers, the relationship between body and soul was analogous to the relationship among practices of knowledge: they were distinct, but also closely connected. Boundaries between them were porous, just as good letters, divinity, and natural philosophy were separate but closely related fields of study. Spirit negotiated the boundaries between immaterial beings (divinities, devils, or human souls), and material, palpable objects (bodily fluids and vapors, or the ambient air).[67] Such semi-material and immaterial spirits were objects of study in natural philosophy. Since spirit was also a significant theological concept, the humoral spirits, addressed by physicians of various persuasions, were also of interest to natural and moral philosophers. A physician might advise on spirits, either as material parts of the body or as causes of the perturbations of the mind; the pastor, as spiritual guide, might suggest amendments to regimen.

The word *spirit* had deep religious roots in English: the *Oxford English Dictionary* shows it entering the language as a translation of the scriptural terms *pneuma* or *ruach* in Wycliffe's 1382 English Bible. The Geneva and King James Bibles followed Wycliffe's practice, substituting *spirit* for the much older word *ghost*. Early modern readers would have been alive to Protestant controversies about the meaning of *spirit* in Paul's epistles, and these senses were certainly active for Burton. *Spirit* had carried medical meanings in English nearly as long as it had religious ones: the first medical citation in the *Oxford English Dictionary* is dated 1387. One of the Latin senses of *spiritus* was *breath*, and for Galen, breath was a primary ingredient of spirit. Since the eighteenth century, we have had a powerful chemical explanation of the animating power of breath: we know about oxygen. Early modern thinkers knew that breath was animating, but *how* breath animated was obscure, and contesting theories explained how the air and other gaseous substances moved through the body. How many spirits were there? Were they produced in the body, or drawn from the air, or both? Were they material or immaterial? How did they relate to the soul?[68] Beyond the simple account of the Galenic spirits I have given, this book cannot give a comprehensive account of how a seventeenth-century audience might have answered those questions, but Burton shows how easily the term *spirit* could support multiple understandings of this subtle substance, and how it could transport meanings from one discursive field to another.

Burton defined *spirit* in conventional terms: spirit was "a most subtile vapour, which is expressed from the *Blood*, & the instrument of the soule, to performe all his actions; a common tye or *medium*, between the body and the soule, as some will have it; or as *Paracelsus*, a fourth soule of it selfe" (1:141). In the "Digression of Anatomy," Burton began with a definition drawn from Galen by way of Melanchthon but also noted Paracelsan revisions of the received doctrine. For Melanchthon, as for medical humanists, spirit was a vapor produced from the blood that linked the body to the world, to demonic and genial spirits, and to the divine principle that ensouled humans. But spirit could also signify an intermediary between soul and body, or the substance that holds the soul in the body, or the principle animating the world and inhabiting the body: it could be wandering or fixed, animist or vitalist, material or immaterial.[69] And Burton also used *spirit* to refer to a divine essence, or to the immaterial part of a person referenced in such scriptural quotations as "*The spirit is willing but the flesh is weake*" (1:372). For Burton, medical uses of spirit merged with religious ones, supporting theories of melancholy as an illness, an error, an affliction, and a sin. Burton was most interested in how the spirits worked on the mind: animal spirits were identified with the mind, and the spirits in general were the immediate causes of passions, vehicles of sensation, and the links between the interior of the body and the external world. For him, the concept of spirit carried with it knowledges and genres—observation, philosophical reflection, textual compilation and exegesis, travel narrative, and clinical report. A natural philosopher speculating on vision had recourse to the concept of spirit; so did a voyager explaining the differing dispositions of the people he met. Burton used all these discourses: contesting concepts are cited as equally credible alternatives or invoked interchangeably, depending on the context of the discussion and the authority he is quoting. The *Anatomy* braids these concepts and practices together, even as they were slowly differentiating.

For Burton, the vaporous spirit was produced by heating bodily fluids, sometimes mixed with air; it operated primarily through the sensitive soul (the faculties of common sense, imagination, and memory) and effected the impulses of the will by operating the nerves and muscles. Burton followed Galen in his account of how spirits were formed: the natural spirits are worked up from blood by the liver; the vital spirits, from the natural, by the heart; and the animal, from the vital, by the brain. Spirits could be compounded with other vapors and gasses in the body; diseases of the stomach send "gross vapours" to the heart and brain, "corrupting humours and spirits" (2:178). The spirits worked, in a material way, on the mind and its passions, and passions also moved and animated the spirits. For Burton, emotions heated, chilled, moved, or fixed the spirits: "*For anger stirres choler, heats the blood and vitall spirits, Sorrow on the other side refrigerates the body, and extinguisheth naturall heat, overthrowes appetite, hinders conconction, dries up the temperature, and perverts the understanding: Feare dissolves the spirits, infects the heart, attenuates the soule: and for these* causes all passions and perturbations must to the uttermost of our power, and most seriously be removed" (2:100). While Burton's advice to avoid the passions is conventional, it was also conventional to observe that all men, even Christ, were subject to passion, and that passions could not be extinguished.[70] Elsewhere in the *Anatomy*, Burton observes that although the Stoics distrusted the passions, "we hold [them] naturall, and not to be resisted" (1:154).

Natural or not, a wise man was expected to contain the passions; moderation could avert melancholy. The literature of moral philosophy drew on Galenic theories of passion, spirit, and humor and instructed readers that philosophic reflection (or, failing that, distraction) could remove the object of passion from the mind and thus calm the perturbed spirits. Books such as Thomas Rogers's *A Pattern of a Passionate Minde* (London, 1580) and Thomas Wright's *The Passions of the Minde in Generall* (London, 1606) drew on Cicero, Seneca, and Plutarch, advising readers to prepare for future hardships by meditating on the inconstancy of fortune. If sorrow and fear overcame them, they should seek the counsel of friends or the distractions of music and travel.[71] Burton drew directly on this tradition, advising not only the moral treatments of stoic reflection and distraction, but also physical remedies, including drugs and bleeding (reflection and distraction, 2:106–207; physical remedies, 2:208–37).

Natural philosophy offered its own advice about the spirits. Among Burton's fifty citations of Philipp Melanchthon in the *Anatomy* is a discussion of the soul and its faculties, offered in the "Digression of Anatomy" which was a substitute for "those tedious Tracts *de Anima*" which "are not at all times ready to be had" (1:147–61, 140). Melanchthon began his commentary on Aristotle's *De anima* with a comprehensive account of Galenic anatomy, including the humors, moving to observations about the vital and animal spirits that effect not only nutrition and reproduction but also sense, motion, and thought. Some consider them to be the soul itself, or instruments of the soul, but Melanchthon put this speculation aside. Instead, he claimed a specific transcendent function for the spirits:

> Et, quod mirabilis est, his ipsis spiritibus in hominibus piis miscetur ipse divinus spiritus, et efficit magis fulgentes divina luce, ut agnito Dei sit illustrior, et adsensio firmior, et motus sint ardentiores erga Deum.

> And what is wonderful, in devout men these same spirits are mixed with that divine spirit, which increases the splendor of the divine light, so that their knowledge of God might be more brilliant, their faith stronger, and their feelings toward God more burning.[72]

Here, a Galenic account of the spirits merges with a Lutheran account of grace, a gift of God that enters the soul to excite religious feeling and confirm faith. By "mixing with the spirits," this divine gift also becomes part of the bodily economy. The passions it causes will stir up other spirits, present further ideas to the understanding, recalibrate the senses, and adjust the balance of the humors. Burton echoed this sense of spirit; he explained that the corrupted will must "be swayed and counterpoised againe, with some divine precepts, and good motions of the Spirit" before it can turn to good (1:160). The understanding of spirit, for both Burton and Melanchthon, begins with anatomy, turns to natural philosophy and theology, and returns to anatomy. The evidence that counts as proof in anatomy, such as the texts of Greek and Roman antiquity or collected observations, is not distinguished from evidence that counts as proof in theology, preeminently the texts of Scripture.

Similar slippage from medicine to philosophy and theology marks Burton's discussions of the spirits as vehicles of perception and affect. Why does music relieve melancholy? For Burton, music acted physiologically on the spirits: "*Scaliger exercit.* 302. gives a reason of these effects, *because the spirits about the heart, take in that trembling and dancing aire into the body, are moved together, and stirred up with it*" (2:114). Burton also mobilizes the sense of spirit as the vehicle of perception in discussions of love melancholy. He speaks of spirit moving to and from the lover's eyes: "The rayes, as some thinke, sent from the eyes, carry certaine spirituall vapours with them, and so infect the other party, and that in a moment. I knowe, they that hold *visio fit intra mittendo* [sight comes from images received within], will make a doubt of this, but *Ficinus* proves it from bleare eyes" (3:88). Sight might come from the object or from the perceiving eye; both theories had their supporters, and although here he sides with those who assign sight to the action of the object, elsewhere in the *Anatomy* Burton had presented both of them evenhandedly (1:150–51; see notes at 4:186–87).[73] Whatever its source, sight moves in the body by means of spirits, traveling in the nerves and presenting an image to common sense and the imagination, potentially exciting love.

The spirit has palpable corporeal effects: Ficino, in his example of "bleare eyes," held that inflammations of the eye are carried from one person to another by the same spirit that carries images. The spirits also carry love, a "Heroicall passion, or rather brutish burning lust" that was for Burton a contagion, like "Plague, Itch, Scabs, Flux, &c. The spirits taken in, will not let him rest that hath received them, but egge him on" (3:89, 90).

No matter how the spirits supported perception, it was clear that they also could distort it. As we have seen, a disturbed or imbalanced spirit produced black fumes that clouded sight, intensifying melancholy, "For *Galen* imputeth all to the cold that is blacke, and thinkes that the sprits being darkned, and the substance of the Braine cloudy and darke, all the objects thereof appeare terrible, and the *minde* it selfe, by those darke obscure, grosse fumes, ascending from black humours, is in continuall darknesse, feare & sorrow" (1:418–19). Disturbed humors could render external objects terrifying and further disturb the mind, recursively generating more dark spirits.

On occasion, Burton forsook Melanchthon's anatomy for that of the neo-Platonist Marsilio Ficino.[74] Ficino's spirits began as Galenic vapors—they were produced by a heating of the blood and connected the body with the soul—but then they swerved into a transcendent relationship with the vital force of the universe. While Melanchthon held that the Galenic spirits mixed with a divine spirit to foster a properly scriptural knowledge of God, Ficino saw the spirits as operating through the senses, opening the well-disposed person to emanations of a World Soul. Objects that attracted a great deal of spirit, or *pneuma*, were especially powerful in establishing this connection—certain images, colors, herbs, music, jewels: "Just as the power of our soul is brought to bear on our members through the spirit, so the force of the World-soul is spread under the World-soul to all things through the quintessence, which is active everywhere, as the spirit inside the World's Body, but that this power is instilled especially into those things which have absorbed the most of this kind of spirit."[75]

Ficino's recommendations for drawing down *pneuma* echo in Burton's recommendations of music, jewels, and herbal medicines as cures. For both Ficino and Melanchthon, the spirit connects an embodied individual with a transcendent realm, animating the body and empowering the mind. They differ radically in their understanding of that transcendent realm, its connection to the humoral spirit, and the method of cultivating that connection. Burton used both theories without a qualm.

Burton's *spirit* also connects the individual to the external world by mixing with other vaporous substances. Spirits could be influenced by material objects, such as airs and gasses; they also opened an individual to the influence of spiritual beings both good and evil. Spirit had a particular affinity for air: "Such as is the Aire, such be our spirits, and as our spirits, such are our humors" (1:233). Air, as a Galenic nonnatural, was an object of regulation in the literature on regimen.[76] In discussing regimen, Burton launched into an expansive subsection, "Ayre Rectified. With a Digression of the Ayre," moving seamlessly from issues of regimen to unsettled questions in natural philosophy and cosmography about air, its influence, its movement over the earth, the diversity of climates, migrating birds, the tides and other movements of water. The imaginary wanderings associated with air could themselves cure melancholy. Burton cheered himself up by his digression: free speculation expanded and warmed the spirits, and such imaginative play was physiologically therapeutic: "I, having now come at last into these ample fields of Ayre, wherein I may freely expatiate and exercise my selfe, for my recreation a while rove, wander round about the world" (2:33). Or, more directly, "But hoo? I am now gone quite out of sight, I am almost giddy with roving about" (2:57).

Spirits were affected not only by air, but by all that the air contained and carried. Air could be a vector of contagion, which early modern physicians understood as the transfer of disease-causing distempers rather than pathogens.

If air were hot, cold, stormy, contaminated with vapors, bad smells, and other noxious elements, it could directly cause disease. Burton was fond of the proverb that the melancholy humor was the devil's bath—he referred to it six times, crediting it to various authors (for example, 1:193–94; 1:231; 3:433). Like the relation between melancholy and darkness, the entrance of the devil into a melancholic's humor was not a metaphor but a physical invasion: "This humor [melancholy] is *Balneum Diaboli*, the Divell's bath, by reason of the distemper of humours, and infirme Organs in us, hee may so possesse as inwardly to molest us . . . hee is Prince of the Ayre, and can transforme himselfe into severall shapes, delude all our senses for a time" (3:443).

As an astrologer, Burton knew that the air carried the influences of the stars and planets. Devils could use these influences to cause all manner of harm, working through the spirit to torment minds and bodies: "For being a spirituall body, he [the devil] struggles with our spirits" (1:193). Burton gives this influence quite precise physiological shape, quoting Jason Pratensis (also known as van der Velde): "*the Divell being a slender incomprehensible spirit, can easily insinuate and winde himselfe into humane bodies, and cunningly couched in our bowels, vitiate our healths, terrify our soules with fearfull dreames, and shake our minde with furies*" (1:193–94). Corruptions or agitations of the Galenic spirits, especially those derived from melancholy humors, could provoke passions, and diabolical spirits could mix with disturbed humoral spirits to produce thoughts, dreams, feelings, and other perturbations. The devil, after all, is a spirit and "hath means and opportunity to mingle himself with our spirits, and sometimes more slily, sometimes more abruptly and openly, to suggest such divelish thoughts into our hearts" (3:433).

Spirit therefore opened the body and mind to both the divine and diabolical influences. It was the mark of a body whose borders were uncertain and porous: spirit presented sensory images, the impulses of divine grace, and satanic temptations indifferently to the mind. In the *Anatomy*, Burton's spirit is connected to the Galenic spirits at one pole and to theological ideas about the spirit and the flesh at the other. As in Melanchthon, the two discursive frames of medicine and theology were not seen as contradictory; Galen's spirits were inducted into Protestant moral and natural philosophy; religious ideas of spirit informed various programs for the treatment of melancholy. Burton also made use of quite different ideas of spirit, based on Neoplatonic connections to an animating world soul, and his remarks on the devil have a medieval cast. He was not especially concerned to reconcile these frameworks but used them when they fit the topic at hand. Galen sponsors the anatomical discussions, and Neoplatonists like Ficino are quoted in the section on love melancholy. Burton selected from the ideas, images, and therapies that seemed most relevant to local topics with little concern for theoretical consistency. Because the physiology of spirit was so closely related to theories of perception, imagination, passion, and affect, medical descriptions of heat, cold, constriction, or violent motion easily became metaphors for states of the mind and spirit. These vivid metaphors could be resolved into physiological accounts of bodily processes for therapeutic purposes and be deployed as descriptions of emotional states in moral literatures. The discourses of medicine, theology, and natural philosophy were mutually porous, tied to each other by multiple recursive lines of influence. Although they all offered distinct lines of proof and conventions for what counted as evidence, these lines were broken and braided. Exegesis of Scripture, reflections on Aristotle, and the maxims of the Reformation all counted as proof in moral philosophy and could be put to use in a medical discourse on the sixth "nonnatural," the perturbations of the mind. Traditional medical genres such as the *consilium* could be mined for moral and ethical teachings.

Since *spirit* was a central term in all these discourses, it enabled ideas to circulate among them. Galen's animal spirit became the redemptive divine spirit of the Reformation, or the Neoplatonic ground of perception, or a late medieval vehicle for demonic manipulation. Unseen but active, spirit was a fertile ground for generating explanations. It is not without justice that William Harvey, in his *Exercitatio anatomica de motu cordis et sanguinis in animalibus* (1628), wrote that "persons of limited information, when they are at a loss to assign a cause for anything, very commonly reply that it is done by the spirits; and so they bring the spirits into play on all occasions; even as indifferent poets are always thrusting the gods upon stage as a means of unraveling the plot."[77] But Harvey's rejection of *spirit* as an explanatory term, itself an ambiguous action, had little force for Robert Burton, for whom, as we have seen, the task of anatomizing melancholy "and that philosophically, medicinally" (1:110) implied a joining of these knowledges.[78] He was not alone in this practice: the physician André du Laurens (1558–1609), who wrote the story of the man who refused to urinate, and who was known for his Galenic orthodoxy, began his treatise on melancholy with two philosophical chapters titled, in Surphlet's translation, "That man is a diuine and politike creature, endued with three seuerall noble powers, as Imagination, Reason, and Memorie," and "That this liuing creature full of the image of God, is now and then so farre abased, and corrupted in his nature, with an

infinit number of diseases that he becommeth all like vnto a beast."[79] The physician Laurens opened a conventional medical text on melancholy as a disease
of the brain with an account of the perfection of creation and the price of sin.
Like him, the scholar of divinity Robert Burton began his philosophical and
medical discussion of melancholy with a compressed version of Laurens's
initial chapters: "Mans Excellency, Fall, Miseries, Infirmities, The causes of
them" (1:121).

Neither Burton nor Laurens saw these sentiments as neat packets of medicine or divinity; for both the bookish physician and the curious divine, the
theological explanation for disease could be connected to motions of humors
and spirits through the economical machinery of Aristotelian causes. What was
lost in this porousness was any hope of scientific parsimony; what was gained
was a dizzying fluidity of explanations, a rich storehouse of possible metaphoric
transfers of meaning, and the possibility of deep connections between the concrete details of physiology and subtle psychological investigations. In this text,
we can find elements of the emerging paradigm of scientific observation and
reflection: consider Burton's reflections on cosmography in the Digression of
Air. Those elements are laid down next to reflections and narratives rooted in
the humanistic practices of textual research, especially as they were mediated in
medical humanism. In return, temporal structures generated by medicine are
imported into learned letters. Taken together, these discursive frames enable
Burton to move fluidly between the body and the mind; between the fragility of
health and the ubiquity of illness; between the unavoidable passions and the
elusive soul that was moved by them.

4

Burton, Rhetoric, and the Shapes of Thought

Burton seldom mentioned rhetoric, but this subject offered him both methods for developing ideas and models for generating texts that resisted conceptual closure and drew readers through the *Anatomy*. Like medicine, which Burton mentioned explicitly and repeatedly, rhetoric was a resource; understanding how Burton used these early modern disciplines poses useful questions for a transdisciplinary rhetoric.

Rhetoric was a staple of early modern education at many levels, including the arts course at Oxford. Peter Mack describes a conventional Oxford humanist curriculum—Aristotle's *Rhetoric* and the rhetorical works and orations of Cicero, especially *De inventione*. These set texts were often supplemented by the *Rhetorica ad Herennium*, Cicero's *De oratore*, or Quintilian's *Insititutio oratoria*, with occasional use of Hermogenes.[1] There are no surviving records of Robert Burton's own rhetorical education, or of the specific curriculum of Christ Church, but we do have the testimony of his library, which included a healthy collection of rhetoric books. Some seventy-three volumes of rhetorical studies that were owned by Burton remain in the Christ Church and Bodleian libraries; many are heavily annotated.[2] They formed a hefty collection of books of rhetorical theory: a 1527 edition of Bede's *De schematibus et tropis sacrarum literarum liber*, a commentary on Cicero's *De inventione*, Erasmus's *De copia*, and a Latin translation of Castiglione's *The Courtier*, which will be discussed more fully in chapter 5.[3] Some are hardy perennials: Rudolph Agricola's *De inventione dialectica omnes* and a collection of passages from Cicero's *De oratore*.[4] Some are technical rhetorics, workaday volumes seldom consulted today, like Gerardus Bucoldianus's *De inventione, et amplificatione oratoria*, a Ciceronian rhetoric published in 1534 that Burton annotated rather heavily.[5] Some are Burton family books: Agricola's *De inventione* was first owned by Robert Burton's older brother William, an antiquarian, who used it and wrote his name in it. Various other readers annotated Agricola, practiced the alphabet on its flyleaves, or wrote marginal comments. Robert Burton dated it "1598," signed it in five places, and

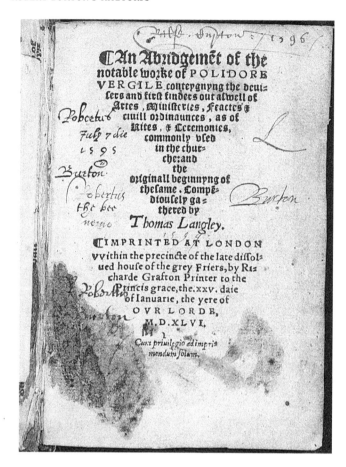

2 | Robert Burton's copy of Polydore Vergil, *An abridgement* [. . .] *conteygnyng the devisers and first finders out aswell of artes* [. . .] *civill ordinaunces, as of rites, & ceremonies* [. . .] (London: Richard Grafton, 1546), title page. This copy includes several versions of Burton's signature, as well as that of his brother (or possibly his father) Ralfe Burton. Photo: Christ Church Library, courtesy of the Governing Body of Christ Church, Oxford.

wrote summaries of key sections in the margin, as well as admiring notes on Agricola's discussion of amplification.[6] The much-used flyleaf of an abridged version of Polydore Vergil's account of the inventors of all the arts, *An Abridgement. . . . conteygnyg the devisers and first finders out aswell of artes . . .* , bears the names of Robert Burton (1594 and 1595), his brother Ralfe (1596), and the final matter-of-fact note "Jan: [Jane] Burton oneth this booke 1596 here is my marke" (figs. 2 and 3).[7] Vergil's compendium includes an account of the origins of rhetoric: "We may be sure that by and by after men were formed, they

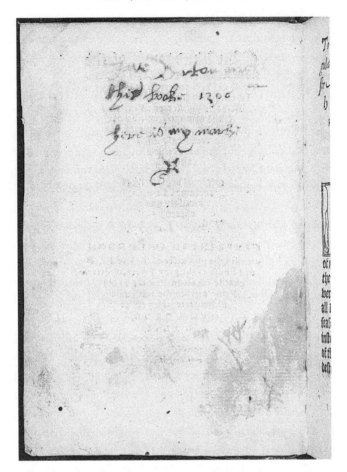

3 | Vergil, *An abridgement*, verso of title page, with inscription by Robert Burton's sister, "Jan: [Jane] Burton oneth his book 1596. here is my marke." Photo: Christ Church Library, courtesy of the Governing Body of Christ Church, Oxford.

received of God the use of speech, wherin what tyme they perceived some words to be profitable, and some hurtefull in uttering of theym: they appointed and gathered an Arte of Speache, or communication called Rethorycke."[8]

While Burton generally collected contemporary books, many of the rhetorics in his library were published in the sixteenth century; they were books that he and his family could have used as school texts. Burton also collected the speeches of John Rainolds, the sixteenth-century Protestant humanist professor at Corpus Christi College.[9] Rainolds was famed for his lectures on Aristotle's *Rhetoric*; the orations Burton owned took up a wide range of topics, and Burton might have learned from Rainolds's frequent comments on oratory and orators, especially in the introduction, but these orations are not works of rhetorical theory.[10] Burton also owned a massive edition of Peter Ramus's works, including his *Rhetoric*; the book is untouched, innocent of markings.[11]

Some of Burton's books are barely recognizable to us as rhetoric, such as Thomas Paynell's 1562 collection, *A frutefull book of the comon places of all S. Pauls epistles*.[12] Such an arrangement of Scripture passages by topic expresses a deeply rhetorical culture, but it would be difficult for us to recognize it as a disciplinary rhetoric. Other books are practical guides to issues of grammar, correct writing, or the composition of letters, such as Edmund Coote's *The English schoole-maister*, a book intended to guide the instruction of very young students, beginning with an English syllabary, moving through dialogues and other models of good language, ending with a catechism, guides to arithmetic, a chronology of the Bible, and a list of hard words (with directions for those who had never used an alphabetical list). *The English schoole-maister* was first published in 1596, but Burton owned the much later 1627 edition, published long after he would have had any active concern with such basic teaching.[13] Many of Burton's rhetoric books are collections of speeches: the orations of Rainolds mentioned above, but also Scaliger's reply to Erasmus's critique of Ciceronianism and the loopy orations of Cornelius Agrippa.[14] He held a handful of technical manuals, such as the delightfully titled book of advice by Albertanus Causidicus Brixiensis (Albert of Brescia), *Libellus de modo loquendi & tacendi*, in which a son is counselled by a careful father to balance his speeches with an equal quantity of silence, but to follow proper rhetorical forms when he did speak.[15]

How did Burton use rhetoric, including the books he owned, the books he would have had access to, and the rhetorical practices of early modern Oxford? Burton's references to rhetoric in the *Anatomy* are infrequent and often dismissive; for example, "Rhetoricians . . . out of their volubility of tongue, will talke much to no purpose" (1:101). But whatever his objections to rhetoricians' chatter, Burton read, studied, and taught the subject. He would have attended the required four terms of rhetoric for his bachelor's degree; later, as a Student at Christ Church, he would have been responsible for offering lectures in the arts program, which included rhetoric. Just as very few figures in contemporary academic life refer to the textbooks they used in their first-year writing class, or to the texts they taught from as graduate assistants, Burton seldom cites a rhetorical text. We have seen similar dynamics in the tacit early modern appropriation of the epideictic (chapter 2).

However, rhetoric offered Burton a broad escape route from the constraint of univocal certainty and from the universalizing deductive power of traditional philosophy. Rhetoric was rich in both methods and models for investigating multiple, potentially contradictory, possibilities. Some of these methods and models anticipate openings that would be adopted by the new sciences; many of them were congenial to Burton's project of exploring the relationships and affinities among early modern practices of knowledge. Since rhetoric offered a wide range of ways to support claims, connect observations, and analyze the arguments of others, it suggested practices of mobility that Burton exploited brilliantly in the *Anatomy*. Since many (but not all) rhetorics assumed a dialogic speech situation, they offered models for an energetic, fully defended argument that did not insist on the closure of discourse. For Burton, multiple voices were situated not only in the marketplace but also in the library; nonetheless, the arguments they advanced, in their contradictory and oblique relationships, demanded their own discursive spaces. Rhetorical models of agonistic speech, as in Aristotle and Cicero, could be read as prescriptions for holding and developing a position, in full recognition that your arguments might contradict, but would not abolish, those of your opponent, who makes his own appeals to the judge. In the world of Oxford, where disputations could offer an afternoon's diversion or determine the freedom of the adversaries, Burton offered a text that exploits some of the possibilities of dialogic rhetoric: holding the question open and embarking on a provisional course of action.

Rhetoric offered Burton a discipline that valued the situational and the contingent. We have seen that early modern university learning valued the permanence and universality of the philosophic sciences. But with the important exception of such Christian rhetoricians as Augustine, rhetoric has never claimed access to either permanence or universality. Even in Augustine, rhetoric relied on the kairotic situation, the well-chosen example, and the skillful adaptation of text to audience. While philosophic knowledge was deductive, rhetoric, like medicine, depended on the collection of observations and the development of *habitus* through imitation and practice.

And rhetoric has traditionally refused disciplinary constraints. Since Plato's *Gorgias*, critics have asked what exactly the rhetorician knows: is there a body of knowledge in this field that can be passed on? Are there any limits to what a rhetorician ought to know? These questions have been investigated perennially in the literature of rhetoric without arriving at any certainty. The melancholy interlocutors of *De oratore* with their inconclusive arguments about whether an orator needed to know the law have had plenty of company. Contemporary theorists, including those who, like me, work to construct a transdisciplinary rhetoric, are the latest but not the last to arrive at Crassus's villa in the country and enter the conversation there. For Burton, whose project in the *Anatomy* transgressed the boundary between religion and medicine, rhetoric offered a model of rigorous study that was, as Aristotle recognized, "not tied to a single defined genus of subject," but which fostered the ability to "find the available means of persuasion in each case."[16] If Burton wanted to show how different practices of knowledge could be brokered, opened to exchange, and mined for provisional advice on the pressing subject of melancholy, then the precepts of rhetoric, which turned on the exchange of arguments, the positioning of evidence, and an orientation to the exigencies of a situation, were as good a model as he was going to find.

These affinities between Burton's practice in the *Anatomy* and elements of rhetorical theory are, of course, very general. To get a clearer sense of how Burton used rhetorical resources, I will focus on two rhetoricians that Burton used freely: Rudolph Agricola, particularly his *De inventione dialectica* (Cologne, 1539), and Desiderius Erasmus, especially *De duplici copia verborum ac rerum commentarii duo* (1512, 1514) and his *Adages* (1500, 1508, 1536). Agricola offered methods for refunctioning the topics as tools of both investigation and development rather than as limited sources of logical figures. Erasmus offered models of polyvalent and unresolved exposition and of associative patterns of arrangement. Both these rhetoricians, like the physicians discussed in chapter 3, suggest models for practices of observation that would mark the new sciences in the last half of the seventeenth century.

Burton frequently cited Erasmus, especially his *Adages*. *De copia* and the *Adages* were widely read in sixteenth-century rhetorical studies; they influenced Burton conceptually and stylistically. Burton did not cite Agricola, but his *De inventione* was central to early modern pedagogy and suggested methods of invention and argument that are interestingly reconfigured in Burton's text. Looking more closely at these two rhetorical theorists can give us a sense of how Burton used rhetoric to make knowledge count. Taken together with discussions of Melanchthon, Aristotle, and Cicero in earlier chapters, these analyses show that Burton had absorbed the most fluid and inventive elements of early modern rhetoric, accommodating new practices of observation and suggesting alternative means of argument about uncertain matters.

Burton owned and annotated both Agricola's *De inventione* and Erasmus's *De copia*. He would have had access to the *Adages* through college libraries.

Erasmus' hefty collection was owned by several Oxford libraries, including the Bodleian, and he was among the authors most commonly owned by Oxford students.[17] These texts offer distinct lines of sight into how rhetoric sponsored not only Burton's distinctive writing, but the new ways of constructing knowledge emerging in the seventeenth century.

Rudolph Agricola and the Topics: Definition

Rudolph Agricola (1444–1485) wrote earlier than Erasmus, completing his *De inventione dialectica* in 1479; it was posthumously published under Erasmus's sponsorship in 1515.[18] *De inventione* is considered the first original work of early modern rhetoric and a central text of Northern European humanism. Agricola replaced judgment with invention as a central dialectical category, focusing on the topics or *loci*. He adapted Aristotle's dialectical treatment of them in the *Topics* into a method of rhetorical invention. Burton had a lively interest in the topics, the focus of many of his books of rhetorical theory, including his heavily annotated copies of Bucoldianus's *De inventione et amplificatione oratoria* (Lyons, 1551) and of Bede's *De schematibus et tropis* (Basel, 1527). When Burton mentioned a rhetorical text in the *Anatomy*, it was likely to be a book on the topics, such as Cicero's *De inventione*.

Medieval rhetoric developed the topics in two directions, following Aristotle's discussions in both his *Topics*, a work on logic, and in his *Rhetoric*. Topics had been separately charged with testing the soundness of arguments and with discovering means of persuasion. Agricola was the first early modern rhetorician to bring these two lines of investigation together.[19] His practice broke with that of Bede, who used the topics solely to generate logical maxims, and with Cicero, who used the topics in *De inventione* solely to generate discourse.[20] For Agricola, the topics raised issues about the grounding of knowledge: were the topics prompts to help the mind recall what it had learned, or did they correspond to underlying structures of reality? Did they indicate lines of argument developed through custom and repetition? How could they guide investigation? This ambiguity made the topics a useful place to negotiate the blurring boundaries of early modern knowledge practices. And no topic bridged the territories of rhetoric and dialectic so neatly as definition.

Agricola's reliance on the topics, particularly definition, accorded with his understanding of the offices of rhetoric. For him, the office of teaching was central, since a speaker could teach without moving or pleasing, but could neither move nor please without teaching. Or, according to the printed marginal gloss in Phrissemius's edition, "Proprium orationis munus esse, ut doceat."[21] Teaching required both the clear presentation of evidence and the deft management of affect, and so a rhetoric that emphasized teaching called for an understanding of the topics that bridged *logos* and *pathos*. Agricola's account of the primacy of teaching would later be taken up in Melanchthon's suggestions for remodeling the epideictic into various teaching genres, as described in chapter 2. It was certainly coherent with Burton's project in writing the *Anatomy*, announced soberly as anatomizing "this humour of Melancholy, through all his parts and species" (1:110). Here, Burton refers to the topics of partition and definition, two basic methods of presenting information. Those topics generate a text that will function to "prescribe means how to prevent and cure so universall a malady, and Epidemicall disease, that so often, so much crucifies the body and the minde" (1:110). To anatomize melancholy was to teach its causes, cures, prognostics, and special forms, thereby benefitting readers who have suffered, or soon will suffer, this universal illness. For Burton, teaching did not mean the transmission of static, depersonalized knowledge. For him as for Agricola, teaching changed readers' dispositions and opened them to a course of action. It could even motivate a general reform of the commonwealth, as in Burton's sketch of a utopian England.

Since he saw it as the foundation of teaching, definition was the first topic Agricola discussed.[22] The purpose of definition was both critical and simple: definition stated what something was. And it was also powerful: no one, Agricola said, seems to be more knowledgeable than the person who can explain what something is.[23] But if the purpose of definition was simple, its accomplishment could be complex. Agricola began by invoking the conventional prescription for definition: it should specify a genus and differentiate it to include all members of the class to be defined and nothing else. He also used the conventional example: man is a rational animal. But Agricola quickly admitted how hard it was to form such definitions. Only by finding out as much as possible about the object being defined can the orator use the topic properly.[24] The word Agricola uses for this investigation is significant—*perlustro*, or "I wander." *Perlustrare* includes senses of wandering through an area, or of examining every part of something; it derives from the priest's circuit of a temple, or from the ceremonies following a Roman census, when tribes of citizens were enumerated. It suggests an investigation in the world of society and nature, an amassing and assessing of examples rather than a deduction from first principles. And indeed, the example of definition that Agricola provided—a definition of law—includes reflections on how the word is used in ordinary speech, what sorts of injunctions would not be called laws, and how law relates to equity—a loose gathering of examples, qualifications, and counter-examples that is not especially concerned with including every possible law.

Agricola did not use the topics, including definition, as doorways to certain knowledge. They were an aid to finding what was *probabile*, or persuasive, not what was always and inevitably true. And Agricola recognized that most of the situations we encounter are uncertain: the topics are useful, he declares, because the greater part of humane studies are uncertain, and different speakers will treat topics differently, according to their own ingenuity.[25] As Peter Mack writes, Agricola saw definitions as constructed by the rhetor rather than inherent in the object; they were useful because they organized "knowledge of things in the world" and gave "the impression of authority," not because they followed logical rules.[26] Agricola's sense of topical investigation as perlustration, a wandering through discourses that is also a careful turning about of the object, evokes very precisely Burton's deployment of the topics in the *Anatomy*.

Burton and the Topics 1: Explicit Definitions

Agricola's *De inventione* has deep affinities with *The Anatomy of Melancholy*: they share a close articulation of argument with affect, an interest in contrary positions, a movement through territories of uncertainty, and a belief that the act of teaching could have its own power. They provide a method for developing discourse through patient but unsystematic investigation that coheres with Burton's procedure in the *Anatomy*. Burton used the topics and Agricola's advice about them without referring to them explicitly as topics: the term was more likely to be cited in reference books like the topical arrangement of quotations from St. Paul noted above than in a text like the *Anatomy*. In works of scholarship or good letters, such a move would have seemed like a child's school exercise. As Obadiah Walker, a late seventeenth-century essayist, observed, the arts of discourse "are but foundations, on which all sciences are built, but themselves appear not in the edifice."[27]

Burton did, however, explicitly refer to definition as a concept rather than a topic of invention, since definitions were conventional openings for early modern treatises. Sometimes, his definition is so elaborate as to be parodic. Consider the short subsection "Definition of Melancholy, Name, Difference," which appears well into the first partition, at the beginning of Burton's systematic discussion of melancholy (1:162–63). Burton collected a staggering variety of definitions of the disease, wandering through the extensive neo-Galenic literature on melancholy. In a page and a half, he quoted no fewer than twenty-three authorities, several of them multiple times. He offered the "common definition" of the disease as "*a kinde of dotage without a feaver, having for his ordinary companions, feare, and sadnesse, without any apparent occasion*" (1:162); he also offered examples that refuted it. Burton discussed the differentiae missing from the common definition and proposed several modifications (1:163). He went, in other words, by the book and thereby demonstrated the limitations of the book. In his account, melancholy has no boundaries: there is no *finis* to be specified. Some cases of melancholy will escape a concise definition, but a definition capacious enough to include them will necessarily include other diseases. Burton's definition of melancholy is certainly a perlustration; it indicates the complexity of the subject, the difficulty of sifting through the authorities who have written on it, and Burton's own brave, but ultimately futile, efforts to make sense of it all.

Even when Burton was satisfied with definitions that specified genus and differentia, he used those topics with a difference. In the subsection on the soul, Burton begins: "According to *Aristotle*, the *Soule* is defined to be ἐντελέχεια, *perfectio & actus primus corporis Organici, vitam habentis in potentiā*: the perfection or first Act of the Organicall body, having power of life, which most Philosophers approve" (1:147).[28] Burton has given us a genus, "perfection or first Act" of the body, which—as Agricola could have told us—is not exactly like placing "man" in the genus "animal." And the continuation, "having the power of life," is an attribute rather than a differentia. Burton is following his source, the first chapter of Aristotle's *De anima* II, but with a difference: in the context of the *Anatomy*, terms like "perfection," "first," and "power" have epideictic force; they are not only logical terms of art. The prescribed form of definition has been adapted to the purpose of praise; Burton celebrates the soul rather than analyzing it. Later in the chapter, Burton used the genus-differentiae form straightforwardly to define the vegetal and the sensible souls (1:148, 150). But when he came to the rational soul (1:155), the perlustrating scholar returned: "In the precedent Subsections, I have anatomized those inferior Faculties of the Soul; the *Rational* remaineth, *a pleasant, but a doubtfull subject* (as one [Velcurio] tearmes it) and with the like brevity to be discussed. Many erroneous opinions are about the Essence and originall of it" (1:155). Given the range of erroneous opinions, it is impossible to be brief, and Burton elliptically references sprawling debates about the substance of the soul, its immortality, the possibility of reincarnation, and the process of ensoulment. After a comprehensive catalogue of authorities both Christian and pagan, Burton settles on a definition:

> This Reasonable Soule, which Austin calls a spirituall substance, moving it selfe, is defined by Philosophers to bee the first substantiall Act of a Naturall, Humane, Organicall Body, by which a man lives, perceives, and understands, freely doing all things, and with election. Out of which definition wee may gather, that this Rationall Soule includes the powers, & performes the duties of the two other, which are contained in it, and all three Faculties make one Soule, which is inorganicall [not divided into parts] of it selfe, although it be in all parts, and incorporeal, using their Organs, and working by them. (1:157)

Burton's definition of the rational soul is a restatement with specifics of the general definition of the soul he had drawn from Aristotle's *De anima*. Burton varied the force of Aristotle's definition, brushing it lightly with Augustine's theory. In this iteration, the definition is more fully differentiated, designating the specifically human categories of understanding and free will. The honorific terms that Burton included in the initial definition of the soul ("perfection," "first," "power") have given way to the narrative of rationality as a motive living force, organizing the arc of human action from perception to action, located in the entire body, itself undifferentiated, but deploying the specialized organs of the body for its own purposes. It is this story that sets in motion the discussions of the understanding and the will, leading to the parodic definition of melancholy as an undefinable illness in the next member of the book. In the space of a few pages, Burton's varied uses of definition constitute a kind of perlustration in themselves. He wrote conventional genus-differentiae definitions, refashioned them, and subverted them. He used definition to frame an object as desirable or laudable, to organize an extended discussion of it, or to demonstrate that it cannot be bounded in any stable way. Later in the *Anatomy*, his definition of heroic love will be framed as a debate about whether or not it is an illness, and if it is an illness, whether it is of body or mind. Burton will treat heroic love as a species of melancholy—an illness that had never been securely located in body, mind, or spirit (2:57). Such deployments of definition are applications and extensions of its treatment by Agricola; they support his practice of tightly organizing ungovernable tendrils of knowledge while drawing attention to the provisional nature of his organization.

Burton and the Topics 2: Digressions

In the *Anatomy*, topics such as definition, cause, and consequence are presented as aspects of the issue under discussion rather than as rhetorical techniques. Sometimes, Burton does not even refer to these issues, let alone name them as topics, but tacitly uses them to organize and develop the text, especially in his marvelous digressions. Let us take the digression on air (2:33–67) as an example. Burton had already discussed air as a cause of melancholy in the first partition; his digression of air appears in the second partition, on cures, which gives advice for the rectification of the nonnaturals. But there is precious little medical wisdom in the digression. Instead, as we saw in chapter 3, it offers a recreation to both author and reader, a free exploration of a free element:

> As a long-winged Hawke when hee is first whistled off the fist, mounts aloft, and for his pleasure fetcheth many a circuit in the Ayre, still soaring higher and higher, till hee bee come to his full pitch; and in the end when the game is sprung, come downe amaine, and stoopes upon a sudden: so will I, having now come at last into these ample fields of Ayre, wherein I may freely expatiate and exercise my selfe, for my recreation a while rove, wander round about the world, mount aloft to those aethereall orbes and celestiall spheres, and so descend to my former elements againe. (2:33)

Recent scholarship by Stephanie Shirilan has demonstrated that such passages were considered therapeutic; they delivered both writer and reader from the obsessive ruminations of melancholy.[29] The digression of air is also a kind of antidefinition. Rather than establishing boundaries, it investigates questions raised in travel literature about the globe and the air itself: How high are mountains? How long are rivers? Why do lakes move? Where do birds go in the winter—mines? riverbanks? the poles? What is at the center of the earth, and is hell there? How and why are the races of humankind different? How do climates differ on different continents? Burton takes up cosmological questions raised by the new sciences: what parts of the "world"—by which Burton means the whole universe—move, and what parts are still? Are there local spirits and do they have powers? Are the newly observed celestial objects in fact new, and if so, what does it mean for the heavens to change? These questions are a radically abbreviated summary of the first half of the digression; they do not give the full sense of Burton's repetition and variation of question forms: "'tis fit to be enquired whether" (2:33); "I shall soone perceave whether *Marcus Polus* the *Venetians* narration be true" (2:34); "I would know for a certaine, whether there be any such men, as Leo Suavius in his comment . . . records" (2:37–38); "how comes it to passe" (2:42). So many ways of asking questions, so many things to ask about, so few answers. So extended and giddy a perlustration.

In fact, these ways of asking questions had been categorized by Agricola's editor Johannes Phrissemius in his ramified diagram of the topics. Following Agricola, Phrissemius listed internal topics, beginning with those substantially connected to the object of investigation—definition, genus, species, differentia, whole, parts, conjugates—and moving to those that inflect its substance— adjacents, acts, subjects. Then Phrissemius lists the cognates, which originate with the object, such as the various Aristotelian causes, effects, time, place, connections, and finally the topics external to the subject—contingents, names, opinions, comparisons, and opposites (fig. 4).[30] This is a lot of ground, and Burton covers pretty much all of it in the digression: he travels from the center of the world to its outermost edges (topic of the whole), he conjectures about the substance of the element air, and its mutability ("If it [the center of the earth] be solid earth, 'tis the fountaine of mettles, waters, which by his innate temper, turns Aire into water" (2:41). He considers adjuncts, such as the oceans, lakes, and rivers, and advances theories about the causes of their motions. He speculates about actions—winds, movements of the stars—and about contingents—the new satellites, the asteroids. Finally, he considers the effects of all this cosmographical speculation: "the World is tossed in a blanket" (2:55). The topics, for Burton, were less a procedure for systematic investigation than a set of suggestions for divagating, wandering, perlustrating. This text adapts the method that Agricola proposed when he advised the rhetor to imagine Virgil searching the topics for material to adorn the narrative of the *Aeneid*, and to do likewise. Of course, the correspondence between Agricola's topics and the themes explored in the "Digression of Ayre" does not mean that Burton actually consulted a list of topics in writing the chapter, still less that he used *De inventione* as a cookbook for *The Anatomy of Melancholy*. Since Agricola's topics were

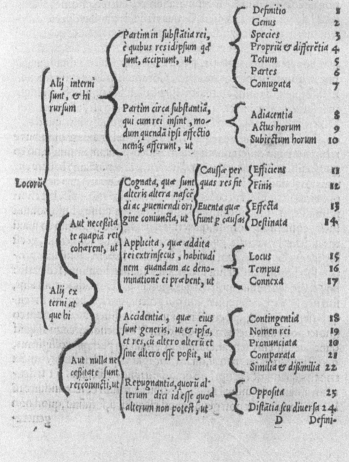

4 | Rudolph Agricola, *De inventione dialectica libri omnes et integri & recogniti* [. . .] (Cologne: I. Gymnicvs excvdebat, 1539), ramified diagram of the topics. Courtesy of the University of Michigan Library (Special Collections Research Center).

intended to apply to any issue, and to discover all that there was to say about it, it would be impossible to write at length about anything at all without deploying many of them. But what is distinctive in Agricola and prominent in Burton's text is the associative, generative development of the topics, their use to construct a practice of knowledge that moved among the fields of cosmography, medicine, and divinity, that included travel literature and natural history and ended with practical advice for building sites.

Burton also used the topics to develop the more discursive sections of the *Anatomy*. They appear, for example, in Burton's discussion of the rectification of exercise, a Galenic nonnatural (2:67–96). This expansive section surveys "labours, exercises and recreations . . . some properly belong[ing] to the body, some to the mind, some more easy, some hard, some with delight, some without, some within doores, some naturall, some . . . artificiall" (2:69)—a catalogue that could have been generated from a commonplace entry, using the Agricolan topics of parts, differentiae, attributes, causes, and places.

Burton begins with "the ordinary sports which are used abroad [outdoors]" (2:70), especially the noble sport of hunting, referencing famous hunters and praise of the sport by Xenophon and Plato. References to foolish, extravagant hunters follow hard behind. Burton takes up the ancient practice which divided hunting into three parts—air, land, and water—to structure the next passage, starting with hawking and ending with fishing, which, although troublesome, is healthy because it offers "good Aire & sweet smels" (2:72). He takes up other outdoor sports, listing twenty-five of them in a short laudatory paragraph, before arriving at the "most pleasant of all outward pastimes" (2:72), travel. Burton describes the things one might see in travel, naming both natural wonders and impressive buildings, ranging the world and returning to England. Burton's recommendations on exercise read associatively but are structured throughout by the topic of place: hunting on land leads to hunting in air, and hunting in water; hunting leads to other outdoor sports; outdoor sports lead to the best thing you can do outdoors, namely travel. And then travel opens up its own associative chain, a perlustration of perlustrating.

For Agricola, such associations were not random; these concepts were human constructions that disclosed the connections among things in the world, connections that supported the very process of making arguments:

So, for example, every thing has a certain substance of its own, certain causes it arises from, certain effects it produces. And so the cleverest men have chosen, out of that vast variety of things these common headings: such as substance, cause, and effect.... As if following these things, when we alert our mind to consider any given subject, at once we shall go through the whole nature of the thing and its parts, and through all the things that are consistent or incompatible with it, and we shall draw from there an argument apposite to the subject proposed.[31]

What are texts like Burton's perlustrations good for? They are certainly entertaining, and Burton was the last to discount the value of entertainment, especially for melancholics. But they also recall the practices of observation that were developing in the late sixteenth and early seventeenth centuries, and the possibilities of negotiating the shifting boundaries among disciplines. In the fifteenth century, Agricola was already aware of these shifts. At the beginning of Book II of *De inventione*, on dialectics, he held that dialectic was essential because of the contemporary confusion of disciplines. Every field of study seemed to be breaking out of its cave and overrunning boundaries, so that nothing was taught in its proper time or place.[32] In Agricola's view, the remedy for this confusion would be for the topics to reenter dialectics, structuring the associative order of texts like the digression of air, providing it with a framework of times and places that gave dispositive weight to rhetorical adornment. Sustained by the topics, the perlustrating investigator ambles but does not drift. The topics would turn the sad story of the *Aeneid* into a richly textured representation of human life.[33] Humanism provided a common store of tropes, authorities, and methods of work that allowed scholars in one field to work with the texts of another; it also provided methods for channeling these overflows, such as the imitation of the texts of antiquity, the production of *copia*, and the dense layering of description and incident.

Burton and the Topics 3: Observation

Twenty or thirty years after Burton's death, interactions among all sorts of scholars, both academic and amateur, would foster networks of correspondence similar to those we encountered among physicians in chapter 3. Savants exchanged specimens, described experiments and reported on singular events, forwarded the letters they received to each other, and established the networks of interlocutors.[34] The development of the nascent republic of letters required two things: a way of compiling and rendering accessible the written record and a way of describing the natural world that was situated, detailed, and potentially replicable. Balancing these two exigencies would be the work of natural philosophers in the late seventeenth century; Burton was among those whose experiments in language constructed the tools that would make their work possible.[35] Burton could have found prototypes for those tools in Agricola's theories of invention, especially as they were mediated in the devices for organizing knowledge described by Ann Blair. In her *Too Much to Know: Managing Scholarly Information Before the Modern Age*, Blair describes the desperation of early modern scholars, faced with the ever-increasing flood of printed books, a desperation that, as we have seen, Burton shared.[36] Blair details the contrivances they developed, including note cabinets and slips of paper fixed in a notebook with reusable glue. Both these devices are extensions of the commonplace book, a means of collecting information recommended by Agricola in both the final book of *De inventione* and in his widely circulated letter *De formando studio.*[37]

The commonplace book was ordered by the associative structures of the topics that Burton used to develop both his digressions and the more discursive sections of the *Anatomy*. Such uses of the topics raise questions about their ontological density; for Agricola, the topics arise from the commonalities among subjects of discourse, as discovered and refined in the tradition of "the cleverest men." Burton's understanding of them was different. In his discussion of exercise, the attribute of place is both an associative link and a real connection among outdoor recreations; mobilized in the topic of travel, it led Burton to other outdoor spectacles, like academic exercises, and then, by way of a shift to seasonal pastimes, to the topic of time. Although each item in the series connects materially to the one before it, the reader moves on a very thin thread of similarity and correspondence; it is a long way from fishing to commencement festivities. Burton's use of the topics, unlike Agricola's, did not depend on a sense of fundamental underlying connections, signatures of a coherent plan underlying the world of nature. For him, fishing is really different from hunting, and lots more trouble. Instead, the topics organize multiple connections at a series of points, links discovered by the writer through the process of invention rather than in contemplation.[38]

The collection of such points of correspondence and the description of the natural objects in which they were found was central to the early modern development of natural philosophy and the emerging new sciences of astronomy and mechanics, to say nothing of fields of study that are no longer part of the scientific canon, such as physiognomy.[39] Observation would be the gateway to the development of the new sciences. It emerged from medieval *experientia* as a practice that trained an individual to place the evidence of the senses within an interpretive framework, to communicate what was seen to other observers, and to present the object of observation clearly to the reader, with full (but as we have seen, not too full) sensory detail. These capacities did not emerge full-blown; they were developed within traditional early modern practices of knowledge. We have seen that, in the second half of the sixteenth century, the case history that might have been interpolated into an earlier text was left to stand on its own as an *observatio*; similar accounts of experience were collected by legal scholars, judicial astrologers, philologists, and astronomers.[40] Fostered in practices of collection, display, and reportage, observation was later elaborated into the signature displays of early experimental science: the air pump, the vivisected dog, the dying dove.[41] Shared practices of observation both supported and directed those boundary violations among disciplines that Agricola lamented; emerging inside and out of the academic *cursus*, organized explicitly or tacitly by topics, they confirmed affinities among members of collaborating groups and established collaborations with distant colleagues.

Observation made use of the techniques of early modern rhetoric: first, the development of ideas and arguments through a commonly shared set of topics, understood as aspects of the objects observed or as representing the consensus of scholars; second, the working up of a textual presentation of those objects through sensory description, using either the rhetorical tools for developing *enargeia* or those used to fashion *paradigmata*.

For Burton, there was little difference between things he had seen or heard himself and the reports of scholars. He used both kinds of evidence in the subsection "Of the Force of the Imagination": "Why doth one mans yawning, make another yawne? One mans pissing provoke a second many times to doe the like? Why doth scraping of trenchers offend a third, or hacking of files? Why doth a Carcasse bleede, when the murtherer is brought before it, some weekes after the murther hath beene done?" (1:254). Reading this series of observations drawn from common knowledge, everyday experiences, and ancient beliefs, all connected with the topic of cause, expanded and elaborated in a circuit through the body from high to low, from life to death, we might imagine Agricola nodding in agreement, only slightly puzzled at this distinctive application of his rhetoric. To our eyes, Burton's next step seems to move from observation to older practices of compiling authorities: "Why doe Witches and old women, fascinate and bewitch children: but as *Wierus, Parcelsus, Cardan, Mizaldus, Valleriola, Caesar Vaninus, Campanella*, and other Phylosophers thinke, the forcible imagination of the one party, moves and alters the spirits of the other" (1:254). But for early modern medicine, and for many of the other emerging disciplines of observation, examples gleaned from history and philosophy seamlessly supported the practice of direct observation. Nancy Siraisi gives an example of a cure effected by the surgeon Ambroise Paré in 1575: by dispersing the fumes of a charcoal brazier, he revived a man who had been given up for dead. Learned physicians confirmed his diagnosis and treatment by referring to the death of the emperor Jovian in 364 CE, as recounted in three sixteenth-century Latin reference works.[42] Nor was this an isolated event: in a book Burton frequently quoted, Johann Schenck's *Paratēr ēseōn sive observantiones medicae, rarae, novae, admirabiles et monstrosae* (1584–97), the *observationes* of contemporary physicians are arrayed with those of Galen and Hippocrates, of Jewish and Arab writers, and with reports of Schenck's own patients and the cases he excerpted from letters.[43] Early modern physicians and natural philosophers were so deeply confident of the evidentiary force of historical texts that the differences between Galen's anatomy and Vesalius's observations were often explained as biological differences between ancient and modern bodies. The collection and collation of authorities supported both Galenic practices of adapting general maxims to individual cases and Hippocratic inductive methods; the relationships, overlaps, and contradictions among authorities textualized practices of repeated observation.[44] Historical texts and direct observation were mutually supportive and confirming, two ways of recording the similarities and correspondences that underlay all of nature, or at least all the practices of the wisest men; the perlustration of writers need not be limited to what they or their colleagues had observed but could wander through the wealth of recorded observations.

In medical *observationes* or in natural histories, these authorities need not be deployed in the serried ranks of for-and-against quotations required for academic disputation; they could be spliced together in fluid, associative chains, disagreements duly noted and suggestive details included. For Burton, rhetoric provided tactics for combining the observation practices of medical humanism and the textual practices of early modern natural philosophy. What was seen and commonly heard could be joined with what was read; this practice allowed Burton the freedom to mix ancient and modern texts, Galenists and Paracelsans, including a striking phrase or a vivid image. In the emerging new sciences, observations were most valuable when they were repeated and sustained; we might think of the twenty-one years of observation performed by Tycho Brahe, an occasional visitor to the pages of the *Anatomy*.[45] In medical writing, the *observatio* could extend to a day-by-day record of the course of an illness; such a procedure is recommended to young doctors by Angelo Vittori in his posthumous collection *Medicae consultationes* (1640), which included case studies of his patients and accounts of his testimony at canonization trials.[46] Observation, report, and reading were all resources for the development of knowledge; *copia* was the path to truth.

But hoo, as Burton would say, how far have I wandered from the sober counsels of Agricola (2:57)? The mention of *copia* is our cue to turn to Erasmus, after summarizing how Burton used Agricola's rhetorical resources. Agricola understood the topics as grounded in material correspondences, confirmed by the common opinion of the learned, discerned in the process of invention. While I see no evidence that Burton understood topics as rooted in substantial identities, he did use them to bridge the domains of dialectics and of rhetoric; the discovery of matter and the construction of argument are founded in the categorical linkages among objects of discourse. This kind of correspondence is quite different from Foucauldian correspondence through signatures: resemblances do not point out the hidden qualities of objects; they are not a language. The discernment of resemblance is a capacity of the rhetor, a connection between the seeking mind and a nature that can, with difficulty, be known. Thus, topics such as definition are not to be contained within Boethian maxims or rules of inference; they are ways of collecting knowledge from the rhetor's experience, from the reported experiences of others, and from the recorded experience of the past. And that collection, although it would ideally be comprehensive, need not be systematic: arguments could be found and presented in a wandering, associative way.

In Agricola's discourse practice, observation is both solicited and contained. The topics offer a way of fluidly organizing empirical knowledge and a way of grounding that knowledge in philosophical categories. The fluidity of argument and openness to observation that characterize the *Anatomy* are constructed through methods that recall distinctive features of *De inventione*. Finally, Agricola's emphasis on teaching offered Burton a way of situating his work in the humanist tradition he so much admired. Like Cicero, like Horace, like Tacitus, Burton collected arguments, images, and testimonies to construct knowledge that was effective and persuasive; it would ease the melancholy it could not cure because layers of observation and testimony preserved the mobility of the sub-ject in the face of the stasis of melancholy.

Erasmus's *Adages*: Animating the Topics

Erasmus claimed a close connection with Agricola, acknowledging him in the *Adages* as the teacher of his teacher: "To the latter [Alexander Hegius] I owe the dutifulness of a son, to Agricola the love of a grandson."[47] Later humanists fondly told stories of an elderly Agricola meeting a very young Erasmus. (But Agricola was only just over forty when he died.) Philipp Melanchthon wrote that Agricola talked to the schoolboy Erasmus, read his writing, and announced, "Tu eris olim magnus," "You will one day be great."[48]

While Burton does not cite Agricola, his debt to Desiderius Erasmus (1466–1536) is recorded in the pages of the *Anatomy*. He cited fifteen works of Erasmus and included him in various lists of edifying modern writers (1:101; 1:244; 2:191, for example). He quoted from Erasmus's *Moriae encomium* ten times; there are scattered references to letters and colloquies. He did not cite *De copia*, although he owned and annotated the book.[49] But Burton returned again and again to Erasmus's *Adages*, a compendious early modern monster collecting over 4,000 proverbs from both modern languages and the literature of antiquity, printed in 163 editions before 1660.[50] In the authoritative University of Toronto trans-lation, the *Adages* fill six hefty volumes; this was a reference book, not a hand-book for ready use.[51] Although the *Adages* is not included in Kiessling's inventory of Burton's library, the book was held in Oxford college libraries as far back as 1556.[52]

Adagia collecteana (1500) was the first book-length text published by the young Erasmus, with 818 proverbs. After a stay with the publisher Aldus Manu-tius in Venice, he expanded the collection to 3,260 proverbs in 1508 under the title *Adagiorum Chiliades* (Thousands of Proverbs). The eighth edition, includ-ing 4,151 proverbs, was published in 1536, the year of Erasmus's death.[53] In each edition, Erasmus expanded his explanatory glosses on the proverbs, adding citations from his ongoing reading or sharpening his observations. Early glosses took the proverbs at face value as prudential advice; later glosses were likely to consider contrary possibilities, or to question the assumptions of the proverb.

For contemporary readers, proverbs are curiosities, decorative tidbits of language, and so a collection of proverbs by the central scholar of northern humanism is a generic anomaly. But for early modern readers, the proverb was a recognized means of persuasion. Aristotle connected the maxim to the enthymeme and recommended its use to older speakers; Quintilian considered proverbs to be concentrated fables, sayings of such antiquity that everyone held them to be true. He included proverbs in his discussion of comparisons, dismissing those that were in common use but false, such as "The generous tree bears fruit as soon as it springs up," criticisms that Erasmus dutifully repeats in his discussion of those proverbs (31:295).[54]

It is hard for us to understand why the proverb, bound up in *doxa*, synonymous with received ideas, could have been so fascinating to Erasmus and to his readers, including Burton. Erasmus intended the *Adages* to serve as a source of wisdom, as a philological resource, and as a record of the lived experience of the ancient world, an early modern analogue to James Joyce's project of describing Dublin so fully that it could be reconstructed from *Ulysses*. And the *Adages* fulfills all of those functions. The proverbs roll by, one by one or in small, loosely associated groups (for example, three proverbs against trusting Thessalians, 31:243–45). They are glossed with lore ancient and modern—we should distrust Thessalians because pirates lurked in caves overlooking their harbor. Erasmus's commentaries include accounts of the habits of farmers or smiths and stories about warriors, birds, and bugs. While we think of proverbs as ways of closing off discussion, of counselling adherence to the way things have always been done, the proverbs in Erasmus's *Adages* are provocations to thought, to seeing things differently.

The *Adages* also served as a philological resource. Like the *Anatomy*, the *Adages* have been compared to scholia, marginal comments on textual and interpretive matters in medieval and early modern books. In proverb after proverb, Erasmus moved into that world of textual disputes, connecting matters of lexis to questions of interpretation, as in his remarks on the proverb "The bull too went off into the wood," which includes, "The current scholia on Theocritus have the particle *ken* instead of the copulative conjunction *kai*; they add that the proverb is used of those who go away never to return" (31:94).[55] He connected the proverbs to his most revered texts: Plato, Cicero, Scripture. Proverbs, he held, were traces of the *prisca scientia*, the most ancient and sacred philosophy (31:14).

The *Adages* would open this resource to any reader who knew Latin. While some early modern scholars like Richard Montagu scorned those who relied upon the "backdoore of an Index," as a help of "Lazinesse and Ignorance," Erasmus, always pedagogically aware, included indexes in all editions of the *Adages* after the Aldine.[56] Since the proverbs were continually cited by ancient authors, Erasmus's compilation of their interpretations offered a vertical section of Greek and Roman thought about such topics as delay, difficulty, or labor, and Erasmus invited his readers to reflect on their range of opinions. In his short gloss on the proverb "From one, learn all," Erasmus first presents Virgil's opinion that one try should teach us all we need to know about an action, and then Suidas's reading, in which the proverb is seen as a caution against overgeneralization (31:214). Neither version is preferred, nor does Erasmus attempt to bring the two distinct senses of the proverb together.

The *Adages* compile the cultural commonplaces of antiquity, accounts of individuals seen as "proverbial" for various events, skills, virtues, or vices: "The eloquence of Nestor" (31:196) or "You are calling for Hylas," after the story of Polyphemus calling after a beautiful drowned Argonaut (31:366). Many of these references were obscure, and some figures, such as "Haughty Maximus" (31:212), survive only in the proverb they inspired. Erasmus asserted in his introduction that the best authors of antiquity could not be understood without knowledge of proverbs: ancient writings are full of explicit or elliptical references to them. Proverbs also reference customs both rare and mundane. So "back to the third line" (31:69–70) referred to the disposition of Roman troops; "to mark with the finger nail" (31:436–37), to the custom of using a fingernail to mark something condemned or unsatisfactory. And still others refer to the lost common knowledge of ancient cultures: "the laugh of Chios" (31:447) for a lascivious game played by Chians; "If only I had what lies between Corinth and Sicyon!" (31:468) for someone who desires wealth. Readers of the *Adages* would learn that "I will move the counter from the sacred line" referenced an audacious move in a Greek game (31:72), and that "They flee from the reddened cord" recalled an Athenian custom of herding reluctant citizens into council with a cord smeared with ochre; anyone found outside the agora bearing marks from the red dye had to pay a fine (31:289). Proverbs, for Erasmus, fulfill functions far beyond those Quintilian described: the adornment of a speech with sayings that seem inexpressibly old, that have no author, and that everyone knows, proverbs like "looking a gift horse in the mouth."[57] In the *Adages*, proverbs reanimate a whole world, showing us everyday life in the great cities of antiquity.

In the *Adages*, reanimation is the name of the game. If, as Aristotle held, a maxim is like the premise of a syllogism, a general statement about how things are, Erasmus's adages put that premise into motion, investing it with narrative energy.[58] In his surprisingly long discussion of the proverb "up and down" (31:302–4), Erasmus quoted from Terence, one of his favorite authors, who used the expression in *Eunuchus* to describe a servant running between two lovers. Then he remarked, "This metaphor seems to be borrowed from the Sisyphus of legend, rolling his stone in the underworld" (31:303). Erasmus compiled stories of people running from place to place, or confusing up and down, or of gods tumbling things back and forth. All of these examples subordinate the logical relationship of opposition between two connected things to the representation of actions, usually physical but sometimes mental, that move on an axis between two poles. Erasmus's strategies for augmenting the adages are legion, and not every proverb receives this treatment. But his transposition of the concentrated expression of the proverb into a vivid narrative is at the center of many of the most celebrated adages; it offered a model for the radical indeterminacy of Burton's *Anatomy*. That indeterminacy escapes the stagnation that, as we saw in chapter 1, horrified Stanley Fish. Nobody (except Burton) was better than Erasmus at presenting a mobile text, and Erasmus was never better at it than in the *Adages*.

Let us consider how this strategy works in Erasmus's treatment of the proverb "a dung-beetle hunting an eagle" (35:178–214), which he glossed as "no one should despise an enemy however humble" (35:214).[59] Erasmus expanded the proverb with a long essay, elaborated over successive editions of the *Adages*. Three quarters of the commentary is devoted to a natural history of the eagle and the dung beetle—and for Erasmus, as for other early modern writers, natural history included not only an account of an animal's name, appearance, habits, and anatomy but also of its mythology and legends.[60] Erasmus identified the eagle with the king (and by extension, the imperial legions)—all, like the eagle, powerful figures, whether as protectors or devourers of the commonwealth. Surprisingly, in the *Adages* both the eagle and the king are ugly and dangerous. Erasmus describes the eagle in an ironic blazon: "Come now, if some honest reader of faces will take a careful look at the features and the mien of the eagle, the greedy, evil eyes, the menacing gape, the cruel eyelids, the fierce brow, and most of all the feature that Cyrus the Persian king found so pleasing in a ruler, the hook nose, will he not recognize a clearly royal likeness, splendid and full of majesty?" (35:183). On the other hand, although the dung beetle is a disgusting beast, foul-smelling, ugly, and in love with feces, in the course of the commentary it morphs into a useful, noble, and even beautiful animal, certainly more beautiful than the eagle. Rather than causing harm, the beetle has curative powers; it was revered by the Egyptians; it can be compared to Silenus, the fig-ure of hidden virtue, and by extension, to Socrates and Christ.

Natural history having been fully ventilated, Erasmus tells how the eagle and the dung beetle became enemies. The eagle was pursuing a hare, who took ref-uge in the dung beetle's hole. Ignoring the dung beetle's pleas for mercy, the eagle killed the hare, violating at once the laws of hospitality, supplication, and friend-ship. "This outrage," Erasmus observed, "sank deeper into the heart of the gener-ous scarab than anyone would have believed," and he plotted a cruel revenge (35:209). Skilled at moving round objects, the beetle pushed the eagle's eggs out of the nest, so that "the unformed chicks were dashed pitifully on the rocks" (35:210). It also destroyed the eagle-stone, a legendary rock without which the eagle could not lay eggs. Facing extinction, the eagle appealed to Jupiter, who agreed to shelter the eggs in his bosom. But the beetle managed to drop a ball of dung among them; Jupiter, disgusted, shook away the dung and the eggs shattered. Since Jupiter needed the eagle as his messenger, he convened a coun-cil of the gods. They could not reconcile the enemies but ordered them to observe a truce for the thirty days when the eagle was nesting.

Even this bare account gives a sense of Erasmus's fluid sympathies: the beetle is noble, and then bloodthirsty. The eagle is rapacious, and then bereft. Their enmity is at first parodic, and then a little frightening.

Contemporary scholars have studied this proverb, focusing on its political salience. For Denis L. Drysdall, in "Erasmus on Tyranny and Terrorism," it tells of the "strife between the ruler and the ruled" as Erasmus saw it play out in conflicts between sovereigns and rapacious foreign mercenaries.[61] Terence J. Martin disputes this identification in "The Intractable Dialectic of Tyranny and Terror: A Reading of an Erasmian Adage."[62] Martin reads the dung beetle as a member of a liberation movement who began as a freedom fighter but ended as a savage killer.

Together, these readings of the enmity between the eagle and the dung beetle capture what is compelling about the proverb and its expansion: Erasmus's fluid presentation of the animals as now repulsive or cruel, now valuable or pitiable; his refusal to present any stable image of virtue or prudence; his constant—and constantly withdrawn—proffer of contemporaneous allegory; his destabiliza-tion of the proverb's allegorical reference (some aspects of the beetle recall mercenaries; others, rebellious peasants). What might be added to these read-ings is a sense of the genre affordances of the commentary: it opens a lapidary concentration of language into an expansive territory where knowledges and narratives can be interrupted, reversed, and reinscribed. Read from the point of view of genre, Erasmus has refigured the domain of the proverb; in his hands, it offers multiple interpretations of vivid actions. This model, available to Burton, could be applied to multifarious early modern practices of knowledge; provisional statements are mobilized so that they can be evaluated kairotically, taken up or rejected by readers. In neither Burton's book nor Erasmus's commentary does the story close in any comfortable way: both present a reader with radical indeterminacy, and with the exigency of choosing, in their own particular case, the best of the contradictory alternatives.

Consider Erasmus's account of Jupiter's dilemma: should he intervene in the war between eagle and dung beetle or not? Erasmus writes, "He was himself, without a doubt, more inclined to the eagle's side; on the other hand, he was influenced by the fact that a very harmful example was set if anyone were to be allowed to hold the laws of supplication, friendship, and hospitality in contempt. So he did what he usually does at critical moments; he called a council of the gods" (35:212). This Jupiter is not an august guardian of the law but a beleaguered functionary, facing the same kinds of contradictory mandates we face in the world beneath Olympus. Erasmus never stabilizes the image of Jupiter: we see him, at one moment, defiled by dung and comically careless of the eagle's eggs; at another, promulgating a sanctuary for the eagles in august language, "Thus he spoke and made all Olympus tremble at his nod. The whole assembly of the gods murmured their assent" (35:213). The expansion of a proverb becomes a way of opening up a narrative, providing multiple points of view, and moving the text through both narrated time and the temporal locations of readers.

Another example of this mobile indeterminacy can be found in the proverb "exchange between Diomede and Glaucus" (31:144–63), drawn from an episode in the *Iliad*. Diomede and Glaucus met in single combat and discovered that their forefathers had been allies. They exchanged armor as a token of their personal separate peace: Diomede took Glaucus's gold armor and gave him bronze armor in return. Homer told this story without judging either character, remarking only that Diomede got the better of Glaucus in this "mad exchange" (31:145). But Erasmus's account presented Diomede as a wily Greek, determined to get the best of a boastful and longwinded Glaucus. He referenced Plato and Aristotle on this story, and then gave Plutarch's reading: there was nothing wrong in exchanging gold for bronze, but it would be foolish to exchange virtue for health. Erasmus criticized Justinian for rationalizing his revisions of Roman law with this proverb—and extended his criticism to the whole legal profession, ignorant of the texts of antiquity. He concluded that the proverb can be used to describe anyone who exchanges something of value for something less valuable, or "the other way round" (31:146). Both the proverb and its opposite are true. These reflections invest someone who "increases his income, but with the loss of honour" (31:146) with the drama of a meeting on the Trojan battlefield, the fragile truce between combatants, the ambiguity of their exchange. A fraudulent contract evokes the golden armor of Glaucus, and subtle questions about the value of what has been gained and what has been lost.

Erasmus's *De copia*: Concentrating the Animation

The *Adages* and the more familiar *De copia* work reciprocally to demonstrate how textual materials can be extended or concentrated.[63] Paradoxically, I will be visiting the *De copia* for examples of concentration. Erasmus saw the *copia* as equally useful in teaching brevity and expansion: he counseled potential critics of the abundant style that "the compressed style and the abundant style depend on the same basic principles."[64] Knowing all the possible words to use in a situation is essential to the writer who wants to choose the single best one. And indeed, in *De copia* Erasmus offers directions for reversing the jubilant expansion of incidents that he had demonstrated in the *Adages*. In *De copia*, the proverb of the eagle and the dung beetle is concentrated into a sentence: "One should not despise or disregard any enemy, however weak and humble, seeing that the eagle in Aesop's tale had to pay for scorning the beetle."[65]

A similar interplay between expansion and compression can be found in Erasmus's treatment of the issues of constancy and change, discussed at length in both the *Adages* and, as we saw in chapter 2, in *De copia*. Erasmus's favorite image for this theme was the ever-adaptable polyp, which changed its color to match its surroundings. Cited in both *De copia* and the *Adages*, the polyp is also mentioned in *De conscribendis litteras* and in Erasmus's correspondence. In the *Adages*, Erasmus radically expanded the proverb "adopt the outlook of the polyp" or "*polypi mentem obtine*" (31:131–36). He cited examples from secular and sacred texts, including Odysseus of the many turnings and the chameleon as described by Pliny and Aristotle. He raised the problem of judging Alcibiades:

was his ability to adapt to the customs of every nation a vice or a virtue? Is there something harsh about a refusal to entertain new customs? How do we avoid giving way to "a disgusting type of flattery" (31:134)?

In other texts, Erasmus recommended imitating the polyp's adaptability. In his advice on writing letters (1522), he urged his reader to imitate the polyp that "adapts itself to every condition of its surroundings," as a way of attending to an audience.[66] In 1527, in a letter to his assistant Nicholas Kass, Erasmus advised him to "imitate the polyp. Bare your head, extend your hand, give way, smile at everyone, but without trusting anyone you do not know." Some readers might call this disgusting flattery, but the polyp knows no absolutes.[67]

In the *Adages*, the proverb becomes a mobile invocation of the pleasures and perils of adapting to circumstances.[68] Alcibiades's and Odysseus's stories are open to interpretation and judgment, to a many-vectored, open-ended exploration characteristic of "living speech," speech that, because of its close adaptation to audience and circumstance, is difficult to represent in a printed book. Living speech, for Erasmus, resembled the intimately modulated style of the letter (31:161). If writing was only an artificial voice, an imitation of a real voice, then the proverb restored to the written text some of the mobility characteristic of life. The more writing approached the mobility of living speech, the less important it was for readers find definitive judgments about the customs of nations or the efficacy of regimens against melancholy. A provisional decision about a particular custom as enacted by a particular person, or a distinctive way of cooking fruit for a specific individual, would suffice.

In *De copia*, as we saw in chapter 2, this mobility is both preserved and compressed. Erasmus includes proverbs and adages in the armamentarium of the abundant style; to illustrate the uses of the commonplace book, he turns again to our friend the polyp.[69] The polyp appears in Erasmus's model commonplace book entry, among ways of expanding the idea of changeableness or irresolution; it is among examples of expansion drawn from science, in this case natural history, taking its place beside the sky in springtime, the chameleon, the shifting images of dreams, and the changeable moods of childhood: "the polyp, whose changeableness has become proverbial."[70] And it reemerges a few pages later, as Erasmus explains that all the material used to criticize inconstancy can be used for an opposite purpose, "praising a man for all seasons, endowed with a versatile and dexterous mind," who can be compared to the "polyp which changes colour according to the surface beneath it."[71] In these citations, grouped with many others associated with the same idea, all the expansion of the *Adages* is latent: in the *De copia*, the polyp's variation also invokes Odysseus and Alcibia-des, the exemplars of the proverb, as well as the metonymic associations of the sea, the sky, dreams. If, as Erasmus claimed, the tools of *copia* are also the tools of compression, then both the expanded proverbs of the *Adages* and the concen-trated references of *De copia* offer ways of inserting narrative elements into a text such as the *Anatomy* that refuses extended narrative. Just as an American rhetor might invoke the story of the fallen cherry tree, the theme of honesty, the policy of avoiding foreign entanglements, and the privations of Valley Forge by mentioning George Washington, the early modern writer who made good use of Erasmus's *Adages* is equipped with references and exempla, drawn from church fathers and the writers of antiquity, that were rich in associations.

In chapter 3, we saw that Burton gathered medical references intended to support a strong inductive inference without elaborating or personalizing them. Both these *paradigmata* and Erasmian interpolated narratives are strategies of compression. The examples Burton used in describing medical cases are pre-sented schematically, the better to gather cumulative force as proofs; the com-pression of the proverb suggests a line of commentary that modifies, amplifies, or even contradicts its point. For example, in his discussion of love melancholy in the third book of the *Anatomy*, Burton opens the treatment of "Heroicall Love, which is proper to men and women" by distinguishing it from the "honest love" of marriage (3:51). Marriage, Burton concedes, is holy and a source of tranquil happiness, as demonstrated by some proverbially happy married cou-ples: "As *Seneca* lived with his *Paulina*, *Abraham* and *Sara*, *Orpheus* and *Euridice*, *Arria* and *Poetus*, *Artemisia* and *Mausolus*, *Rubenius Celer*, that would needs have it ingraven on his tombe, hee had lead his life with *Ennea* his deare wife 43 yeares, 8 months, and never fell out" (3:52). This is not an edifying list. Every reader would recall Sarah's refreshing but unseemly laughter at the thought that she might have a child in old age, her exile of Hagar and Ishmael, and Abraham's habit of passing her off as his sister. The story of Orpheus and Eurydice is one of needless and irreparable loss. Some of Burton's readers would also have known about the disputes about whether Paulina voluntarily opened her veins when Nero ordered Seneca's suicide, or was stabbed by Seneca to insure a joint suicide, or accepted Nero's order that her wounds be bound up, or some combi-nation of these grim endings. The story of Arria and Paetus is also one of joint suicide: Pliny reports that when Paetus hesitated to follow Nero's order that he commit suicide, Arria stabbed herself, handed him the dagger, and told him that it didn't hurt. Artemisia, an emblem of chaste widowhood, not only built a (proverbially) splendid tomb for her husband Mausolos but mixed his ashes with her daily drink. Rubenius Celer, also known as Rubrius Celer, seems to have been known only for the funeral inscription that Burton quotes. Taken together, this group does not exactly confirm Burton's summary comment on marriage, "There is no pleasure in this world comparable to it" (3:52). These are certainly love stories, and some of them are indeed proverbial—although not as examples of marital bliss. Indeed, many of these examples are concerned with death, including violent and suicidal death, and all raise questions about constancy or the lack of constancy. Was Abraham right to pass Sarah off to the Pharaoh as his sister? Do we believe Rubenius Celer's inscription? Should Paulina have allowed her wounds to be bound up? Was Artemisia a model widow or a disgusting cannibal? Burton does not linger over these questions, or even raise them explicitly; the text of the *Anatomy* hurtles on into a discussion of heroic love melancholy. But for a reader who lingers over these proverbial examples and has entered into a long, rambling conversation, the text has become Erasmus's living speech.

Burton sometimes quoted Erasmus's proverbs straightforwardly—he was especially fond of "one nail drives out another"—but other references to the *Adages* are floridly polyvocal. In "Democritus to the Reader," Burton pleads guilty to the charge of taking material from other writers without adding anything of his own: his only defense is that all writers do the same. He imagines a reader saying "that this is *actum agere* [to do what has been done], an unnecessary worke, *crambem bis coctam opponere*" or "to set out twice cooked cabbage" (1:8). The reference here is to Erasmus's rather more threatening "crambe bis posita mors" (31:417–18), "twice served cabbage is death," glossed in the *Adages* with multiple citations praising the health-giving effects of cabbage, emphasizing that it is a cure for drunkenness. Erasmus explained that because the Greeks found overcooked cabbage repulsive, the phrase can be used to criticize boring, repetitive speeches, but that it should not be applied to a beautiful speech that could be repeated over and over. It is even possible, Erasmus suggested, that aversion to cabbage was based on a feeling that the plant was sacred and worthy of veneration. Here, a wide range of possible responses to textual borrowing is compressed into a proverb: is such borrowing, and therefore Burton's book, a stale rehash of other writers; is it health-giving; is it boring; is it sacred? Erasmus demonstrated to Burton the power of multivoicing, and the possibilities of inserting points of contradiction and controversy within the text as it rolled forward in "ambages" (1:18). In these moments, the reader could be drawn into a long, quiet, and unresolvable conversation with the writer. Both writer and reader speculate about their object of reflection, whether overcooked cabbage or golden armor, entertaining the possibilities that it was good, bad, useful, harmful, useful in certain circumstances, or harmful if used unwisely. Such speculations are neither direct extensions of the story nor rigorous arguments; if anything, they recall the ancient Greek custom of discussing epideictic discourses and traditional poems over dinner, debating the merits of various actors and actions. For Jeffrey Walker, these discussions formed beliefs and ideologies; they were the seedbeds of civic arts of speaking.[72]

I argue that Burton found in Erasmus a model for producing a text that, while it did not shrink from assertion, also opened spaces for contrary views and qualifications; this way of writing prompted a reading practice that accommodated both the novice student who might ask whether it was really a good idea to drive out one nail with another and the learned reader for whom every classical reference trailed a tradition of commentary and controversy. If, for Burton, the conversation of friends was among the most effective cures for melancholy, he found in Erasmus a rhetorical model for writing such conversation, a way of grafting it into the compendious structure of the early modern treatise.

Adages, Copia, and the Shapes of Ambages

Nor was the proverb the only structural device that Burton learned from Erasmus. He could have found in the Adages and the first book of De copia the wandering shape of his "ambages," the associative textual form barely contained within the orderly scheme of the Anatomy. Erasmus did not order either his proverbs or his suggestions for expanding ideas in any conventional way, but both of these congeries continually suggest connections and provisional progressions. Only in the index—and Erasmus's Adages was among the first books to offer one—could a curious reader search for proverbs on a specific topic. Even here, a reader searching for a proverb on constancy had to simply browse the list, since the index organized the proverbs under 257 topics but did not order the topics alphabetically.[73] In the main text of the Adages, the numbered proverbs morph from theme to theme, teetering on the edge of intelligibility. Take, for example, these proverbs:

89. The tunic is nearer than the cloak.
90. The knee is closer than the calf.
91. Everyone wants things to go better for himself than for others.
92. Self-lovers.
93. Out of range.
94. Behind the front rank.
95. Far from the horse's hooves.
96. Away from Jove and from the thunderbolt. (31:89–114)

This sequence opens with the theme of caring for what is closest to you, and extends to wanting things to go well for oneself, a disposition that Erasmus pillories in "self-lovers," as "shameful" (31:311). Destructive self-love turns to other kinds of self-preservation, both base and noble: in Erasmus' commentary being out of range of an attack is a reasonable stratagem, but deliberately taking a place behind the front rank is "suitable to a cowardly wretch" (31:312), while avoiding the horses' hooves or Jove's thunderbolt is an act of prudence. The first four proverbs deal with proximity; the second four, with distance. Each proverb is linked to the one before it, but they do not form a coherent class.

The seldom-read first book of *De copia* offers similar associative structures. In that book, after his celebrated list of variations on "I was happy to get your letter," Erasmus collected in short chapters possible expressions and turns of speech for specific topics; for example, chapters 55–58 offer ways to say that something is "customary."[74] Erasmus also listed various phrasings of discourse functions, as in the sequence of chapters 35 to 37, which suggests ways of presenting negative statements of either equal or unequal weight.[75] By far the most common lists of variants are synonyms for specific nouns and verbs—134 chapters in all. Like the adages, these chapters seem miscellaneously arranged; like the adages, they modulate slowly among loosely associated topics. The chapter expanding "before time," for example, lists nine expressions for various premature events, such as an early death or marriage. These are followed by three *sententiae* about the folly of making hasty decisions; the chapter ends with a quote from Ovid's *Heroides*, "your corn is still in green leaf."[76] In the *Adages*, these materials would have been expanded in an essay; here, they are presented in a bare list. In both *De copia* and the *Adages*, Erasmus collected varied expressions for specific situations, prudential *doxa*, and quotations from good authors. Both texts are organized in associative series; in *De copia* the expansion of "before time" appears in a series that deals with all kinds of temporal relations:

187. In time, etc.

188. Before time.

189. After time, late.

190. Haste. (42:552–57)

Like the proverbs dealing with proximity and distance in the *Adages*, each phrase connects to the one that precedes and follows it. But the changes are so constant and incremental that it is impossible to describe the overall structure of the 206 chapters.

In chapter 3 of this book, we saw that the temporalities of regimen offered Burton a way of structuring text that avoided the drive toward closure of early modern fictional narratives. This temporality, alternately dilated and compressed and punctuated with irregular crises, was an instructive model for the tempo of the *Anatomy*. But how do we account for its momentum, its ability to pull the notorious slugabed Samuel Johnson out of bed two hours early?[77] What attracted the enthusiastic contemporary readers that Stephanie Shirilan studied?[78] I propose that Erasmus's associative structures offered Burton ways of connecting ideas that continually drew readers forward into a relentlessly plural text.

Burton could have found in Erasmus's associative lists a way of loosening the constraints of the *Anatomy*'s overall structure, with its relentless ramified *divisio*. Writing over a century after Erasmus, with the intention of offering comprehensive, useful information, Burton did not write a book as sprawling as *De copia*, let alone the *Adages*. But he did engraft the associative structure of these works onto the orderly development and division presented in the tabular list of contents that introduces each book of the *Anatomy*. Take, for example, a subsection in Book 3, "The last and best Cure of Love Melancholy, is, to let them have their Desire" (3:242–72), expansive in both its development and its concept. Preceding subsections had argued for the containment or reversal of love by persuasion, by reflecting on the general nastiness of women, or by offering medicines, but here Burton offered permission to love, a loosening of restraints. He began with the encompassing invitation, "let them goe together, and enjoy one another" (3:242), augmented with noted physicians' advice to marry. But almost immediately, Burton swerves into a long discussion on impediments to marriage such as unrequited love, the fickleness of women, the opposition of parents, severe laws, and rash vows of chastity. These impediments, each of them liberally expanded, take up nearly half the chapter: the imprudence of forbidding monks and nuns to marry leads to stories of clergy who died because of their celibacy, citations of church fathers who advised against celibacy, and quotations from Chaucer set in gothic type. Somehow this leads to stories of generals who provided prostitutes for their troops. After his exhaustive treatment of impediments, Burton offers a list of reasons to marry imputed to Jacobus de Voragine, but actually drawn from *Loci communes* (1545) by Urbanus Rhegius, who himself drew from Erasmus's *Encomium matrimonii*.[79] Then Burton's own quite Erasmian Anti-parodia reverses each of the reasons to marry. The subsection ends with a flurry of quotations from love poems, and a list of references in untranslated Latin for those "qui volet de remediis amoris," those who wish a remedy for love (3:272).

This expansion is congruent with Erasmus's procedures in both the *Adages* and *De copia*. Burton listed as specious arguments against marriage exactly the traditional counsels to lead a single life that he had developed with all seriousness in the immediately preceding subsection. He embellished the text with examples of marriages that were imprudent, or delayed, or too hasty. He quoted liberally from both ancient and modern authors. Like Erasmus, then, Burton spoke both for and against marriage.[80] Like Erasmus, he used associative structures of arrangement to support a polyvocal text. That text developed in the interstices of textual divisions mandated by both Agricola's structures of definition and the customary divisions of the early modern compendium. The subsection does not relinquish the authority of the treatise, but it refuses to subside into a static compilation of past authorities. Instead, it contains its own possibilities of reversal, its own acknowledgement that offering general rules for the myriad exigencies of life is impossible, its own demonstration of a form of reasoning oriented to the contingent and provisional: in short, the necessity of rhetoric. Although Burton was an expert player with words, the force of his rhetoric did not depend on his fluency in tropes and figures. Although he understood the subtleties of argument, Burton's rhetoric was not simply a set of strategies for developing *logos*. Rather, it was rooted in Burton's situation, in the *kairos* of an early modern academic culture with one foot in neo-Latin scholarship and the other in emerging national markets for vernacular print. That situation presented him with the dual exigency of compiling and making accessible the growing resources of knowledge, including specialized knowledges such as medicine, and the equally pressing exigency of constructing a textual practice that replicated the fraternal, mobile tempo of learned conversation, disseminating those relationships among diasporic communities of readers. It was a practice that looked backward to the scholarship of northern humanism and forward to the development of specialized knowledge domains. It was a practice that grappled with problems that our culture, and our rhetorical tools, have never fully resolved: how can we freely talk about things that are at the limits of our collective knowledge, things that many of us will never fully understand, but which all of us must make some sense of? If, as Bruno Latour has claimed, Greece produced for us "one invention too many" in giving us both democracy and science, Burton's *Anatomy of Melancholy* offers a model of how these inventions could, in fact, be yoked together, of how their contradictions could be contained within rhetoric's capacious openness to varying conditions of truth, its embrace of the provisional, its willingness to work with propositions that are avowedly positional.[81] These issues were Burton's bread and butter: the problem he set himself was to make them work together under rapidly changing conditions of knowledge, on a topic in which he was himself deeply invested.

The solutions of the *Anatomy* are themselves provisional. Although Burton worked on problems faced by the new sciences—representing observations, weighing the authority of experience, reasoning about probabilities—the *Anatomy* was no model for the scientific prose of the late seventeenth century. It barely retained authority as a model of English prose, although it earned the affection of generations of readers. Neither does Burton's deployment of rhetoric give us a model for transdisciplinary writing. Unlike Burton, we do not have active access to the knowledge practices of humanism; unlike him, we contend with fully differentiated disciplines. New ways of knowing are surely on our horizon, but they are not the sciences of observation and experiment developed late in the seventeenth century. Burton does offer us provocative models for thinking about transdisciplinary discourses, for focusing on the possibilities of exchange rather than on rendering boundaries less permeable. His text beckons us in and then invites us to lose our way, to emerge with a handful of new connections. It presents the question of whether a twenty-first-century *Anatomy* would look something like Thomas Pynchon's *The Crying of Lot 49* or Octavia Butler's *Fledgling*, books that have created communities of readers who speculate about what is appropriate in the text, how it could be extended, what its displaced representation of our social world might mean, and what openings for change it suggests.

5

Translingualism | The Philologist as Language Broker

We have seen that *The Anatomy of Melancholy* sponsored exchange and mobility on the levels of genre and discipline. In its genre structure, the *Anatomy* fashioned a textual domain open to various embeddings and border crossings, a space for the refunctioning of languages hatched in porous disciplines. When Burton discussed the learned practice of medicine, he left open questions of therapeutic practice, modeling how the medical literature could be adapted to individual circumstances. Medical knowledge and other forms of humanist learning, including religion and good letters, were active sites of exchange and transposition, although these disciplines retained their identity and their distinct norms of demonstration. Burton used rhetoric as a generator of textual forms that taught and persuaded without closing off inquiry; it offered models of allusion and inclusion that held disparate materials in a kind of textual suspension. In this chapter, we come to the issue of language, and of the exchanges among languages effected by Burton.

No one who reads or teaches *The Anatomy of Melancholy* in this century can ignore its florid mixture of Latin and English. Burton glosses his observations with Latin quotations, mixes Latin with English in the same sentence, and from time to time, when his topic is too sensitive for the vulgar tongue, drops into Latin for several paragraphs. Although those extended passages are not translated, most of Burton's Latin quotations are immediately paraphrased into English. The text requires a nimble reader, and either a learned or a trusting one; the laborious task of tracing and checking Burton's quotations is one reason why the magisterial Oxford edition of the *Anatomy* was twelve years in publication and god knows how many in preparation. Scholars routinely acknowledge the *Anatomy*'s wealth of Latin quotations, but what happens when we take Burton's language practice as itself an object of investigation? We might profitably consider the *Anatomy* as establishing a communicative relationship between two languages; translingual theories, which see languages as repertoires of varied practices rather than as freestanding systems, help frame this understanding. Sociolinguists call such texts *code-meshed* and have found that they are surprisingly common, especially in sites of cultural exchange.[1] As the writer of a code-meshed text, Burton can be seen as a language broker, a third party who facilitates overall communication among speakers of different languages—or, in terms his contemporaries would have recognized, as a philologist.[2] As a language broker, Burton negotiated complex asymmetric relationships with his readers and their sponsoring institutions.

We associate the current role of English as global language with both increased communication and the tragic loss of local languages. Latin worked differently. To understand how, we need an account of translingual theory. We also need a fuller picture of the language culture of mid-seventeenth-century England, specifically at Oxford, that house of many languages, and of how Burton worked in that world.

Translingual Theory

We see languages as discrete entities; a text is in one language or another; speakers have competencies in a native tongue and acquire other languages; a "language question" is nearly always posed as a choice between two languages, each carrying historical and cultural freight. But what if languages were seen not as discrete and stable but as fluid and emerging? If languages are viewed through the lens of communicative practice rather than as expressions of national unity, speakers can be understood as using varied codes, whether or not they are themselves fluent in different languages. The boundaries among languages become permeable as individuals move among registers of different languages; in the case of Burton, this movement produces a text that combines multiple versions of English and Latin. Such code-meshed texts combine languages and language varieties; they accommodate readers with varying competencies in the range of languages they deploy and negotiate collaborative relationships among readers in a variety of social locations. For Burton, the shapes of English and Latin in the *Anatomy* establish a relationship between academic cultures and a broader literate public; they enact a public version of Burton's language practices in restricted academic and religious settings.

Translingual theory assumes that languages are practices rather than possessions, and that their norms are continually being modified by speakers. These changes happen in specific historical, social, and political contexts; they are shaped by asymmetrical social relations as language users negotiate and transform language practices. Mary Louise Pratt has vividly described those interactions: "Every minute of every day, in public, private and institutional spaces, the residents of globalizing social worlds are at work exploring and explaining their differences, creating clashes and resolving them, negotiating ethics, desires, spaces, manners, meanings, and the assumptions of mutual responsibility that make collective life work or fail."[3]

While translingualism recognizes that languages are distinct—a speaker of English does not automatically understand Latin—it considers speakers heteroglossic by default. Even monolingual speakers know multiple dialects, registers, and styles of their first language. Sociolinguist Jan Blommaert observes that, seen from the perspective of translingualism, language competence "should not be seen as a collection of 'languages' that a speaker controls, but rather as a complex of *specific* semiotic resources, some of which belong to a conventionally defined language, while others belong to another 'language.'"[4] Relations and interrelations of languages take place in both time and space; at any moment, a language practice includes embedded historical interactions that are themselves transformed in multiple zones of contact. To study a language is to take a snapshot of those interactions, so that "sociolinguistic reality is never synchronic, but is always made synchronic."[5]

Most research in translingual theory has been oriented to either contemporary literature or to second language pedagogy.[6] Controversies about this theory, particularly in the pedagogical literature, raise problems beyond the scope of this book.[7] My interest is not in the pedagogical use of translingual theory, but in investigating its analytic power as a tool for historical research in rhetoric. Translingual theory is a potentially useful frame for understanding early modern practices of knowledge as they were carried out in exchanges throughout Europe and the Mediterranean world. These exchanges were mediated by Latin, which had been in common use for centuries. As a spoken language, Latin reflected the syntax and vocabulary of its speakers' birth languages. It functioned in multiple prestigious and contested forms, all of which were deeply affected by the arrival of the printing press.

Scholarly exchanges also took place in the context of a complex system of overlapping vernaculars. Consider the demonstrative, if exceptional, case of Montaigne. According to his own account, Montaigne's father sent him to nurse with a local peasant family so that he would learn their way of life, including their language, a variety of Occitan.[8] We also know that his mother, who was probably Jewish, had come to France from Spain; she might have added to the home languages Ladino, a language that combined a Spanish vocabulary with elements of Hebrew, Aramaic, and Turkish. Montaigne's enterprising father wanted to give him a leg up on Latin, and so he engaged a Latin tutor who knew no French and ordered that the young Michel be addressed only in Latin, ensuring not only his son's precocious fluency but the survival, in neighboring villages, of Latin names for tools and artisans.[9] At school, where Latin was compulsory, Montaigne set it aside in favor of French, the language in which he wrote his *Essais*.[10] Montaigne is, of course, a French writer, but we miss something if we see him *only* as a French writer, without taking into account his access to a range of languages, from the most prestigious varieties of Latin and French to various consigned ways of speaking.

Robert Burton did not enjoy so broad a linguistic repertory as Montaigne: he favored Latin and English. But he wrote in a university that had become a crossroads for language exchange. This context, I argue, was alive in both the *Anatomy* and in Burton's other works, but to trace their influence will require more specific discussion of the languages in play in Burton's world.

Languages and Nations

We associate the development of vernaculars with the formation of early modern nation states, but in the sixteenth and early seventeenth centuries, nationhood, including English nationhood, often spoke Latin. Latin signified empire, and during the Reformation, imperial status was central to a country's claim that it should control its church.[11] Lively commerce in many languages was an audible and visible sign of imperial power. Even if within England's own borders minority languages such as Welsh were ever more firmly marginalized, it was considered a matter of national integrity and security that the English monarch have access to all the learned discourse, which is to say all the Latin discourse, of Europe.[12]

Other forces fueled a desire for the vernacular. The Reformation sought to lift the Babylonian yoke of the Vulgate and abolish Latin church services, and later reformers sought to purge the courts of law French, a remnant, in their eyes, of Norman domination. (After the Norman Conquest, English legal proceedings were carried out in French; over time, this language incorporated many

English words and followed the norms of English pronunciation. Law French persisted until after the Restoration, when it was replaced by Latin and English.) Carrying out legal proceedings in English was seen as a way of opening them to all citizens, loosening aristocratic control, and asserting the sovereignty of the nation. It was a step in satisfying Philip Sidney's longing for "a kingdom of our own language."[13] Other linguistic developments and reforms, both restrictive and expansive, were supported by analogous arguments: Henry VIII's decree of 1535 outlawing Welsh in court cases, Mulcaster's and Ascham's development of a humanistic pedagogy oriented to public life, and the printing of English dictionaries and grammars were all seen as efforts to build an English nation. But just as Ascham saw teaching classical Latin as the way to develop English prose, the adornment and perfection of English also required an active translingual practice. Few of these projects could be accomplished with English alone; as Steven Mullaney wrote in *The Place of the Stage: License, Play, and Power in the English Renaissance:* "Learning strange tongues or collecting strange things, rehearsing the words and ways of marginal or alien cultures, upholding idleness for a while—these are the activities of a culture in the process of extending its boundaries and reformulating itself."[14]

Language questions could emerge in any corner of public life. Should public inscriptions be carved in Latin, which would presumably render them intelligible for all time, or in the vernacular, so that the citizens who saw them could read them? When physicians spouted Latin, were they protecting their patient's sensibilities or just flimflamming them? Should botanists use the Latin nomenclature developed by Pliny the Elder and systematized by Leonhard Fuchs, or the vernacular of books such as John Gerard's *The Herball or General History of Plants,* which Burton owned and bequeathed to a woman friend?[15] Latin plant names connected the botanist to all of Europe and to thousands of years of collections and catalogues; the vernacular, to the vast corps of amateur botanists.

The foundation for all these questions was the uncontested importance of Latin and Latin learning as a sign of a cultivated, advanced country. A writer who aspired to produce work that counted as knowledge was more likely to write in Latin than in the vernacular. To read Latin was to have access to the prestigious literature of Roman antiquity, as well as to the writings of the church fathers and nearly all the literature of the emerging sciences. To write in a Ciceronian Latin rather than medieval scholastic Latin was a sign of cultivation. Italian humanist educators aspired to promote Latin literacy; this aspiration also animated Jesuit schools and Melanchthon's German Protestant universities. As

Jürgen Leonhardt observes, "the attempt to model Latin on the spirit of antiquity and the notion advanced by the humanists—that writing and speaking beautiful Latin perfected the person—set up a peculiar interaction with the national consciousness that was emerging in the various European countries."[16]

We should not imagine that every Latin speaker from Russia to Mexico could make himself flawlessly understood throughout Europe. Scholars' Latin was anything but perfect, and writers improvised both words and syntax; regional pronunciations could render one country's Latin unintelligible to visitors. Travelers commonly complained that they could not understand the Latin of other countries, or that they could not make themselves understood: the Latin spoken in England, which was relatively isolated, was especially difficult to follow.[17] For every Hungarian innkeeper who readily spoke Latin, there was an English academic who mistook a foreign scholar's Latin for beggar's cant, which was, after all, a distinctive language practice in its own right. But that did not stop either the Hungarian innkeeper or the visiting scholar from making their way in this supposedly dead language, nobody's mother tongue but everybody's resource.

The importance of Latin to developing national cultures is expressed in the production of Latin translations from modern languages; 1,140 such translations were printed before 1799.[18] Among them was Bartholomew Clerke's *De curiali*, his Latin translation of Baldassare Castiglione's *Book of the Courtier*, which he saw as a way of protecting the prestige of England. He wrote in Latin, he explained, lest the English court be shamed by being found less worthy than that of Urbino, and thereby insured that Elizabeth's court would excel by many degrees the courts of the Medicis and Gonzagas.[19] Clerke's purpose was not to render the text accessible to those who did not read Italian: Sir Thomas Hoby's wonderful English translation of Castiglione had been published thirty years earlier, in 1561. (In England, Clerke's Latin translation would be reprinted more often than Hoby's English.) Translation into Latin stabilized and dignified the text; it also identified the English court with the wealth and culture of the Italian city-states.

There is no more dramatic example of the use of Latin to establish national standing than Francis Kinaston's Latin translation of Geoffrey Chaucer's *Troilus and Criseyde* (fig. 5). Published in 1635 as *Amorum Troili et Creseidae*, Kinaston's rendering of the first two books of the poem was intended to convert its antiquated language, subject to "the accidents of humanity, which we see daily," into a text that would "remain invariant, fixed, and lasting."[20] English changed,

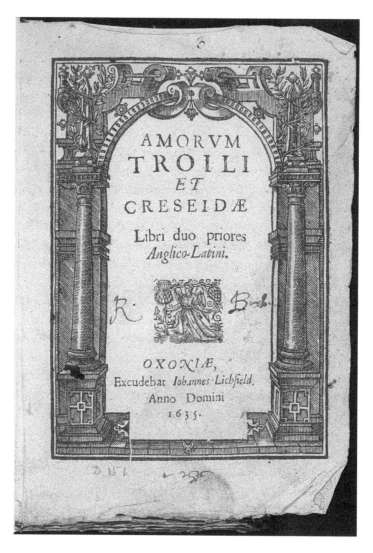

5 | Robert Burton's copy of Geoffrey Chaucer, *Amorum Troili et Creseidae libri duo priores Anglico-Latini*, translated into Latin by Sir Francis Kinaston (Oxoniae: Excud J. Lichfield, 1635), title page. Photo: Christ Church Library, courtesy of the Governing Body of Christ Church, Oxford.

and Chaucer's language had become archaic; nobody outside of England could be expected to read it, and nobody could be certain that it would be accessible to English readers in the future. Putting this national treasure into Latin, therefore, secured it, made it mobile in time and space. If the dedicatory verses praising the translation for producing a Chaucer *"revidivus"* are any indication, a

Latin translation also somehow modernized Chaucer. Robert Burton owned copies of both Clarke's *De curiali* and Kinaston's *Amorum Troili et Creseidae.*

Writers and scholars have been expected to contribute to the glory of the nation since Cicero's *Pro Archia.* In early modern England, those contributions included epideictic exercises, especially the verse collections that both universities and their associated colleges produced to mark important national occasions. The first such collection at Oxford commemorated Elizabeth's visit in 1566, and the form reached full expression in 1587 with *Exequiae illustrissimi equitis D. Philippi Sidnaei,* a collection mourning Philip Sidney's death. As the story goes, devastated scholars wrote memorial poems that they pasted on their doors and walls; these were collected and published by the dramatist William Gager, of whom there will be more to say.[21] *Exequiae* was followed by a series of volumes marking the university's participation in the events of national life: the births, marriages, and deaths of the royal family and of other national figures. These collections were prime venues for the display of multilingual virtuosity. A collection for James I's coronation, *Panegyrica. In auspicatissimam pientissimi ac potentiss. Regis Iacobi inthronizationem* (the title itself demonstrates the flexibility of the neo-Latin lexicon), included not only poems in Latin, Greek, German, and Italian but also three labeled "Bohemia," "Russiaca," and "Polonia," written by "I. B. Ex tribu Levi, Italus."[22] A volume mourning the death of Prince Henry opened with three poems by Joseph Barbatus in Chaldean, Syriac, and Turkish.[23] Barbatus was a pen name for Yusuf Ibn abu Daqan, a teacher of Arabic who was sponsored by Burton's nominal tutor, Richard Bancroft, and who taught Arabic at Oxford in 1610.[24] These volumes eloquently speak of the intersections between university learning as a practice of collating and interpreting the languages of the ancient and modern world and as a vehicle for constructing national events as moments of global significance.

Burton was a frequent contributor to the commemorative and memorial volumes published by Oxford and by Christ Church. (We will look closely at Burton's memorial verses for Thomas Bodley later in this chapter.) Burton contributed such poems as *"Vade quid in media struis oppugnacula campia"* to a 1603 volume celebrating James I's accession, *"Lampedo Spartana suo celeberima saeclo"* to a memorial volume for Queen Anne in 1619, and *"Mentitus formam quod Princeps Carolus exit,"* to a 1623 collection for Charles I.[25] These poems were gathered among Latin acrostics, short verses in Hebrew or Spanish, and scattered English poems in the commemorative volumes, which were distributed to patrons and donors. Burton's contributions to translingual political discourse may have included deliberative as well as epideictic texts. It is possible that

Burton collaborated with that inveterate language broker John Florio on his translation of a work of Italian republican theory by Traiano Boccalini, *The New-Found Politike*.[26]

Languages and the Reformation

While the rejection of Latin for certain religious purposes was an important aspect of the Reformation, other aspects of Protestant thinking encouraged the study of ancient languages. If England were to control its own church, and if that church would no longer be tied to the Vulgate and its many distortions, then England had need of Hebrew, of Syriac and Chaldean, and therefore also of Arabic. Latin was the language that organized these exchanges, since dictionaries and grammars would be written in Latin.[27]

Latin and the vernaculars influenced each other, and the choice of language could be a conscious strategy to advance a religious agenda. Latin was both a vehicle for sociality among the learned and a gatekeeping device, protecting knowledge deemed too dangerous for wide distribution. These tensions were especially acute in religious controversies, where Latin was praised for stability and universalism; vernaculars, for accessibility and broad usage. These values lead us to associate Protestants with vernacular worship, and Catholics with the universalism and tradition of Latin.[28] But since the exigencies of stability and accessibility were salient to both Catholics and Protestants, these broad outlines need cross-hatching. Until the Council of Trent, Catholics in countries with strong vernacular traditions had celebrated religious services in those languages.[29] Humanist Roman Catholics held vernacular services and worked toward vernacular translations of Scripture: remember Erasmus's hope that "the farmer sing some portion of [the Scriptures] at the plow, the weaver hum some parts of them to the movement of his shuttle, the traveler lighten the weariness of his journey with stories of this kind." Also remember that Erasmus wrote these words in Latin, in the *Paraclesis*, a preface to his Latin translation of the New Testament.[30] Both Catholics and Protestants carried on religious controversies in Latin and corresponded in Latin, sometimes with each other. Philipp Melanchthon, the Lutheran "schoolmaster of Germany," wrote extensively in Latin and promoted the study of Greek and Hebrew.

In England, these controversies were sharp, even bloody, especially in the middle of the sixteenth century. John Jewel proudly asserted, in his 1562 *Apology* or *Answer in Defence of the Church of England*, that "We make our Prayers, as is fitting, in a language understood by the whole Congregation . . . lest, as St. Augustine says, we seem, like Jays and Parrots, to speak what we ourselves do not understand."[31] For Jewel, the Latin liturgy debased and dehumanized those who performed it; it offended against reason. The Roman Catholic polemicist Thomas Harding answered Jewel from Antwerp, countering his charge that only Protestant churches promoted the diffusion of Scriptures: "We [Roman Catholics] gladly suffer [Scriptures] to be had in every place of Christendome in the lerned tongues, Hebrewe, Greke, and Latine. Neither were they altogether forbidden to be had in some vulgare tonges, before the fancy malepertnes of heretikes forced the governours of the church for the saveguarde of the people to take other order."[32] But things were not as simple as this polarization suggests. Jewel's Protestant apology was published simultaneously in English and Latin; the Latin version had been revised and translated back into English by Lady Anne Bacon. Harding dismissed Anne Bacon's renderings as examples of the danger of letting women meddle in church affairs.[33] In this controversy, Latin could signify ignorance, learning, safety, transparency, and the maintenance of masculine order. Bitter as it was, it was less bloody than the Cornish Prayer Book Rebellion of 1549, an uprising provoked by the imposition of the *Book of Common Prayer*. The rebels demanded that the Latin liturgy be left in place, since "we the Cornyshe men (whereof certen of us understand no Englysh) utterly refuse thys newe English."[34] Thousands of people died in that conflict.

For both Roman Catholics and Protestants, the choice of language was an issue of pious observance and doctrinal regularity. After Trent, Latin was not merely a convenient means of communication; it had become a sacred language, redolent with the virtues of tradition. The council decreed in 1546 that the Latin Vulgate, "which, by the lengthened use of so many years, has been approved of in the Church, be, in public lectures, disputations, sermons, and expositions, held as authentic, and that no one is to dare, or presume to reject it under any pretext whatsoever."[35] In a later session, the council asserted the validity of the Latin mass: "if anyone says that the . . . mass ought to be celebrated in the vernacular tongue only . . . let him be anathema."[36]

Equally stern assertions of the signal value of the vernacular appear in the preface to the 1549 *Book of Common Prayer*: "wheras s. Paule would have suche language spoken to the people in the churche, as they mighte understand and profite by hearing the same, the service in this Churche of England (these many years) hath been read in Latin to the people, whiche they understand not; so that they have heard with theyr eares onely; and with their hartes, spirite, and minde, have not been edified thereby."[37]

The Reformation prompted deep reflection on the significance of language choice, an outpouring of religious writing in Latin, and an equal outpouring of religious writing in the European vernaculars.[38] While the development and translation of ecclesiastical texts in English were central occupations of theologians and religious scholars through the sixteenth and the first half of the seventeenth century, both theological controversy and devotional life remained multilingual throughout that time. Religious controversy took place across national lines and supported a translingual practice that relied heavily on Latin.

At Oxford, sermons were delivered in both English and Latin, and both languages were used for controversial writings. Burton, as a Student at Christ Church, would have been expected to preach in the cathedral, and we have a sparse but linguistically interesting record of one of his sermons. The Bodleian holds a small manuscript book that contains summaries of sermons preached in Oxford. It has a single entry for Robert Burton:

> Burton of Xt Church
>   Text: John: 15.14
> Yee are my friends, if you doe whatsoever I command you.
> The words divide themselves into 2 parts
> { 1 obligation or contract; you are my friends
> { 2 the condition of the obligation, if you doe whatsoever
> {   I command you.[39]

This text was drawn from a passage full of uplifting sentiments: Jesus's promulgation of a law of love and his promise to send a comforter. Burton's sermon did not focus on these ideas but on the word "obligation," which does not appear anywhere in the chapter on which he was preaching. He located obligation within the vocabulary of legal obligations, speaking of contracts and conditions. Such choices may explain why Burton did not gain fame as a preacher. But "obligation" and "contract" may have had other resonances when spoken in the context of a translingual culture: they suggested duties that were also connections, constraints that were promises, and ties that drew people together. These senses of obligation collocate with "friends," implying ties of both affection and kinship. Perhaps Burton played with the connections between two kinds of bonds: those that express affinity and those that constrain to duty. His sermon was given in English, but it was not for that reason monolingual.

Language and Scholarship

For those devoted to good letters and academic scholarship, Latin had significance beyond the expression of national pride: it was the language of the republic of letters. But Latin was not the only language studied at Oxford, where, as we have seen, both ancient and modern languages fulfilled critical functions, supporting scriptural study and preparing students for international trade. As in the commemorative verse collections, languages could be deployed indexically, to signal learning or global connections rather than to communicate. (In linguistics, *indexicality* refers to the elements of a text or utterance that refer to its context in time and space, or to the relations between writer and reader, or that invoke the context in any other way. For translingual theory, a language is used indexically when its primary function is not to communicate content—indexical expressions may be unintelligible to the reader—but to refer to the values associated with the language and its culture. A Latin university motto suggests learning; a dress shop with a French name suggests fashion.) Quotations or inscriptions in the languages of the ancient and modern world indicated scholarly or imperial ambitions, just as inscriptions in kanji or Greek now index cultural sophistication.[40]

While Latin could function indexically, in the university its main use was to support scholarly communication.[41] A Latin text was transferable and permanent; to render a text into Latin was to bid for its place in a European canon. A text in Latin could count as knowledge; writing in Latin was a way of making knowledge count.

More than one Latin circulated in academic, religious, legal, and diplomatic cultures. Medieval academic Latin had developed an extensive vocabulary for discussing people and things, such as popes, artillery, and feudal legal relations, that had been unknown to the Romans.[42] When humanist scholars launched a general reform of the language, their desire to return to the language of Cicero did not obliterate that medieval vocabulary. Medieval Latin texts were in continued use in some (but not all) disciplines. Not all Latin documents were polished: many were workaday case records or legal notes, written in haste and heavily abbreviated, often conjectural in their grammar.[43] Other texts showed the pressure of the writer's vernacular: correct enough in their vocabulary and syntax, they followed the word order of a modern language. Latin served as a medium of exchange among some disciplines, and as a barrier in others. Medical writing, for example, could be shared among learned physicians throughout Europe, but radical shifts in philosophical Latin, as we shall see, meant that scholastic texts were closed books to early modern scholars.

We must put equal weight on both words when we characterize academic Latin as the language of a "community of scholars." Students and teachers came to the universities with diverse goals, stayed for various lengths of time, and used Latin with varying levels of skill and commitment. Latin names a whole group of academic practices, deployed in a shifting relationship to various vernaculars and other learned languages. In the translingual world of Oxford, Latin served to disseminate meaning, to confirm personal relationships among the learned, and to protect secrets. It maintained a shifting relationship with other ancient languages, and also with English, particularly as the vernacular developed in prestige and flexibility in the first half of the seventeenth century. Burton's *Anatomy of Melancholy* sits at the boundary between an academic culture saturated in Latin and a growing culture of vernacular literacy; in its pages, these two practices speak to each other. Burton thereby brokers a relationship between learned literacy and vernacular literacy, between the Latins of good letters and of medicine and the many registers of written English.

On the surface, Latin was the only language of the university, and university rules specified that students speak to each other only in Latin. Other languages were valued—students could also speak in Greek or Hebrew. From its foundation, Christ Church offered frequent lectures in these languages, whose distinctive grammars troubled the assumed universalism of Latin.[44] Knowledge of Hebrew, especially, was considered the mark of an ambitious young man. Arabic, Chaldean, Syriac, and Turkish, with their salience to both the study of Scripture and the promotion of trade, could be studied with private tutors or the manuscripts at the Bodleian. But Latin—fluent Latin—was the price of admission to higher learning; the Laudian statutes of 1636 specified that each candidate for a degree be examined to be sure that he "could deliver the thoughts of his mind in Latin."[45] Of course, there would have been no need for Laud to write such a statute if it went without saying that all entering students were fluent in Latin. The need to regulate language continued: a hundred years after Burton's time at

Christ Church, we read of a Professor of Rhetoric rebuking a student: "*Abi et disce latine loqui,*" "Get out of here and learn to speak Latin."[46]

And for good reason. Everything an Oxford student learned—humanities, philosophy, natural philosophy, and divinity—would be studied in Latin. The basic works, whatever their original language, would almost always be read in Latin; lectures were in Latin, and at academic exercises, students listened to Latin and spoke in Latin. If they went on to study law or medicine, Latin would become, if anything, more pervasive. If they corresponded with other scholars, they would write in Latin; if they traveled, they would find that Latin was the common language of learned Europe. The ability to converse in Latin was the mark of their legitimacy as scholars, and of their future usefulness to aristocratic employers.

University Latin included not only the prestigious Roman and humanist registers, but other forms of the language. We have seen that medieval scholars added to the ancient vocabulary; anyone who has attempted a text in medieval Latin can attest that their work with suffixes was especially inventive. Ann Moss has shown that the turn from medieval Latin to the more or less Ciceronian Latin of the humanists rendered scholastic philosophy unintelligible to students who had cut their teeth on a more refined Latin.[47] In other fields, such as law and medicine, this rupture was not as radical. For philosophy, medieval Latin had been developed as a technical language, suited to the conduct of formal disputes, while humanists aspired to create a culture of Latin speakers and writers who could animate the language, using it to serve all the needs of the republic of letters. It therefore makes sense to speak not only of the Latin of the learned in the sixteenth and seventeenth centuries, but of multiple learned Latins: scholastic documents, intelligible but marginalized in some fields; the cultivated humanist Latin of Valla or Erasmus; and the serviceable workaday Latin of the many scholarly treatises written in the late sixteenth and seventeenth centuries, inculcated by a humanist curriculum but adapted to the needs of scientific and philosophical scholarship.

Unstable relationships among Latin words, vernacular words, and familiar objects could emerge in any field. The growing interest in such natural sciences as botany raised questions about the relationships among natural objects and their names in Latin and the vernaculars. These problems were especially pressing for physicians, who, as we saw in chapter 3, were eager to replicate the medicines of ancient physicians. As scholars grappled with immense numbers of new plants and animals from the new world, critical readers of Greek and Roman natural histories sought to reconcile the inconsistencies among their sources and to connect the descriptions in Pliny and Dioscorides to plants they knew. What plant, exactly, was the Asiatic rhubarb that the ancients valued so highly? Did it have any relationship to plants that early modern physicians called by a similar name?[48] Sorting out these issues required careful practices of observation, extensive correspondence, and exchange of specimens among natural historians.

Philipp Melanchthon offers an example of the difficulties of negotiating the translingual work of botany in his final dialectical treatise, *Erotemata Dialectices* (1558); he is discussing the topic of definition:

> Definitio nominis est, cum pereginae linguae vocabulum interpretaris notiore vocabulo nostrae linguae, et genus dominas, ut si dicat, Centaurium est herba, quam vocamus tausent gulden, vel Aurin, genus et nomen audis minus peregrium, ac fieri potest, ut res adhuc ignota sit.

> It is the definition of a word when you interpret a word from a foreign language with a familiar word from our language and you name the genus, as when you say: Centuary is a plant which we call "tausent gulden" or Aurin; the genus and the name you hear is less strange, and yet it can happen that the thing itself is still unknown.[49]

The gaps between familiar names, everyday objects, and passages in ancient texts drew attention to the need for observation, lest *"res adhuc ignota sit."* Latin intersected with the vernaculars, both facilitating and complicating the movement of knowledge, prompting both acute attention to texts and the collection and exchange of specimens.[50]

The fortunes of both Latin and English were tied to the diffusion of the printed book. By the late sixteenth and seventeenth centuries, books, including books in Latin, became more readily available, and there was a substantial market for them. In England, one in ten of the books printed from 1540 to 1650 was in Latin; this number includes many of the works of serious scholarship printed in that period.[51] More than half the books sold at the Frankfurt Book Fair were in Latin until well into the 1680s, and during the same period, so were more than half the books published by Oxford presses.[52] Oxford had been late to enter the market for Latin books. Until 1584, Oxford would enjoy the services of a press only intermittently; the international book trade, significantly called the "Latin trade," passed it by.[53] When the university secured a press in 1584, it published works of scholarship in divinity, law, and philology, and editions of Latin classics with commentaries and of Greek classics translated into Latin. As books became cheaper, books in Latin also became more common. By the 1590s, the college libraries of Oxford had abandoned the chained rows of horizontally stored books for vertical shelves, and the canon of Latin classics had become available in relatively affordable editions.[54]

In the seventeenth century, the library had become a central point of exchange in this translingual culture. Oxford libraries worked through local booksellers to purchase books from the biannual Frankfurt Book Fairs and to import texts from France and Italy. Thomas Bodley followed a program of aggressive acquisition in ancient and modern foreign languages; as early as 1603, the Bodleian had begun collecting books in Chinese. Although their numbers were small, foreign scholars, most of them from the Netherlands and Germany, visited the Bodleian, and the library ordinances made specific provisions for admitting them. Students and alumni donated books in various languages to the library, either as bequests or as gifts at graduation.

Latin in all its variety existed in a dynamic relationship with English. Jürgen Leonhardt has shown that the development of neo-Latin writing was an incentive rather than a hindrance to the development of vernacular forms.[55] Readers who admired the urbanity of Cicero's letters might aspire to polished English speech; vernacular imitations, parodies, and adaptations of Latin literary forms spurred the development of European languages and literatures. Recent work has demonstrated that both Latin and the vernaculars existed simultaneously in speech and reading communities for hundreds of years, shaping each other reciprocally. Tom Deneire summarized this line of research: "It appears that rather than interpreting the question of neo-Latin and vernacular culture within a cultural dichotomy with predetermined historical, social, religious, aesthetical or other values for Latin or vernacular practices, recent scholarship now recognizes the matter as a highly complex and dynamic process of cultural poetics ... which needs to be carefully examined with much sense for nuance."[56]

Robert Burton was deeply imbricated in this complex cultural process. As Christ Church librarian, he had daily responsibility for the college's access to good letters. From 1624 until his death, he was responsible for gathering resources in the languages that were becoming important to Christ Church scholars; as we have seen, he also accumulated a remarkable personal library.[57] Christ Church, like many other Oxford college libraries, was supported by gifts. The custom of the college, later formalized as a rule, required a student to give the library a book or the money to buy one on leaving the college. The library's donation book records these gifts, and shows that students sometimes clubbed together to make a substantial gift. Burton himself would leave Christ Church library 780 volumes at his death, the remains of his library after some individual bequests and the Bodleian's exercise of its right of first refusal. Taken together, these bequests supplied the university with multiple learned Latins; they made available the texts of Greek antiquity in both Latin translation and in increasingly accurate Greek. Christ Church was also especially known for its resources in Hebrew. John Gregory, a Hebraist who wrote on Scripture, law, and the Kabbalah, came to Christ Church in 1624 and remained until 1643; he collected many versions of the Kabbalah and other Hebrew texts. Gregory was also an Arabic scholar, and used sources in Syriac, Persian, Ethiopic, and Armenian.[58] Burton's colleague John Selden, an even more noted scholar of Hebrew, was quoted three times in the *Anatomy*.[59]

Burton's own library was an avant-garde collection. Three quarters of his books had been published during his lifetime. He collected literature and divinity, but also history, government, mathematics, travel, and science. His library is much more diverse than those of other Oxford scholars, especially since he collected contemporary literature, including plays and joke books.[60] The library is evenly divided between English and Latin books, with a very light sprinkling of volumes in French, Italian, Hebrew, German, and Spanish.

Many of Burton's books are concerned with languages and the exchanges among them. There is a book of French dialogues, ostensibly designed for law students, more or less untouched (Claudius Holyband, *The French Littleton: The Most Easy Perfect, and Absolute Way to Learne the French Language*).[61] There are dialogues in Greek and Latin, printed on facing pages.[62] Henri Estienne's *De latinitate falso suspecta*, a book in aid of "those speakers who fall silent for shame, lest they use a barbarous term," offered advice on Latin usage.[63] And there is Petrus Gyllius's monumental Greek dictionary, a hefty folio offering Latin translations of Greek terms, with sources and commentaries.[64] Whether or not Burton directly engaged these books, all of them treat languages as active, social, communicative practices, with possibilities for travel, commerce, advancement, and humiliation. They are cut from the same cloth as Burton's copies of the Latin translations of Castiglione and Chaucer; they are material concentrations of the intense exchanges among languages that structured his world. Burton's library speaks of the desire to collect into one place a wealth of language practices; it speaks of both the conviction that Latin was the medium of exchange that could stabilize such a collection and the recognition that such stability might be difficult to achieve.

The exhilaration of early modern translingual culture and the importance of the library in organizing it are expressed in Burton's poem for one of the memorial volumes commemorating Thomas Bodley. The first part of the poem is worth quoting:

> *Quae tam seposita est, quae gens tam barbara* voce
> Ex quā non librum *Bibliotheca* tenet?
> *Indus, Arabs,* quicquid *Graeci, scripsere Latini,*
> Aethiopes, quicquid, *Persa* Camaena dedit,
> Aut olim *Hebraei,* aut *Syri,* quod eunque vetustas,
> *Galli, Itali, Hispani,* quod nova lingua dedit:
> Omnes BODLEIUS Thecam congessit in unam[65]

> Who are so remote, so barbaric,
> That the Library does not have a book from them?
> India, Arabia, anything the Greeks or Latins wrote,
> The Ethiopians, anything that the Muse Camaena gave to Persia,
> Or formerly the Hebrews, or Syria, whatever of antiquity,
> Gallic, Italian, Hispanic, what the new languages gave:
> All these Bodley heaped together in one library.

Burton's poem echoes an epigram from Martial's *De spectaculis*, commemorating the opening of the Roman colosseum:

> Quae tam sepostita est quae gens tam Barbara, Caesar
> ex qua spectator non sit in urbe tue.

> What race is set so far, what race so barbarous, Caesar,
> wherefrom a spectator is not in your city?[66]

Martial's poem ends by celebrating the unity Roman rule imposed on different languages:

> Vox diversa sonat popolorum, tam tamen una est
>   Cum verus patriae dicens esse pater.

> Diverse sounds the speech of the peoples, yet then it is one
>   When you are acclaimed your country's true father.

There could have been no clearer illustration of how language diversity could establish a powerful, centralized nation than Martial's poem; Burton's adaptation positions the Bodleian as a learned, Christian, colosseum. The desire to *"congregare in unam"* that provoked Burton's admiration and his emulation was a passion for language collection that crossed space and time, bringing together the work of antiquity with texts that were *"barbara."* This scholarly wealth was not ideologically neutral. The *"unam"* constructed within the walls of the Bodelian was an expression of British power and influence. At the same time, these languages were also sources of pleasure; a sanctioned and celebratory game. They indexed an experience of liberation that echoed Burton's wild flight in the "Digression of Aire." The language of scholarship had not yet become distinct from the language of recreation.

Ludic Latins

Plays were one of the chief ways that universities sought to cultivate fluent Latin as a means of communication. Both Oxford and Cambridge followed the humanist practice of fostering urbane Latin speech by encouraging students to put on plays—typically, for humanists, the comedies of Terence. During the late sixteenth century, Terence gradually gave way to new Latin plays written by members and friends of the university, including Nicholas Grimald (1519–1562); William Gager (1555–1622), who had collected the memorial verses for Philip Sidney; and Matthew Gwinne (1558–1627). They wrote Latin plays in the genres that would become familiar on the vernacular stage—chronicles, comedies, revenge plays, and tragedies.[67] Some plays were dignified representations of Roman history; others, like William Alabaster's *Roxana*, were bloody and lurid. In the first half of the sixteenth century, Oxford was especially associated with tragedies, such as Grimald's plays on the lives of Suleiman the Magnificent and of Tuman Bey. J. W. Binns characterizes these plays, with their tight plotting, rich language, and supple verse as "a body of drama which until about 1585 was in advance of anything the London popular stage could offer."[68]

Just as London theaters had their opponents, so did the Latin dramas at Oxford, including John Rainolds, rhetorician and dean of Corpus Christi College, who refused to attend Gager's Latin play in 1592. In response, Gager defended drama from Rainolds's charge of immorality: "We . . . doe it to recreate owre selves, owre House, and the better parte of the Vniversytye, with some learned Poeme or other; to practyse owre owne style eyther in prose or verse; to be well acquaynted with *Seneca* or *Plautus*; honestly to embowlden our yuthe; to trye their voyces, and confirme their memoryes; to frame their speeche; to conforme them to convenient action, to try what mettell is in evrye one, and of what disposition thay are of."[69] Gager's defense balanced the practices of humanistic learning and of competitive display that were hallmarks of university Latin, asserting that somehow these two spurs to anxiety were also sovereign recreations.

The fun continued; Latin plays for students were performed until the Civil Wars. Gager's plays were followed by Gwinne's in the first years of the seventeenth century. Gwinne, a London physician, was a close friend of both Giordano Bruno and of John Florio; he was a member of the Sidney circle and a coeditor of *The Countess of Pembroke's Arcadia*. For the visit of James I and Anne to Oxford in 1605, Gwinne wrote the allegorical piece *Vertumnus, sive, Annus recurrens* and *Tres sibyllae*, a sketch in which three undergraduates praised James for his virtues and his descent from Banquo.[70]

These were not bare-bones productions. Royal and aristocratic visitors expected to see plays, and they expected to see them lavishly produced. The colleges aimed to please, with performances in college halls or chapels, ornamented with elaborate machinery. At James I's visit in 1605, Inigo Jones first demonstrated perspectival scenery, to the general puzzlement of the audience.[71] Rivalries and grudges played out at university performances. Students at St. John's College and at Christ Church battled it out during the Christmas holiday performances of 1607–8. Windows were broken, two people were stabbed, and the Hilary term was delayed for a week—to allow for more plays![72] Much more decorous were the dramatic performances marking the four royal visits to Oxford between 1566 and 1636, all but one of which was staged in a lavishly decorated hall of Christ Church, the largest common space at Oxford. By 1636, the plays for royal visitations were written in English by university writers, overseen by the Office of Revels and performed by professional actors: they became quasi official state functions.[73]

Latin drama would have been thriving at Oxford throughout Burton's life at the university. It was anything but a pious exercise: these plays consciously mixed genres, stretched time frames, and exploited the possibilities of topical reference. They were performed in style, at festive occasions, to audiences of both academics and townspeople. Although such performances were the most public university displays of Latin, Latin also served as a language of comity at academic ceremonies. At the University Act, a public commencement ceremony also known as the *comitia*, Latin disputations and verses were combined with a comic oration by the *terrae filius*.[74]

Burton wrote two Latin plays; the text of only one, *Philosophaster*, survives. *Philosophaster* was both in and about Latin. The title page documents a long road to performance: it was written in 1606, finished in 1615, and performed at Christ Church in February 1619.[75] *Philosophaster* confirms the sociality of the college and its adherence to the king as demonstrated in the rigor of its Latinity. A satire on bad scholarship and false learning, the play is also a celebration of the virtues of true scholarship and a confirmation of the ties between the sovereign and the university: all these issues are joined in a battle between good Latin and bad Latin.

Philosophaster gives us star-crossed young lovers and clever servants straight from Roman comedy. References to Terence, Ovid, and Erasmus's *Adages* are frequent. This play established and confirmed the bonds of scholarly community: it also defined what scholarship was and was not. It features false scholars, each speaking a distinctive bombast associated with a register of academic Latin. *Philosophaster* put specialized Latins that might have echoed in the halls of Christ Church into the mouths of the fraudulent scholars who flocked to the play's fictional University of Osun. These charlatans praised the scholastic Latin that had been roundly criticized for decades:

> Tuum est disputare de Infinito, Ente, Vacuo,
> Naturā Naturante et Exietate Scoti,
> De causalitate causae et quidditatiuā materiā,
> De Gabrielitate Gabrielis, et spiritali animā. (1.1.81–84)

> Now your job is to discuss infinity, being, vacuity,
> Natura naturans, and the haecceity of Scotus.

Talk of the causality of cause and the materiality of matter,
the Gabriclity of Gabriel, and the spirituality of spirit.

But the philological practices of humanism fared no better. The fraud Peda-
nus meets the true scholar Philobiblos and criticizes as barbarous his use of
such words as "*splendesco*," "*liquesco*," and "*tabescco*." Philobiblos laconically replies
"*Ciceronem authorem habeo*," or "I have Cicero as my author" (3.1064–65). Other
characters satirize the terms of art that may have been used in Oxford lectures
and disputations, and the specialized languages of divinity, medicine, and law.
In the course of its satire, *Philosophaster* inventories the multiple forms of academic Latin circulating at Christ Church at the beginning of the seventeenth
century.

Sometimes, Burton strings together incongruous terms; sometimes he con-
cocts his own parodic words. This small sampling needs (and really, can have),
no translation:

> Disputabus de parimiro, lili, tartaro, mummia,
> Elixir extrahendo, caementis, gradationibus. (1.1.89–90)
> Dicor, vocor, salutor, appellor, habeor, existimor. . . .
> Per antiphrasin ludimagister, per periphrasin
> Maior iuuenum castigatorque minorum . . .
> Gymnasiarcha, Pedotriba, vel Hipodidasculus,
> Magister, Magistellus, siue Magisterculus. (1.2.185–92)
> de radice zanzenique, zinzizanzizeqique et huiusmodi. (1.1.64)

Fraudulent scholars are forever teaching each other strange words intended to
confuse and impress; they are forever correcting the perfectly good Latin of the
true scholars. In the academic broil of competing languages, all the studied
forms of Latin become ridiculous; only steady application to humane letters and
a modest, sociable spirit of collaboration save the good scholars from the grisly
punishments imposed on the frauds at the end of the play.

Philosophaster also performed an important function of early modern Latin:
setting boundaries—in this case, those between the city of Oxford and the
university. Citizens of Oxford attended the Latin plays in great numbers. In
Philosophaster, they would have heard, but perhaps not understood, the prostitutes' speeches complaining that they were worse customers than students (4.6).
This scene not only jibed townsmen in a language they could not follow, but it
also mockingly flattered students for their generosity to prostitutes.

Burton's other neo-Latin play, *Alba*, a pastoral for which no text has survived, had been presented on the first night of James I's visit in 1605, quite possibly with Inigo Jones's scenery. *Philosophaster*, however, was performed in February, in the middle of the Hilary term, and therefore for a local audience. And indeed, the play is one long inside joke: while we will never know whether any of the scholars were recognizable portraits of university professors, we can still feel the force of the play's insistence that the university, a worthy enterprise, is also easy prey to pedants, and that language is the vehicle for both its corruption and renovation.

Secrecy

There was little controversy, however, about the need to protect sensitive information by keeping it in Latin, safe from the prying eyes of the vulgar. Especially in medicine, Latin restricted access to knowledge.[76] The division between Latin and vernacular works was gendered; vernacular guides to health and compendia of remedies were kept in a health closet or stillroom with medical supplies and simples, where they were available to the women responsible for the health of the household. Medical texts in Latin were kept in the library or a private study. James Primrose, in his *Popular Errours of the People in the Matter of Physick*, argued that women should confine their medical work to nursing, since "they usually take their remedies out of English bookes" without making the required Galenic adjustments to the individual patient.[77] When Laurent Joubert published a book on obstetrics in French in 1578, he was roundly criticized for writing about such a delicate subject in French rather than English, especially since the book was dedicated to Marguerite, Queen of Navarre.[78] Even late in the seventeenth century, when books about sexual and reproductive matters were more freely translated, translators hesitated to render Latin words for sexual organs or acts into English.[79]

Latin was also a support for secrecy in private documents. In diaries, delicate matters were often written in Latin, safe from the eyes of women and servants. In the private manuscript collections favored by students, aristocrats, and members of the Inns of Court, erotic poetry in Latin and English was interleaved with devotional texts and comic verse. These collections could be collaborative documents, including contributions from several authors, verse copied from other collections, and various ephemera.[80] Latin could be used to arouse lust or to confess sin, to reassure patients or to deceive them, to circulate or restrict knowledge; an individual's facility with Latin, his ability to speak about ordinary matters in the language and to use it in various specialized performances, was the signal sign of membership in the community of scholars.

Burton in His World of Tongues: Philologist as Language Broker

While Latin organized festivity, recognized guests, or established networks of correspondence across national and confessional boundaries, it was also a spur to the development of vernacular literacies: English genres developed in emulation of Latin texts, and the resources of Latin offered models for the expanding literate practices of the vernacular. Writing in refined Ciceronian Latin was a way of asserting the excellence of British culture; so was writing in polished and copious English. For an Anglican divine, the cause of the Reformation was equally advanced by a stinging critique of the Jesuits in Latin or by a moving sermon in English: it is not accidental that John Donne wrote both the Latin *Conclave Ignati* (1611), the initial version of *Ignatius His Conclave*, and a collection of brilliant English sermons.

This was the complicated web of language practices that Burton entered, a carnival of language practices he wholly embraced. We have seen that Burton worked with Latin as a librarian and scholar, and that his poetry and drama were written in that language. If we also consider the many levels of his language practice in the *Anatomy*, his role as philologist and language broker emerges. Taken together, Burton's neo-Latin verse, neo-Latin drama, and work as a librarian and collector of books would have occupied a fair percentage of his time. These activities, all of which required a deep engagement with language, were oriented to the relationships among various forms of Latin, among Latin and other languages, and between Latin and the material and social relationships of the university. Burton moved among language practices in much the same way that he moved among knowledge practices.

We might use the term "language broker" to describe this work; it was originally derived from Clifford Geertz by contemporary sociolinguists to describe individuals, like the children of immigrant parents, who manage interactions between two parties who have no common language.[81] Unlike the translator, the language broker is not limited to accurately transferring meaning between speakers of different languages; the broker's work also includes organizing successful conversations. Brokers can animate a conversation, intervene in it on their own authority, and redirect or revise the utterances of any of the parties involved.[82] The broker has his or her own stake in these matters, and the control exercised by the broker can become an independent source of power.[83] While most of the sociolinguistic research on language brokers has been carried out in family settings, language brokers can be found in hospitals or clinics, in workplaces where one worker manages conversations among others of differing languages, in online settings, and among scientific specialties.[84]

While many language brokers find the role satisfying, it is rife with potential conflicts: How does the broker negotiate conflicting rules of politeness? How can sensitive information be conveyed by a broker who has a stake in the conversation?[85] Brokering can be uncomfortable: as someone who stands between two language systems, the broker can attract all the opprobrium associated with either of them. This practice requires solid language skills, the ability to identify and perform speech or writing that moves all participants forward in the conversation, and facility in moving among differing language contexts and lifeworlds. It is a role immersed in relationships of mobility and exchange.

We might find traces of a broker's shame in Burton's apology for writing the *Anatomy* in English:

> It was not mine intent [In 1621, Burton wrote "it went against my Genius"] to prostitute my Muse in *English*, or to divulge *secreta Minerva*, but to have exposed this more contract in *Latin*, If I could have got it printed. Any scurrile Pamphlet is welcome to our mercenary Stationers in *English*, they print all.
> —*cuduntque libellos*
> *In quorum foliis vix simia nuda cacaret;*
> But in Latin they will not deale. (1:16)

Nicolas Kiessling is skeptical of the claim that Burton could not find a printer for a Latin volume (1:xxxv). Indeed, the *Anatomy*, with its florid interleaving of English and Latin, would be a poor accommodation to the market. Even Burton's apology for writing in English is double-sided. The untranslated Latin verse directed against "mercenary Stationers" speaks of a libel so foul that monkeys would not shit on it. His reference to "secrets of Minerva," like a proverb in Erasmus's *Adages*, recalls a concentrated narrative. Ovid used the phrase in the *Metamorphoses*, recounting the story of Mercury bribing a woman to help him seduce her sister, who had been dedicated to Minerva. Mercury's accomplice falls in love with him, gazing at him with "the same avaricious eyes with which she had recently peeped at the hidden secrets of fair-haired Pallas."[86] Burton has written an apology for using English, that is not exactly in English: a reader would need knowledge of Latin, and of the racier passages in Latin poetry, to appreciate his satire and savor his profanity. It is as if, for Burton, the act of publishing in English has implicated him in an exchange of uncertain propriety that could only be rectified with impropriety in Latin. He was embarking on a project that entangled him and his readers in a series of language exchanges; he was becoming not simply a monitor of good Latin but an active language broker.

The work that engaged Burton, in the *Anatomy* and his other writings, created what Galina Bolden has called "a party of language experts," a group for whom language expertise is not the possession of a single individual but an aspect of constructed and negotiated social interaction.[87] For Burton, the first site of such negotiation was Oxford: from there, he connected university Latin to the court, established and repaired norms of academic Latin, and framed the translingual collections of the college and university libraries as a nationalist project. This work would be extended by the publication of the *Anatomy*.

There was, of course, no such term as "language broker" in mid-seventeenth-century England. But the puzzling title given to Burton, "philologist," serves as a rough equivalent. The first biography of Burton, a very short mention in Thomas Fuller's *History of the Worthies of England* (1662), observes, "Scarce any Book of Philology in our Land hath in so short a time passed so many Impressions [printings]."[88] Thirty years later, Anthony Wood would describe Burton as a mathematician, astrologer, and "a general read Scholar, a thro'-pac'd Philologist, and one that understood the surveying of lands as well."[89] How would Burton's readers have understood the philologist's work with language?

To us, a philologist is someone engaged in critical language study, like Lorenzo Valla's exposure of the Donation of Constantine, or Erasmus's frequent corrections of textual errors in Latin or Greek. Burton never writes like that. But the contemporaneous sense of philology was much broader, as summarized by Fuller in the early pages of his *History of the Worthies of England*, where he described philology as "Terse and *Polite Learning, melior literatura*, (married long since by *Martianus Capella* to *Mercury*) being that *Florid skill*, containing onely the *Roses* of learning, without the *prickles* thereof, in which narrow sense *thorny Philosophy* is *discharged* as no part of *Philology*. But we take it in the *larger notion*, as inclusive of all *human liberal Studies*, and preposed to *Divinity*, as the *Porch* to the *Palace*."[90] Burton's philology, like Fuller's, is an immersion in language and literature, a pleasant wandering (or should we say perlustration?) in the domain of good letters.[91] This wandering, learned recreation is the proper occupation of the language broker and his interlocutors, who gather bits and pieces of language from various sources. Burton brings to the mix Roman Latin, medical and scientific Latin, and theological Latin and combines them with various forms of English—Middle English, inkhorn terms, satirical language, religious language—to enable readers to move among these texts, to join him in his perlustrations.

The resulting text is a deep mixture of languages. Latin words appear in twenty percent of the printed lines in the Clarendon *Anatomy*, and in nearly all of the marginal glosses.[92] And Latin was not the only foreign language Burton used. He imagined Athenian onlookers urging on Socrates and Xantippe with "*Eia Socrates! Eia Xantippe!*" (1:50), transliterating the Greek into Roman letters; he referred without translation to κακοξηλιαν (1:53; unhappy rivalry). He quoted lines of Chaucer in Middle English, setting them in Gothic type to mark them as archaic. He frequently used words that are not exactly English: *peccadillo* (1:49), *ambodexters* (2:53), *otacousticon* (1:55), *Anti-parodia* (3:267).

On the level of lexis, Burton imported so many words from Latin to English and collected so many other distinctive terms that he is cited 1,350 times in the *Oxford English Dictionary*. His is the first cited use of *allspice*, and of the delightful word *gubber-tush*, meaning a projecting tooth. He is also cited for words derived from Latin, such as *coll*, to throw one's arms about someone's neck, from Latin *collus*, neck. Often, words for which Burton's is the first citation are listed as obsolete or rare; they are more or less transliterations from Greek and Latin. Here is a representative list: *corrivate* (cause liquids to run together), *dementate* (demented), *immund* (unclean), *opiparous* (rich), *sacculus* (small bag for medicines), *ardelio* (meddler), *anfractuous* (winding). While Burton did not succeed in bringing these words into common use, he did construct an English prose whose boundaries with Latin, and with its own local dialects, were blurred. *Abbreviate* was clearly an English word; why not *immund*?

Burton generally translated or paraphrased both difficult terms and Latin expressions, but these paraphrases can be very loose: "To see a Foole-hardy fellow like those old *Danes, Qui decollari malunt quam verberari*, dye rather than be punished" (1:54); "If young, she is likely wanton and untaught, if lusty, too lascivious, and if she be not satisfied, you know where and when, *nil nisi jurgia*, all is in an uproar" (3:236). From time to time, Burton left a Latin phrase untrans-lated: "which *Mercury* did by *Charon* in Lucian, by touching of his eyes, to make him discern *semel & simul rumores & susurros*" (1:55). This untranslated phrase would have been within the grasp of many readers; the context—Burton's wish that men had windows in their breast so that their thoughts could be seen—clarified the words.

Other untranslated bits of Latin are less easy to decode. Untranslated Latin passages are frequent in Burton's treatment of love melancholy, as in his list of the illicit loves of the ancients, with special emphasis on lust for animals (3:49–50). He leaves untranslated both short quotations and longer lyrics praising sweet nights of married love in his advice to cure love melancholy with marriage (3:262, 264, 265). Neither the prescriptions for increasing nor those for lessen-ing sexual desire are translated (3:63–65, 206–7). Elsewhere in the *Anatomy*, Burton thought it best to keep his extended complaint against corruption in the university in "The Misery of Schollars" in the family by leaving it untranslated (1:324–27). Just as the contemporary language broker silently elides difficult or transgressive speech, Burton fenced off sensitive passages, admitting only other scholars to full understanding.

Burton's commerce with languages is mobile and dynamic. For his contem-poraries, reading the *Anatomy* meant coming to terms with a lot of Latin and a few other languages with a fair amount of help. If the reader were learned, he would be welcome to browse the marginal glosses, rife with untranslated Latin quotations. The less assured reader was guided by Burton's careful intercalation of languages. In most cases. Latin does not overwhelm the text; paraphrases help, and many of the untranslated phrases are rich in cognates or clear from their context. A reader whose Latin was rusty would also be supported by Bur-ton's habit of copious repetition. For example, in his treatment of love melan-choly Burton writes, "For such men ordinarily as are throughly possessed with this humor, become *insensate & insani*, for it is *amor insanus*, as the Poet calls it, beside themselves, and as I have proved, no better than beasts" (3:97). Nothing in this passage would present problems to readers who had any Latin at all. A reader with no Latin skills might puzzle it out from English cognates and the context. Even one unfamiliar with the Latin of medical texts would have little trouble making sense of "*Senes etiam decrepiti cerebrum habent concavum & aridum, ut imaginentur se videre* (saith Boissardus) *quae non sunt*, old men are too frequently mistaken and dote in like case." (1:424). In his "Digression of Anatomy," Burton makes it clear that his philological brokering is a deliberate

accommodation to readers. He offers the digression "for the better understanding of that which is to follow; because many hard words will often occurre,
as *Myrache, Hypochondries, Hemrods, &c. Imagination, Reason, Humours, Spirits, Vitall, Naturall, Animall, Nerves, Veins, Arteries, Chilus, Pituita*; which of the
vulgar will not so easily bee perceaved, what they are, how sited, and what end
they serve" (1:139). For Burton, exchange between English and Latin is a project
to be facilitated, a matter of making available the words that give access to critical
ideas. Burton's philology opens the resources of learned disciplines to his readers:
materials from Scripture, Latin antiquity, learned medicine, and humanist texts
become accessible when they are scaffolded with paraphrases and offered in context. Access to Latin offers readers access to practices of knowledge; that access is
afforded by Burton's ingenious device, a translingual text.

The Code-Meshed *Anatomy*

Burton inducts his readers into the translingual world of early modern learning:
as a philologist, he ranges freely among the many language practices available to
him; as a language broker, he opens those languages to curious readers, remov-
ing or erecting barriers to understanding according to the sensitivity of the
topic. Sociolinguists call this kind of diglossic writing a code-meshed text;
Burton called it "this my *Maceronicon*" (1:11).[93] Recent research has identified
code-meshed texts in many cultures. Suresh Canagarajah has described the
manipravala, or "pearl and coral" texts written in eleventh-century India, mixing
Sanskrit (pearl) and Tamil (coral): "By mixing [quotidian] Tamil [with the
prestigious Sanskrit], the Tamil upgraded their regional language, making it a
suitable medium for serious community relations. By appropriating Sanskrit
for their purposes, Tamils were democratizing a learned, literary, and elite
language. Resources from Sanskrit were made more widely available to the
local community. . . . Tamil was gradually being made a suitable medium for
religious, political, and learned discourses, elevated from its regional and local-
ized status."[94]

Code-meshed texts were found in the ancient Mexican Oaxacan Federation;
British colonial officers wrote them by mixing indigenous languages with English.[95] In early modern Europe, code-meshed texts included letters, minutes of
meetings, university lectures, and sermons.[96] Not all examples of code-meshed
texts speak of hurried writing composed under pressure: code-meshing is also a

writerly practice, a way of exploring the resources of different languages. In contemporary literature, we have the writing of Gloria Anzaldúa, especially *Borderlands / La Frontera: The New Mestiza*, which combines various versions of both English and Spanish, and the work of Minae Mizumura, who wrote a fictionalized autobiography, *Shishōsetsu from left to right* [*An I-novel from left to right*]. The book was written in Japanese with frequent excursions into English, printed horizontally rather than in Japanese vertical columns.[97] Both Anzaldúa and Mizumura saw their writings as interventions into language politics; as Mizumura put it in a later book, "By juxtaposing the two languages what I hoped to convey above all was the irreducible materiality of the Japanese language. . . . I tried, through the bilingual form, to make a case for the irreducible materiality of all languages."[98]

Nor were code-meshed texts absent from early modern good letters. Lope de Vega wrote bilingual scenes that mixed Latin and Spanish. Thomas Browne, whose work I discuss in chapter 6, included short Latin quotations in his *Religio Medici*, and Latin glosses are frequent in his *Hydriotaphia, Urn Burial*. The churchman Jeremy Taylor's *Holy Living and Holy Dying* was written in a vigorous vernacular, but his technical controversial works were written in elaborately code-meshed English and Latin; in his book defending the episcopacy, he followed a philological discussion of the relation between feeding and governing with quotations from Scripture in English and Greek and references to Homer and Euripides in Greek.[99] And of course there were the *Essais* of Montaigne in John Florio's English translation. An Italian Protestant refugee, Florio lived for decades at Burton's Oxford; he rendered into English both Montaigne's affinity for Latin and his playful blurring of the boundaries between quotations from Roman writers and his own prose. In either case, the choice of language is anything but casual; at a moment of passion, Latin could be more expressive than French. As Montaigne wrote, and Florio translated, "The Latine tongue is to me in a manner naturall; I understand it better then French: but it is now fortie yeares I have not made use of it to speake, nor much to write; yet in some extreame emotions and suddaine passions, wherein I have twice or thrice falne, since my yeares of discretion, and namely once, when my father being in perfect health, fell all along upon me in a swoune, I have ever, even from my very hart uttered my first words in latine: nature rushing and by force expressing it selfe, against so long a custome."[100]

These code-meshed texts effect, to varying degrees, linguistic and rhetorical exchanges: they broker the relative prestige of the two languages and support mobility between them; they express the diglossia of a specific community of readers and writers, opening its practices to other readers; they facilitate the movement of linguistic and rhetorical resources. The exchange of languages fosters an exchange of knowledge practices. The pearl dignifies the coral; the coral grounds the pearl. Quotations or paraphrases from writers of antiquity function as maxims: they are taken as true on their face, or they insert condensed narratives into the text. And just as the development of university neo-Latin plays spurred that of English vernacular drama, code-meshed texts in ancient and modern languages facilitated the adoption of new words and the adaptation of Latin syntactical patterns. Such texts also may have served to reanimate the language capacities of readers. A clergyman or solicitor whose daily use of Latin was thin could have refreshed his fluency if the Latin text were supported by the surrounding English. The high standing, persuasive power, and literary development of Latin literature and learning thereby become available to writers addressing mixed audiences and to readers whose primary working language is English.

The capacities of the code-meshed text unfold, page by page, in the *Anatomy*. We have seen how Burton borrowed Latin words, or inserted them into his sentences with translations, and how he scaffolded other Latin passages with contextual helps or paraphrases—unless the canny language broker had reason to limit some readers' access. Burton's text also meshes codes on the levels of genre and rhetoric. These relationships are more complex, as demonstrated by his "Consolatory Digression," a series of subsections in the second partition of the *Anatomy* (2:125–207). This digression, the longest in the *Anatomy*, offers comfort against all the possible misfortunes of life; a mourner who accepted consolation would be less subject to melancholy. While Burton conceded that it was unlikely anyone suffering serious injury would be helped by these counsels, he was fairly certain that they would do no harm. In the meantime, they cheered him up, and they were a warning to the complacent. Burton's consolation takes up the vast Latin and neo-Latin literature of consolation, including Plato, Seneca, Plutarch, and other writers of antiquity up to Boethius and the neo-Latin writers Cardan, Petrarch, and Erasmus. These texts are full of matter, and Burton made that matter available to readers: "As *Hierome* in like case said, *si nostrum areret ingenium, de illorum posset fontibus irrigari*, if our barren wits were dried up, they might be copiously irrigated from these well-springs: And I shall but *actum agere* [do what has been done]; yet because these Tracts are not so obvious and common, I will Epitomize, and briefly insert some of their divine precepts, reducing their voluminous and vast Treatises to my small scale, for it were otherwise impossible to bring so great vessells into so little a creek" (2:125).

Burton's language of philological accommodation echoes his introduction to the earlier "Digression of Anatomy," a summary of "those tedious Tracts *de Anima* [which] are not at all times ready to be had" (1:140). The "not so obvious and common" writings that Burton epitomizes here included an array of genres: the *consolatio* could be written in prose or verse, as a letter, a dialogue, an oration or an essay. It could be written for any misfortune—sickness, loss of office, exile, the death of a loved one, one's own impending death.[101] Burton's consolation is a unique example of this tradition, since it is, according to Angus Gowland, the only developed Humanist *consolatio* specifically focused on melancholy.[102] Like other humanist consolations, Burton's adapted Greek and Roman themes to Christian beliefs. Alone among writers of consolation, he attempted to remedy mental distress caused by a physical ailment, crossing the border between the body and the passions. Burton drew heavily on Latin texts: Cardan and Lemnius, as well as the more satirical works of Agrippa and J. V. Andreae's *Menippus*, which could supply reasons for taking lightly the loss of worldly goods (4:206–7).

In the "Consolatory Digression" Burton embedded seeds of narratives from Scripture and from Greek and Latin antiquity. These stories are folded into the exposition, each suggesting elaboration: "How did *Achilles* take on for *Patroclus* departure? A black cloud of sorrowes overshadowed him, saith *Homer. Jacob* rent his cloathes, put sack-cloath about his loines, sorrowed for his sonne a long season, & could not be comforted, but would needs goe downe into the grave unto his sonne, *Gen. 37.34*" (2:177). Often, these concentrated narratives are given in Latin, as in the opening of the digression, which includes a marginal gloss from Ortelius about mourning customs and quotations from Catullus and Vergil. Gerolamo Cardano had cited these authors in his *De consolatione* (1542); Burton imports not only Cardano's topics but also his Latin authorities.

Later sections of the digression juxtapose sacred with secular literatures, Scripture with Horace. Burton mobilizes these authorities to shape an anthology of consolatory forms, tropes, and arguments, offering English models drawn from a Latin genre. Those texts offered Burton ways of inducting readers into the literature of antiquity; they offered lexical possibilities, models of genre and tone, and *topoi* that could be developed to meet varied exigencies. Burton brought these resources, drawn from medicine, good letters, and divinity, into the domain of English prose, shaping the possibilities of the language as he prostituted his genius to it. Burton's consolatory digression makes available to its readers texts, narratives, figures, and ways of writing that would have been the common property of the international republic of letters. These pieces of language become available for exchange in their varied forms, some in English and some in Latin. They open to readers a culture that aligns Christian patience with Roman fortitude, laced with the astringent distance of satire, inflected with endless variations of form.

If one of the central actions of the *Anatomy* is to facilitate exchanges among genres and disciplines, two of the most powerful tools that Burton used to organize such exchanges were the resources of rhetoric and his ability to move from Latin to a copious and expressive English. The translingually rich environment of English culture, especially of university life, at the beginning of the seventeenth century enabled such fluency and created readers who needed, understood, and valued his text. Burton's translingualism bridged the world of Latin and neo-Latin learning and the emerging practices of vernacular scholarship. As a language broker, he imported the lexical, generic, and rhetorical resources of Latin into vernacular contexts; he opened doorways into Latin literature and science by framing those texts with translations, paraphrases, and contextual clues while drawing on the traditional resources of Latin for restricting access to sensitive information. Jan Blommaert observes that "Multilingualism . . . should not be seen as a collection of 'languages' that a speaker controls, but rather as a complex of specific semiotic resources, some of which belong to a conventionally defined 'language' while others belong to another 'language.'"[103] Burton had access to the semiotic resources of two rich languages, and he was interested in putting those resources in conversation with each other, using the semiotic possibilities of Latin to enrich English, and animating the Latin resources by making them available to English readers.

6

The Anatomy of Melancholy and Transdisciplinary Rhetoric

Each chapter of this book has placed Burton at a busy crossroads where knowledges, discourses, genres, and languages moved through and around each other, tracing irregular but not random paths, crossing or obstructing each other, handing off bits of language in passing. Burton, in a roadside café, followed these patterns while sipping a glass of wine (or perhaps dark beer). Sometimes he looked down on traffic from the Paradise of Singular Writers, where Walter Benjamin kept him company. Or Burton was a wary pedestrian, dodging traffic on his way to a safe haven. Or he was a traffic cop, trying to make the most productive and least dangerous use of this fraught space. Now is the time to think about how rhetoric supported and enabled those patterns and what they have to say to us as rhetoricians in search of transdisciplinary theories. In this discussion, I will treat rhetoric as a broad study of the discourses that organize knowledge, underwrite cooperation, and contain conflicts, and secondarily as a specific academic discipline, the school subject that Burton, and many readers of this book, learned and taught. Finally, as promised in chapter 1, I will discuss Burton's understanding of melancholy.

The *Anatomy* is an exacting demonstration of the importance of rhetoric as it organizes multiple practices of exchange and circulation. It is one long celebration of the pleasure and usefulness of movement, of the work of the roving philologist; rhetoric is a map of those movements, a rubric for the rituals of perlustration, and a framework for the exigent work of the philologist. Rhetoric provides the *topoi* that organize objects of investigation for nascent disciplines; it offers a taxonomy for the tropes and figures that ornament and augment Burton's prose. Rhetoric orients the texts' many addresses to the reader; it names and directs the affective currents that the book puts in motion.

The rhetorical orientation of Burton's writing distinguishes it from the work of other seventeenth-century writers who shared Burton's Latinity and who, like him, worked the porous seams of early modern disciplines. For example, Thomas Browne (1605–1682) wrote on religion, natural history, and ancient history; current scholarship sees his work as a textual connection between traditional learning and the new sciences.[1] Browne, a physician, was an omnivorous student of ancient texts and a close observer of nature. Unlike Burton, he was a sometime experimenter and active in learned societies. His essays, beginning with *Religio Medici* (1642), and continuing with *Pseudodoxia Epidemica* (1646), *Urne-Buriall* (1658), and *The Garden of Cyrus* (1658), are full of questions, doubts, and debates, but those uncertainties are generally settled, however provisionally.

The Anatomy of Melancholy offers no such stable resolutions. Browne's reflections are contemplative; Burton's, oriented to exigency, the need to undertake a cure of melancholy. Both uncertainty and exigency are distinguishing marks of rhetoric; both are central to the *Anatomy* and rare in Browne's writing.

Two passages from *Pseudodoxia Epidemica* and their counterparts in the *Anatomy* demonstrate these differences. In his discussion of the mandrake, Browne dismantles a brace of popular errors: mandrakes do not grow from the fat of executed men, they do not scream when uprooted, and they are not fatal to dig up. Browne's evidence against these beliefs is drawn from various sources. Like many other seventeenth-century scholars, he believed that living things could arise from decay: bees from the corpse of an ox, lice from human sweat. But while the bee does not resemble the ox, or the louse a man, mandrakes famously take human shape. For Browne, this shape could not express a human origin because nature distinguishes beings produced by corruption from "seminal productions." Beings produced from seed always resemble their parents, while those produced from corruption never do.[2] The belief in the shrieking mandrake is dismissed as "false below confute," an exaggeration of the "small and stridulous noyse" that any pulled root might make.[3] Finally, digging a mandrake cannot be deadly, since the mandrake is a useful plant. To make its harvest dangerous would be to "introduce a second forbidden fruit," which the providence of God would never allow.[4] Popular errors can be refuted by referring to the principles of natural philosophy, common experience, or religious reflection, and all these resources are credible and applicable to a wide range of questions.

Burton has little to say about mandrake; it is mentioned, along with many other simples, in the chapter on medicines to provoke sleep (2:255–56). A reader seeking a cure for insomnia would be hard put to distinguish mandrake from the score of other plants he recommends, or to puzzle out whether it should be taken internally, used as a pillow, or reduced to an oil. Burton is not after a cure, but an exchange of knowledge practices—in this case, moving from the sciences of the soul, which treated the effects of sleep on the mind, to medical practices, including the quotidian herbal remedies in the hands of every housewife. Like many of the exchanges in the *Anatomy*, this one leads to unsettled alternatives rather than confirmed conclusions.

But Burton, unlike Browne, worked with questions that called for resolution; he dealt with questions of therapy and cure. This difference is evident in the two writers' discussions of diet. Browne takes up this question in his chapter on eating meat.[5] He argues from Scripture that humans can live without eating meat and gives evidence from both the literature of Greek and Roman antiquity and from early modern travel literature that people have eaten all kinds of animals with relish. Food preferences are shown to be arbitrary, so that there can be "no solid rule of selection or confinement," but "necessity, reason, and Physick, are the best determiners" of diet.[6] Browne balances skepticism of received ideas about which meats are unclean with a serene invocation of the authorities that will decide which meat is best for each individual. For Burton, as we have seen, the question of diet required two long sections of the *Anatomy*, discussing at length vegetables, meats, drinks, cooking methods, and times for eating, drawing on the writings of physicians ancient and modern. None of Burton's discussions is conclusive; in the *Anatomy*, it is not clear that necessity, reason, and physic do indeed provide authoritative, univocal advice. Burton and Browne, divided by a generation, both wrote in the world of traditional academic practices and emerging sciences; the malleable knowledge practices of early modern learned cultures were central to both their writing practices. But Burton, unlike Browne, saw all disciplines as uncertain, while readers' needs for knowledge were urgent. Burton used both these affordances of rhetoric—arguing about uncertain matters and making decisions on the basis of partial evidence—to structure the movement and exchange of the *Anatomy*.

We can trace the effects of these affordances on three levels. First, rhetoric fosters exchanges among knowledge practices and thereby allows for the circulation of new knowledges and new means of producing knowledge. A rhetorical understanding of genre assumes that genres are nested and that they interact; it offers an alternative to understanding genres as unchanging forms or as hybrids that repeat with variation. Rhetoric supplies methods of textual organization that respond to differentiated exigencies of evidence and proof: the fully realized narrative that presents vivid images to the readers of history can be condensed and multiplied to show readers of medicine what can be expected to happen for the most part. These variations were salient to Burton's readers, who could move from history to medicine with some frequency. They are even more salient to us, as readers for whom history might be a rare indulgence and medicine a site for panicked information-gathering.

Having sponsored the movement of knowledges and knowledge practices, rhetoric allows us to trace and understand those movements. On this second level, rhetoric demystifies disciplinary claims of privileged access to knowledge while recognizing the efficacy of specialized language practices. Rhetoric disposes the scholar to experiment with mobility, to enjoy rather than reprehend the transgressive wandering of some bit of knowledge from one discipline to another. Rhetoric played that role for Burton, writing when the boundaries among disciplines were still quite porous; it can, perhaps, also play that role for us. Rhetoric forms a disposition toward mobile language practices; it also forms the subject who can entertain that disposition, who does not worry that crossing disciplinary boundaries will necessarily produce something called "mush." But our encounter with rhetorical exchanges will necessarily differ from Burton's: for us, disciplines are not the traditional or emergent discourses Burton encountered, but deeply institutionalized and highly differentiated knowledge practices. The *Anatomy* moves among loosely formed knowledge practices, following Burton's perlustrating patterns of thought. Our movements among disciplines are necessarily more deliberate and programmatic.

On a third level, rhetoric orients us to the contradictory impulses of deliberation: the need to entertain multiple perspectives, even when they are fundamentally irreconcilable, and the equally pressing need to decide on a course of action. As an educational method, rhetoric shapes collectivities capable of deliberation that is both open and engaged; as a political practice, it forms publics that can weigh evidence, consider, and act provisionally. Again, these orientations operate differently for us than they did for Burton; deliberative discourse was vexed in the attenuated public sphere of Burton's England, while we face both developed structural constraints on deliberation and sharp exigencies for making decisions.

Rhetoric and Exchanges Among Knowledge Practices

Let us begin with the issue of exchanges among knowledge practices. I have presented the *Anatomy* as an investigation of early modern ways of knowing as they move and condense themselves into disciplines. While academic disciplines as we know them had not emerged in Burton's Oxford, and would not for a good two hundred years, he was certainly aware that divinity was a hegemonic knowledge practice, while Paracelsan medicine was not. That did not lead him to publish religious treatises or to forgo reading Paracelsus. Although Burton studied theology and practiced his clerical profession, for him divinity was a resource rather than a framework for writing. As he said in reply to an imagined critic, he was diverted from "the maine Channell" of his religious studies by the "Rillet" of melancholy: "Not that I preferre it before Divinity, which I doe acknowledge to be the Queene of Professions, to which all the rest are as Handmaids, but that in Divinity I saw no such great neede. For had I written positively, there be so many Books in that kinde, so many Commentators, Treatises, Pamphlets, Expositions, Sermons, that whole teemes of Oxen cannot draw them" (1:20).

Burton rejected the stabilized genres of theological discourse; he would not participate in controversies that shaped the discipline; he would instead watch the contentions and rivalries and the associated polemics and treatises that mark a mature knowledge practice. He found the same limits in medicine, and indeed "in all Sciences" (1:21). His remedy did not dismantle those disciplinary structures, which he relied on even as he ridiculed them. Instead, by bringing the disciplines of theology and medicine into conversation around the topic of melancholy, he established routes of exchange and motion: "I could not find a fitter taske to busie my selfe about, a most apposite Theame, so necessary, so commodious, and generally concerning all sorts of men, that should so equally participate of both [disciplines], and require a whole Physitian. A Divine in this compound mixt Malady, can doe little alone, a Physitian in some kinds of Melancholy much lesse, both make an absolute cure" (1:22–23). The promised "absolute cure" turns out to be illusory, but Burton's attention to the circulation and movement of knowledges sidesteps disciplinary rivalries. His practice recalls Kenneth Burke's proposal that rhetoric worked *ad bellum purificandum*; it transposed potentially violent disagreements into the less dangerous field of discourse. Burton's practice of movement and exchange made disciplinary rivalries productive; it established relationships between and among distinct knowledge practices.

This work of connection is essentially rhetorical. Burton tracked the movements among disciplines with flexible attention, as if he were following the courses of a stream from its main channels to the tiniest rivulets. He followed the movements that knowledge practices perform behind the backs of their practitioners: the migration of genres, the adaptation of tropes and figures, the slippage between a text and its subsequent citations. And he tentatively traced new channels that could bring disciplinary streams together to water new fields.

And so he produced a book that drew on the central resources of early modern scholarship but never left them undisturbed. The laws of genre were opened into practices of genre embedding, embellishment, and layering: the cento supports the treatise, the treatise includes an embedded consolation that gives way to a satire. Such busy crossing of borders promotes the exchange of resources among genres and disciplines: the religious teachings of the consolation mingle with the sage, quotidian advice of the medical treatise; all that solemnity is enlivened by a jolt of satire.

Disciplinary practices were exchanged as well as genres. Academic medicine offered inset case histories that imported the resources of medical observation into received medical genres; Burton modified them to comply with Aristotelian canons of proof. Such narratives torque the norms of medical discourse to establish plausible relationships between specific events and general laws. Such movement among discrete modes of argument allowed Burton to remain skeptical of medicine's claim to knowledge while taking seriously the exigency of relieving melancholic suffering.

We are deep in rhetorical territory here, and nobody mapped this area better than Kenneth Burke, the rhetorical theorist of motion and change. Burke's observations in *Permanence and Change: An Anatomy of Purpose* suggest that actions can be understood by considering the perspectives of those who perform them, especially when those perspectives are rooted in cultural norms or reinforced in daily work.[7] Burke named the expertise that supports some understandings of action occluding others "trained incapacity." He broadened the concept by borrowing a term from John Dewey—"occupational psychosis"—to name the norms of understanding that permeate a culture or historical period. (For what it's worth, Burke claimed that by "psychosis" he meant *"pronounced character* of the mind."[8]) These observations remind us that Burke wrote *Permanence and Change* during the postwar development of formal interdisciplinary programs: the book was published four years after the founding of the American Studies Association in 1950. Burke recommended shifts of interpretation as a remedy to trained incapacity: "We try to point out new relationships as meaningful—we interpret situations differently; in the subjective sphere, we invent new accounts of motive."[9]

Early modern academic culture, which did not enforce disciplinary segregation, restricted the movement of knowledge practices less than Burke's, and certainly less than ours. Early modern scholars were not members of departments, were not expected to publish in a single field, and were admired for expertise in multiple knowledge practices. Burton developed and advanced this fluidity of practice, moving discursive resources from one field of knowledge to another, the better to grapple with both the unruly nature of melancholy and the development of new forms of learning. Burke's counsel to shift frames was anticipated in *The Anatomy of Melancholy*, which connected learned discourses, mobilized them, and facilitated readers' movement among them. Burton uncoupled the efficacy of the text from the stability of its truth; readers' movements among contraries, tracing the perlustrations of writers, were themselves mental "changes of ayre" (2:64). He offered a model of interdisciplinarity that is ludic rather than dutiful, concerned with producing something new rather than with bowing at every disciplinary shrine.

How can we learn from these practices and deploy them in a world where disciplines are much more strictly segregated? Our first step might be to call on a theorist who has navigated this world, Jürgen Habermas. In *The Theory of Communicative Action*, Habermas speaks of the irreversible disenchantment of the world.[10] His analysis, drawing on Max Weber, sees the modern knowledge practices of science, philosophy, ethics, and government as uncoupled from transcendent ideas of the creation or divine law that had grounded them. Elsewhere in *Theory of Communicative Action*, Habermas asserts that, while our survival depends upon coordinating our activities by reaching agreement through communication, that work is complicated by the conditions of modernity that have led to the "decentration of our understanding of the world and the differentiation of various universal validity claims."[11] Habermas has variously identified those differentiated validity claims at different stages in his career; generally, he has distinguished a claim of truth and rational consistency intrinsic to theoretical discourses, a claim of normative rightness intrinsic to moral discourses, and claims of sincerity and truthfulness intrinsic to self-expression. We can extend this logic by observing that the claims of truth and rightness that operate in contemporary disciplines are supported in distinctive ways: academic theology has relationships to both the moral counsel of denominational religious discourse and the conceptual work of ethics, but each of these closely related discourses uses distinctive ways of reasoning. The process of differentiation was beginning in Burton's world, where arguments in astronomy were settled by repeated observations while those in metaphysics required demonstrations leading to intuitively certain conclusions. Still, in Burton's university, the central methods of critical humanism supported common practices in many disciplines: philologically informed reading; consultation of authorities ancient and modern; analysis by division. Observation, a scandal for scholastic knowledge, could be recuperated in the general framework of study under Aristotelian concepts of demonstration.

Habermas's analysis suggests that connections among disciplines might best be constructed by considering the structural implications of their implicit claims rather than by calibrating their rules of evidence and demonstration. The scientific claim to truth can be variously understood as generativity or representation; whatever our understanding of this claim, it supports practices in natural sciences whose procedures and rules of evidence are opaque to each other. The theory of differentiation directs us to drop down to the fundamental interests of disciplines in order to establish connections among them.

This position is very useful in understanding foundational commonalities and distinctions among disciplines, and in framing general discussions about the relations among them. It could be of help, for example, in thinking through the relation between STEM disciplines and the humanities. But despite its impressive consistency, it is of limited use in establishing connections among specific discourses. On the level of fundamental assumptions, the relations among disciplines are so general as to be amorphous. A theory that supports transdisciplinarity would need to follow Habermas in recognizing both the distinctiveness of discourse practices and their profound connections at the level of discourse claims. But an effective theory of transdisciplinarity would also need to connect disciplines by establishing relationships among the propositions they advance and the resources of language they use to construct such propositions. Transdisciplinarity, therefore, needs rhetoric. Rhetoric is deeply concerned with propositions but recognizes no transcendental claim to truth or rightness; it attends to language as a practice constituting and connecting discourse communities. It offers room for the discussions that Habermas's theory of differentiation sponsors; it offers rich resources for the inventional shifts that Burke recommends.

Burton's text is useful to rhetoricians as a model for a certain kind of rhetorical production, a suggestion of how disciplinary boundaries might be negotiated and disciplinary distinctions related to common assumptions. Although Burton could still speak of divinity as the "Queene of Professions," as if all modes of study were connected in an interdependent hierarchy, he enacted the possibilities of disciplines that were not so neatly arranged, that traded among themselves without regard for their traditional rankings. If all disciplines were foolish, controlled by their individual learned incapacities, it was better to simply absorb their resources: Galenic medicine's pulsating temporality; theology's subtle connection between the divine spirits and the air we breathe.

Among the disciplines that Burton used was formal rhetoric, including especially the rhetorics of humanism and of Greek and Roman antiquity. Rudolph Agricola's expanded *topos* of definition supported a practice of collecting materials from a range of sources, refined to persuasive force by the rhetor's integration of them rather than by externalized logical regularity; definition could be employed in any discipline. Erasmus's practice of concentrating polyvalent narratives in proverbs offered Burton an alternate function for his narrative illustrations, which could be placed like easter eggs in the dense, busy, body of the text. Following Agricola and Quintilian, medical cases could be truncated, grouped, and cited as evidence drawn from observation; following Erasmus, the mention of a name or the citation of a few lines of poetry could connect to centuries of debate. All of these strategies share with both Habermas and Burke a heady reliance on the relations between writers and audiences, a central concern of rhetoric. While Habermas has never, as far as I know, had a kind word to say about rhetoric, the theory of communicative action rests on an implicitly rhetorical recognition of the assumptions that support the relation between writers and readers. In *Theory of Communicative Action*, Habermas explained that "both ego, who raises a validity claim with his utterance, and alter, who recognizes or rejects it, based their decisions on potential grounds or reasons."[12] These shared reasons permit the negotiation of differences in experience and point of view; the possibilities for collaboration or exchange are not based on the sorting out of transcendent truth claims, but on mutual recognitions that all parties have grounds for their positions and that those grounds are open to discussion. That position, whether Habermas would like it or not, is essentially rhetorical.

Agreement on propositions and norms of truth, however, is not the only basis for relationships among disciplines. Burke describes how concepts can be refunctioned, reevaluated, and transformed: they can be placed in new contexts, compared to disparate objects, or classified in new ways. Such movements are not a matter of systematic argument; they are performed outside the line of argument rather than constructed on its face, and thereby support the movement of language resources from one domain to another. Burke recommends the cultivation of such perspectives by incongruity by developing contradictory concepts, or presenting ideas through metaphors rather than abstractions.[13] Long before Burke,

Burton practiced such exchanges and refunctionings of disciplinary terms, tropes, genres. Like Habermas—and this is the only way that Burton is like Habermas—Burton distrusted academic rhetoric, and he had harsh words to say about what he saw as the petty distinctions of academic rhetoricians. But just as Habermas understood the relation between speaker and audience as the basis of all validity claims, Burton saw the rhetorical movement and reconstitution of language as a method for engaging the reader in an encounter with realities that cannot be stabilized.

Rhetoric Forms the Mobile Thinker

The *Anatomy* educates readers in a broad practice of rhetoric: it requires a nimble movement among practices of knowledge; it forecloses the possibility of unreserved commitment to any single discipline. Many contemporary critics have seen the *Anatomy* as a therapeutic text; to read the book cures the disease of melancholy.[14] Certainly, the text invites such a use. But it has a more profoundly curative rule: it forms a subject who can read the discourses of modernity from the inside out, tracing their subterranean connections. The reader of the *Anatomy* has been well schooled in the construction of Burke's perspectives by incongruity.

For such a reader, the nonnatural air becomes a metaphor for mobility and then metonymically connects to the space of the cosmos, the center of the earth, and all that the air contains. Classifications intersect and comment on each other. For example, in Burton's discussion of amusements as cures for melancholy, he organizes his extensive lists of diversions by location, place in the social hierarchy, and suitability to different kinds of melancholy. Burke showed how such contradictory classifications can capture the movement of changeable objects, and no object was more changeable than melancholy. In Burton's deployment of multiple classificatory systems—melancholy characterized by bodily locations, by objects of obsession, by humoral complexions—we can read a preference for knowledge that works on the bias. A reader who follows Burton on these journeys has uncoupled knowledge from stability. This reader might locate authority—the authority of the text, their own authority, or institutional authority—in mobility and adaptation rather than universalism or permanence.

Burke observed that "some people write their poems on paper, and others carve theirs out of jugular veins."[15] In *The Anatomy of Melancholy*, we read a text carved out of the jugular veins of early modern knowledge; this text uses its own difficulty, its own movement through genres, disciplines, and languages, as a way of delaying our rest, alternating rebarbative authorities with amusing stories that do not lend themselves to settled conclusions. To read the *Anatomy* is to approach the construction of knowledge as an affective process: passion and knowledge are cut from the same cloth. The structures of the *Anatomy* orient us to mobility and to fluid relations of exchange; we find there the knowledge practices that Burke recommends, practices that direct us to the production of new relationships and the cross-hatching of disparate classifications rather than the routine elaboration of a received paradigm.

Rhetoric and Democratic Deliberation

A subject whose deliberations are conditioned by these rhetorical values is ready to participate in debates about knowledge and its uses. In moving to this third affordance of rhetoric in the *Anatomy*, we build on the question of relations among practices of knowledge to consider how agreement is secured, action is motivated, and decisions are made in spite of imperfect knowledge. Since all disciplines produce only partial and provisional forms of knowledge, the reader of Burton will welcome the insights of mixed methods in addressing dilemmas that, like melancholy, are "mixt" and intractable. Such an early modern sensibility cannot be called transdisciplinary, since there were no early modern disciplines in our sense. But in its fluidity and in the fruitfulness of the exchanges it sponsors, the *Anatomy* offers a model of what a transdisciplinary deliberation might look like. It would include both the expansive expression of desire of Burton's utopia and the dour realism of his criticism of the university. The goal of such mobile deliberation is itself mobile.

For the monarchist Burton, deliberation was the province of the prince: "where good government is, prudent and wise Princes, there all things thrive and prosper, peace and happiness is in the Land, where it is otherwise, all things are ugly to behold, incult, barbarous, uncivill, a Paradise is turned to a wildernesse" (1:74). In his Utopia, Burton describes a "good government" balanced between mobility and stability and expressed in multiple relationships of exchange. Burton's Utopia is governed by a monarch, but while noble rank is hereditary, it requires continued achievement: commoners can become nobles, and nobles can lose their rank. The good government promotes industry and commerce, within and outside its borders; it rewards and supports the discovery of knowledge; and it appoints scholars to offices of trust.

Burton saw bodies, families, and nations operating analogously; since the Utopia of "Democritus to the Reader" was a prescription to correct the "common grievances of the body politicke" (1:68), it rests on the assumption that both the state and individual bodies are subject to melancholy. General remarks on good government morph into a discussion of the family, and then of the various conditions of men; the deliberative strategies that identify cures for melancholy bodies suggest corresponding rhetorical practices in civic and interpersonal deliberation. The *Anatomy* traces the contours of those practices, beginning with the collection of opinions and experiences from the widest array of sources. (Recall that Burton quoted from Protestants and Catholics, Muslims and Jews, ancients and moderns.) If these sources are sufficiently broad, they are likely to include contradictions; those contradictions are not to be resolved, since they are inherent in complex situations. Rather, Burton looked for the preponderance of evidence, or searched out a way of making a choice that allowed for multiple resolutions of a problem, depending on the exigencies of time and place.

Consider his discussion of whether melancholics should eat fish, especially carp (1:214–15). Burton quoted an ancient medical authority who held that carp was "no better than a slimy watery meate," followed by several modern authorities who approve of it. (Does a single colorful rejection outweigh many bare mentions of supporting authors?) Burton cited the practice of contemporary country gentlemen, who fill their ponds with carp. And then he presented the counsel of the French physician Bruerinus, who held that the fish was healthy if it came from a clear, sweet pool, and harmful if it came from a muddy one. Burton suggested that this rule of thumb could be extended to all freshwater fish, but he cautioned that too much fish of any sort can cause melancholy, as proved by the state of the Carthusians, "whose living is most part Fish," and who are all too subject to the disorder. Burton brought together a broad array of contradictory opinions and experiences. None of them has been discounted because, in given circumstances, any of them can be salient. Carp can be harmful if it comes from a muddy pond or if it is eaten too often; at other times and places, it can be healthy.

This passage offers a model for thinking through problems that require choice rather than contemplation: either we eat carp, or we don't eat carp. Burton's weighing of the evidence accommodates situations in which contrary courses of action can be successful: we could follow the practice of jovial country gentlemen who eat carp or heed the warning of the dour Carthusians and avoid it. Burton refuses any promise of certainty but offers guidance that can be applied prudently and modified when conditions change.

This is not at all a bad model for making complicated decisions, although it does not guarantee that things will go well. But Burton's model does open space for deliberation: a reader who can tolerate the contradictory messages that drove Stanley Fish crazy will, perhaps, tolerate being contradicted or confronted in discussions of civic problems. As Jeffrey Walker argued in *Rhetoric and Poetics in Antiquity*, alternatives must be discussed, and choices must be made even in the most autocratic of political systems; democratic alternatives to authoritarianism cannot arise without the practice of rhetoric. Rhetoric is "democracy's condition of possibility."[16]

Rhetoric, Mobility, and Melancholy

Although melancholy has not been the subject of this book, my investigation of rhetoric and its transdisciplinary affordances does have implications for that topic, and it is time to spell them out. As Burton showed, an understanding of melancholy requires moving among systems of knowledge: medicine cannot be neglected, but neither can divinity, politics, or good letters. Mobilization and exchange are central to Burton's understanding of the causes and cures of melancholy. Over and over, the cause of melancholy is found to be obstruction of movement by blockages, whether physical, mental, or emotional. On a cosmic level, Saturn, slowest of the planets visible to the early modern world, could dispose a patient to melancholy; even a palm marked on the mount of Saturn portended danger (1:200–202). On the level of family and nation, melancholy passed unbroken from parents to children; only periodic movements of populations would prevent the settlement of bad humors (1:206–7). On the level of the individual body, "nothing begets [melancholy] sooner, encreaseth and continueth it oftner than idleness" (1:239).

The danger of immobility was especially great for bookish readers, who led "a resty life" (1:212). They should avoid strong or heavy foods that could corrupt blood. The air they breathe, like the water they drink, should be mobile (1:234–37). While they should avoid excessive exercise, they should also remember that "Idlenesse as a Tempest, drives all vertuous motions out of our mindes, & *nihil sumus*, on a sudden, by sloath and such bad waies we come to naught" (1:242). Burton's paradoxical comparison of idleness to a tempest suggests that stasis and immobility include their opposites, the disordered and destructive motions that endanger both body and mind.

Although Burton conceded that no human being can withstand the first onslaught of a passion, he asserted that we can avoid prolonging passionate thoughts and feelings. These extended disturbances of the mind work physiologically, preventing calm interchanges of fluids and spirits in the humoral body: "they overwhelme reason, judgement, and pervert the temperature of the body" (1:248). Even benign passions, if prolonged, will wear away at the mind, "*as the raine* (saith *Austin*) doth a stone" (1:248). Those who do not govern their passions but "give all encouragement unto them, leaving the raynes, and using all provocations to further them" (1:255–56), will sooner or later be consumed by melancholy. For Burton, it was dwelling on emotions, rather than the passions themselves, that caused melancholy; passions became immovable states of the soul, the static tempests of settled melancholy.

All kinds of melancholy are treated by restoring mobility and sponsoring exchange, especially social exchange. In a preface to the second partition, on cures for melancholy, Burton directed the sufferer to pray for divine help, willingly pay for treatment, eagerly hope for a cure, and confidently trust a single physician (2:14–16). The melancholic cannot even enter treatment without establishing a minimal practice of exchange, fluidity of affect, and openness to influence. Burton's discussion of rectifying the nonnaturals is a paean to mobility: melancholics must exercise, keep bodily fluids moving, eat foods that are easily digested, and, by implication, become as mobile and porous as the air that inspires Burton's most lyrical digression. They should guard against any blockage of evacuation—constipation, sexual abstinence, amenorrhea, or blocked hemorrhoids (1:229–33). We can let Burton's recommendations for drinking water stand as an example (2:21–22). The best drinking water is pure, thin, and light, easily heated or chilled. Ideally, it is collected from newly fallen rain, or a fountain with its source in the east, presumably so that it catches the rays of the rising sun, as Hippocrates had recommended.[17] Fast-flowing springs and rivers are also beneficial, but Burton warns against thick or muddy rivers, still waters, or stagnant lakes.

This advice is extended in Burton's recommendations for calming the perturbations of the mind—music, merry company, the advice and comfortable counsel of friends. To become aware of the mobility of the world is to forestall settled
melancholy. The recognition that change and movement are inevitable, indeed
universal, is a consolation for a universal malady; Burton quotes Epictetus: "*If
thou lovest a pot, remember 'tis but a pot thou lovest, and thou wilt not be troubled
when 'tis broke: If thou lovest a sonne or wife, remember they were mortall, and thou
wilt not be so impatient*" (2:186). He observes that a person who ignores this
advice "makes a cord to bind himselfe and pulls a beame upon his owne head"
(2:186). For Burton, participating in this universal motion is therapeutic. The
vibrations of music set in motion the spirits about the heart (2:114); study
encourages perlustration among the endless variety of animals, plants, stars,
territories, histories, exempla, and theories (2:84–86). And there is "no better
Physicke for a melancholy man then change of ayre and variety of places, to
travel abroad and see fashions" (2:64).

We can trace an analogous relationship between mobility and melancholy in
the scholarship on Burton and melancholy. Although critics do not agree in
their evaluation of melancholy, they consistently associate beneficial melancholy
with mobility and harmful melancholy with stagnation. Angus Gowland, in *The
Worlds of Renaissance Melancholy: Robert Burton in Context*, shows us an increasingly skeptical Burton, less persuaded by learned discourse in each edition, and
especially dismissive of controversial writing.[18] Burton came to advocate a *phi-
losophia practica*, a philosophy that renounced controversial speculation in favor
of advice to both individuals and nations on the proper conduct of life, synthe-
sized from theological, moral-philosophical, and neo-Galenic wisdom. For
Gowland's Burton, melancholy anchors a cosmic chain of causes, reaching from
the fall of Man, through the depravity of human will, to the passion-ridden
body. This omnivorous humanist Burton, skeptical but not cynical, pessimistic
but not fatalist, constantly recommending amendments of both body and mind,
is certainly to be found in the pages of the *Anatomy*.

A very different Burton can be found in Jennifer Radden's *Melancholic Habits: Burton's "Anatomy" and the Mind Sciences*, which connects Burton's account
of melancholy with contemporary cognitive sciences.[19] Radden avoids any easy
identification of early modern melancholy with contemporary depression. In
her reading, melancholy begins with indulgence in the delights of the imagination, idle fancies divorced from action or labor. These reveries entrench habits of
solitude and idleness, leaving the melancholic defenseless when the imagination

inevitably presents sad or fearful images. The natural history of melancholy moves from freedom to relentless confinement. Radden focuses on Burton's concern for melancholy habits rather than passing melancholy indispositions.[20] Habitual melancholy brings obsessions: "still, still, still thinking of it . . . still that toy runnes in their minde, that fear, that superstition . . . that agony, that crotchet."[21] Melancholy is prevented by avoiding solitary, idle habits; it is cured by disrupting such habits with diverting occupations, the advice of friends, and rectification of the humors. Radden's Burton is a worldly wise Stoic, too pessimistic to hope for the elimination of all passion but entirely convinced of the need not to let passions settle into immovable obsessions.

Other scholars follow similar paths of association. Drew Daniel, in *The Melancholy Assemblage: Affect and Epistemology in the English Renaissance*, reads the *Anatomy* through Gilles Deleuze's concept of the assemblage.[22] In Daniel's account, the assemblage is a constellation of actions, bodies, and discourses organized along the contrary vectors of stabilizing territorialization and disorganizing deterritorialization. In this view, melancholy is an assemblage of physical states and symptomatic performances. Daniel places the *Anatomy* within the canon of early modern melancholy texts as "both the highwater mark and the vanishing point of a certain historical trajectory."[23] He refuses to let go of either Burton's references to Galen, who saw melancholy as an illness, or of his interest in the pseudo-Aristotelian *Problemata* 30.1, which associates melancholy with genius. Melancholy, for Daniels, is productive because it is mobile; it is textually absorbing insofar as it sponsors exchanges among incompatible systems of knowledge.

If Daniel locates melancholy in the individual psyche, for Douglas Trevor in *The Poetics of Melancholy in Early Modern England* it is the incurable occupational disease of scholars. He reads the *Anatomy* as a response to the isolation of scholars as the the patronage system collapsed. Since melancholy is a necessary condition of scholarship, and scholarship is vitally necessary to social order, plenty, and peace, it would be harmful to rectify melancholic distemperature, even if that were possible. For Trevor, melancholy produces knowledge essential to the nation, and melancholy scholars should be supported by generous patrons. Just as wealth circulated to scholars, scholars would disseminate knowledge to better their country.

These readings are remarkably diverse. The analytic tools they use range from scrupulous historicism to psychoanalytic theory. They vary in their scope of analysis, in their evaluation of melancholy, and in a host of technical issues, especially the possibility of cure. What is constant—and, I have been arguing, what is constant in *The Anatomy of Melancholy*—is an orientation to movement, fluidity, and the porous exchange of knowledge, dispositions associated with a rhetorical approach to the production and reception of knowledge. A writer who sees the *Anatomy* as a praise of melancholy holds that melancholy elevates the soul to higher Ficinian realms. One who reads melancholy as a disease understands it as a settled habit, the confinement of the soul by passions or vices, or the stagnation of corrupt overheated humors. If melancholy is incurable, it is immovable; if it can be cured, the treatment requires exercise, distraction, changes in the sufferer's habits and attention, and friendly instruction in consoling religious ideas. If melancholy has good social effects, then those effects must circulate with the suitably supported scholars; if it is a blight on the nation, then swamps must be drained, cities must be built, trade encouraged, and universities supported.

These themes are so insistent in the criticism because they resonate with the text of *The Anatomy of Melancholy*, which invokes ideas of mobility, exchange, and fluidity on multiple levels, including the questions of melancholy's causes and cures. If melancholy can be known, however provisionally, through a fluid exchange of discourses among knowledge practices, then the same habits and dispositions that render melancholy and the rest of the natural world knowable are also central to its therapy.

Rhetoric has been associated with mobility and exchange since Greek and Roman antiquity. In the *Gorgias*, Plato criticized the orator who was not an expert in military strategy or shipbuilding or law for presuming to suggest policies in all those areas; he condemned the orator even more severely for changing his opinions with the crowd's and trying to please all kinds of people, including immigrants, women, and slaves.[24] Plato, aspiring to permanence and transcendence, could only see rhetoric as a scandal. Aristotle, absorbed in the topics of motion and change, was less offended. He pointed out, early in the *Rhetoric*, that premises that form rhetorical syllogisms are seldom true for all times and places. "People deliberate and examine what they are doing, and human actions are . . . none of them, so to speak, necessary." Deliberators must be satisfied with searching out useful analogies and weighing possible courses of action. Arguments in rhetorical settings, therefore, are "sometimes necessarily true but mostly true only for the most part."[25]

Melancholy is not a part of rhetoric, and rhetoric is not a part of melancholy, but both melancholy and rhetoric are praised and blamed proportionately to the writer's orientation toward mobility, change, and exchange. Both are promiscu-ous practices, in the early modern meaning of the word: shared, common, unsys-tematic, offered without distinction. (Recall the nineteenth-century American horror at women speaking to "promiscuous audiences.") Physicians inveighed against the changeable nature of melancholy; humanist neo-Platonists praised it as a tool of transformation; the *Gorgias* presented rhetoric as a knack rather than an ordered body of knowledge; Aristotle's *Rhetoric* offered guidelines for adapting rhetorical maxims to constantly changing situations. Burton reveled in just these indeterminacies: "Democritus to the Reader" is an exuberant *divisio* showing that melancholy is everywhere, and similar explorations of instability mark every subsection of the book.

In all of these practices, Burton's opinion about the specific propositions advanced in various disciplines is less important than his deployment of their resources to establish a fluid field of knowledge. Observation, reported experi-ence, and canonic texts are laminated in the *Anatomy*: no authority is discounted or accepted without question. Burton described his own practice best. Immedi-ately after his famous comparison of the style of the *Anatomy* to the various course of a river, Burton compared the reader to a traveler who encounters a variety of terrain: "sometimes faire, sometimes foule; here champion, there inclosed; barren in one place, better soyle in another: by Woods, Groves, Hills, Dales, Plaines, &c. I shall lead thee *per ardua montium & lubrica vallium, & roscida cespitum & glebosa camporum*, through variety of objects, that which thou shalt like and surely dislike" (1:18). (The Latin quotation, from Apuleius, can be translated "over steep mountains, through hazardous valleys, dewy lawns, and ploughed fields.") Burton conceded that he was prone to error, to mangling and approximating quotations, and to meddling with disciplines such as medi-cine that were not his own. But these are admissions, not apologies: Burton would do anything—transgress disciplinary boundaries, mingle sacred with profane authors, annoy his readers—to keep his text moving. Only a mobile text could do justice to early modern practices of knowledge as they addressed the fluid condition of melancholy.

If we follow Burton into these woods, groves, and plains, taking the rough and the smooth as they come, he can offer us examples of knowledge practices that are not radically divorced from each other and suggest that it is possible to establish relations among distinct knowledge claims without establishing false equivalences among them. Taken up consistently, these practices could form a transdisciplinary rhetoric. Beyond its utility in sponsoring new research methods, our look at the seamy side of the *Anatomy* suggests that such transdisciplinary practices could cultivate exchanges among various decentered subject positions.

Burton's mobile practice was oriented toward embodied subjects, each vulnerable to specific modulations of melancholy as it was associated with a body part, a way of life, or a nation. Race, gender, and class studies have given us more subtle tools than those available to Burton for understanding how the experience of embodiment is socially, culturally, and historically inflected; those understandings can extend a practice that values the exchange of understandings across social as well as disciplinary differences. If a practice of deliberative democracy is to be constructed for the twenty-first century, it will be in the work of such exchanges.

Notes

Chapter 1

1. Burton, *Anatomy of Melancholy* (1961–64).
2. Burton, *Anatomy of Melancholy* (2001).
3. Fish, *Self-Consuming Artifacts*, chapter 6, 303–32.
4. Hans Schäufelin, *Melancholiker*, 1511, oil on limewood, Kunsthistorisches Museum Vienna. Schäufelin painted a suite of four images portraying the humors; according to the Metropolitan Museum of Art, these were the first visual representations of the four humors produced after antiquity. See the notes on *The Choleric Temperament*, 1511, oil on limewood, Metropolitan Museum of Art, New York, http://www.metmuseum.org/art/collection/search/693948.
5. Burton, *The Anatomy of Melancholy* (1989–2000). All subsequent quotations from the *Anatomy* will be from this six-volume edition, given parenthetically by volume and page. I have followed this edition in reproducing Burton's italics and spelling. Unless otherwise noted, translations of Burton's Latin are taken from this edition.
6. Robert Burton, note on the flyleaf of James Shirley, *The Wedding* (London: J. Beale, 1633); Burton's copy is in the Bodleian, 4° T 38 (11) Art.
7. Maclean, *Logic, Signs and Nature*, 118–21, 174–77.
8. Mobility and exchange are most frequently investigated in the contemporary scholarship by researchers in rhetorics of place. See, for example, Dingo, *Networking Arguments*; Olson, "'Raíces Americanas'"; Olson, *Constitutive Visions*. See also Stuckey, "Forum on Rhetorical Circulation," especially the introduction by Stuckey, "On Rhetorical Circulation."
9. Gowland, *Worlds of Renaissance Melancholy*; Lund, *Melancholy, Medicine and Religion*; Shirilan, *Robert Burton*.
10. Colie, *Paradoxia Epidemica*, 453.
11. Ibid., 453.
12. Jones, "Hannah Arendt's Female Friends."
13. Fish, *Self-Consuming Artifacts*, 323.
14. Ibid.
15. Ibid., 330.
16. Breitenberg, *Anxious Masculinity*, 35–68.
17. Aristotle, *Problemata physica*; Ficino, *Three Books on Life*, 117.
18. Breitenberg, *Anxious Masculinity*, 35.
19. Shirilan, *Robert Burton*, 98–99, 163–67.
20. Williams, "Disfiguring the Body of Knowledge."
21. Burton, *Description of Leicester Shire*.
22. Bamborough, introduction, 1:xiv.
23. Traister, "New Evidence About Burton's Melancholy?," 67.
24. Traister, *Notorious Astrological Physician of London*, 67. However, J. B. Bamborough and J. C. Eade observe that "the evidence is not really strong enough to support this speculation," in "Robert Burton's Astrological Notebook," 280.

25. I am grateful to Angus Gowland for information on academic ranks at Christ Church.

26. For a good short biography, see Bamborough, "Robert Burton." Bamborough offers a fuller account in his introduction to the Clarendon edition of *Anatomy of Melancholy* (1989–2000).

27. McConica, "Elizabethan Oxford," 696–99.

28. Kiessling, *Library of Robert Burton*, 373–76.

29. Kiessling, *Legacy of Democritus Junior*, 66–69.

30. Vicari, *View from Minerva's Tower*, 10.

31. Kiessling, *Library of Robert Burton*, 371.

32. Flannery, *Emperor's New Clothes*.

33. Kusukawa, *Transformation of Natural Philosophy*, 24–28.

34. Newton, *Mathematical Principles of Natural Philosophy*, 387–93.

35. Joy, "Scientific Explanation," 70–105.

36. Melanchton, *Initia doctrinae physica* (original publication 1543), 13: column 179; translated and quoted by Daniel M. Gross in "Melanchthon's Rhetoric," 7.

37. Maclean, *Logic, Signs and Nature*, 234–76.

38. Struever, "Petrarch's *Invective contra medicum*"; see also Struever, "Rhetoric and Medicine."

39. Newman, "From Alchemy to 'Chymistry,'" 496.

40. Kiessling, *Legacy of Democritus Junior*, 28.

41. Rutkin, "Astrology."

42. Kiessling, *Legacy of Democritus Junior*, 29–31.

43. Wood, *Athenae Oxonienses*, 1:626.

44. Kiessling, *Legacy of Democritus Junior*, 38.

45. Kiessling, *Library of Robert Burton*, viii–ix. Rouse wrote "Comoediarum, Tragediarum, et Schediasmatum et Ludicrorum praesertim ideomate vernaculo, aliquot centurias, quas propter multitudinem non adjecimus" in the *Benefactors' Register*, Bodelian Library, Library Records, 358 and 360.

46. Kiessling, *Library of Robert Burton*, 335. The items mentioned are numbers 222, 452, and 1349.

47. Kiessling, *Legacy of Democritus Junior*, 99.

48. Daston, "Ideal and Reality"; Goldgar, *Impolite Learning*; Yoran, *Between Utopia and Dystopia*; Mayhew, "British Geography's Republic of Letters."

Chapter 2

1. For early modern genre theory, see Colie, *Resources of Kind*.

2. Fuller, *History of the Worthies of England*, 2:134: "Scarce any book of *Philology* in our Land has in so short a time passed so many Impressions"; Gowland, *Worlds of Renaissance Melancholy*, 296. For readings of the *Anatomy* as a book of counsel or encyclopedia of psychology, see Fowler, *Kinds of Literature*, 40–44.

3. Frye, *Anatomy of Criticism*, 311; Vicari, *View from Minerva's Tower*, 144; Trevor, *Poetics of Melancholy*, 146; Colie, *Resources of Kind*, 79; Gowland, "Rhetorical Structure and Function"; Gowland, *Worlds of Renaissance Melancholy*, 116–18; Gowland, "'As Hunters Find Their Game'"; Lund, *Melancholy, Medicine and Religion*, 5–6.

4. Fowler, *Kinds of Literature*, 40–44.

5. Moretti, "Graphs, Maps, Trees 3," 9.

6. Pethes, "Telling Cases."

7. Aristotle, *On Rhetoric* 1.3.1 (trans. Kennedy, 47); W. Rhys Roberts translates *eidos* as "division" in his *Rhetoric and Poetics of Aristotle*, 1358b. Eugene Garver uses "kind" in "Aristotle on the Kinds of Rhetoric."

8. Aristotle, *Poetics*; Genette, *Architext*, 60–72; Jameson, *Political Unconscious*; Cohen, "Travelling Genres."

9. Farrell, "Classical Genre in Theory and Practice."

10. *Rhetorica ad Herennium* 1.2 (ed. Marx, 188). Translation from *Rhetorica ad Herennium* 1 (trans. Caplan, 5).

11. Cicero, *De partitione oratoria* 20.68–69 (trans. Rackham, 360–63). Quintilian, *Institutio oratoria* 4 (ed. Butler, 3–4).

12. But for an account of the divergence between Roman critical theory and Roman poetic practice, see Farrell, "Classical Genre in Theory and Practice."

13. Shepherd and Watters, "Evolution of Cybergenres," 2.

14. Moretti, "Graphs, Maps, Trees," 39.

15. Fowler, "Formation of Genres," 185.

16. My discussion of temporal and spatial genre frames is indebted to the workshop on emerging genres led by Carolyn Miller and Victoria Gallagher at the Rhetoric Society of America Summer Institute, June 2011.

17. Jacobus, "Law of/and Gender."

18. Sidney, *Defence of Poetry*, 99–110, 87–88.

19. Derrida, "Law of Genre."

20. Menander Rhetor, "Division of Epideictic Speeches," and "On Epideictic Orations," in *Rhetores graeci* (ed. Aldus). These treatises were later published in Latin in *De genere demonstrativo libri duo* (trans. Conti). In this essay, I have used "Division of Epideictic Speeches" and "The Imperial Oration," the treatise that is sometimes titled "On the Epideictic," in *Menander Rhetor* (ed. Russell, 1–75 and 76–225 respectively). I am grateful to Laurent Pernot for his seminar on the epideictic in 2012, sponsored by the International Society for the History of Rhetoric, at the convention of the Rhetoric Society of America in Philadelphia.

21. Menander, "Division of Epideictic Speeches," in *Menander Rhetor*, ed. Russell, 3.

22. Colclough, "Verse Libels and the Epideictic Tradition."

23. Scaligero [Scaliger], *Poetices*, 1:5.

24. Scaliger, *Poetices*, poetry as persuasion, 1:1; figures, 1:5.

25. Wilson, *Arte of Rhetorique*, 11.

26. Puttenham, *Arte of English Poesie*; Plett, *Rhetoric and Renaissance Culture*.

27. Melanchthon, *De rhetorica libri tres*, xxx; see also Melanchthon, *Philip Melanchthon* (ed. Kusakawa).

28. Melanchthon, *Elementorum rhetorices libri duo*, 421; Fahnestock, "Stylistic Core of Rhetoric and Dialectic." I am grateful to Prof. Fahnestock for her generous help with all issues related to Melanchthon in this book.

29. Fowler, *Kinds of Literature*; Colie, *Resources of Kind*.

30. Flannery, *Emperor's New Clothes*.

31. Spies, "Scaliger in Holland," 22.

32. Scaliger, *Poetices*, 3:25.

33. This tradition is not dead. For example, Joseph Farrell's statement that "most [Roman] poetic genres can be regarded to some extent as derivatives of Homer," in "Roman Homer," 254.

34. Meek and Sullivan, introduction to *Renaissance of Emotion*, 15.

35. Clement, "Art of Feeling."

36. Pender, "Rhetoric, Grief, and the Imagination."
37. Wawrzyniak, "Pity as a Political Emotion," 51.
38. Sidney, *Defence of Poetry*, 91; Olmsted, *Imperfect Friend*, 54–75.
39. Olmsted, *Imperfect Friend*, 71.
40. Sidney, *Defence of Poetry*, 95.
41. Vickers, *In Defence of Rhetoric*.
42. Aristotle, *On Rhetoric* 1.9.40.
43. Menander Rhetor, "Epideictic Speeches," 135–47.
44. Mack, *History of Renaissance Rhetoric*.
45. Erasmus, *De copia* (ed. Thompson).
46. Ibid., 647.
47. Puttenham, *Arte of English Poesie*, 2:148; Roe, "Rhetoric, Style, and Poetic Form."
48. Cave, *Cornucopian Text*, 182–87.
49. Rebhorn, *Emperor of Men's Minds*, 23–29.
50. Murphy, "Welcome to Our Readers," 2.
51. Guillén, *Literature as System*, 122.
52. Siraisi, "Oratory and Rhetoric," 202.
53. Ibid., 200.
54. Ibid., 192.
55. Gowland, "Rhetorical Structure and Function."
56. For a full discussion of amplification and *copia* in Burton, see Schmelzer, *'Tis All One*. This absorbing study, based on a 1988 dissertation, speaks of the moment when deconstruction began to negotiate a historical turn. Schmelzer therefore rejects any closed, determinate reading of the *Anatomy*, arguing that it should be understood in the context of the early modern affinity for *copia*.
57. Erasmus, *De copia* (ed. Thompson), 572.
58. Sawday, *Body Emblazoned*, 2–3.
59. Fish, *Self-Consuming Artifacts*, 303–32; Fox, *Tangled Chain*.
60. Cave, *Cornucopian Text*, xi.
61. Conley, "Vituperation in Seventeenth Century Historical Studies."
62. Bazerman, *Shaping Written Knowledge*.
63. Smith, *Common-wealth of England*.
64. Ainsworth, *Communion of saincts*.
65. Du Terme, *Flovver de luce*.
66. Furdell, *Publishing and Medicine*, 50; Siraisi, *Medieval and Early Renaissance Medicine*, 49.
67. For lectures as commentaries, see Siraisi, *Medieval and Early Renaissance Medicine*, chapter 3. For an example of Burton's use of natural history, see Bacci's *De natura vinorum historia de vinis italiae*. Even though the natural history of wines is not a topic usually associated with melancholy, Burton quotes Bacci twice. For the significance of the natural history tradition, see Pomata and Siraisi, *Historia*.
68. Kiessling, *Library of Robert Burton*; Bamborough, introduction, 1:xxii.
69. Eisenstein, *Printing Revolution*, 70–74, 94–99.
70. Gross, Harmon, and Reidy, *Communicating Science*.
71. Daston and Galison, *Objectivity*.
72. Siraisi, "Oratory and Rhetoric."
73. For readings based on the rearrangement of classic texts, see McGill, *Virgil Recomposed*, and Okáčová, "Centones." For readings based on compilations of quotations, see Tucker, "Justus Lipsius and the Cento Form."

74. McGill, *Virgil Recomposed*; Okáčová, "Centones."
75. Williams, "Medievalism in English Renaissance Literature."
76. Lipsius, *Politica*, ed. Waszink, 56.
77. For Ashbery's cento, see "Dong with the Luminous Nose." For the cento as a school verse form, see Stohr-Hunt, "Monday Poetry Stretch." For the cento as appropriative form, see Rubinstein, "Gathered, Not Made."
78. Ausonius, *Works*, 1:371.
79. Tucker, "Justus Lipsius and the Cento Form," 179.
80. Milowicki and Wilson, "Measure of Menippean Discourse."
81. Blanchard, *Scholars' Bedlam*; Sherbert, *Menippean Satire*; Bakhtin, *Rabelais and His World*.
82. Milowicki and Wilson, "Measure of Menippean Discourse."
83. Frye, *Anatomy of Criticism*, 311.
84. Miller, "Genre as Social Action," 159; Bawarshi and Reiff, *Genre*, 4.
85. Hume, "Some Capacities and Fallacies."
86. Derrida, "Law of Genre," 224.
87. Ibid.

Chapter 3

1. Kiessling, *Library of Robert Burton*, vii.
2. Prosperus Calanius, *Paraphrasis in librum Galeni de inaequali intemperie* (London: S. Gryphium, 1538), Christ Church library. The inscription is on the frontispiece. The quotation is identified by Kiessling in *Library of Robert Burton* as from Ovid, *Amores* 2.4.5 (p. 55). Kiessling's transcription of Burton's note differs from mine; he separated "*antidotum vitae*" so that the Ovidian tag begins "*sapientia odit*."
3. Ovid, *Amores* 2.4.5 (ed. Henderson, 390–91).
4. The Vulgate has, "*non enim quod volo hoc ago sed quod odi illud facio*."
5. Kiessling, *Library of Robert Burton*, 80.
6. For differentiation of knowledge practices, see Habermas, "Social Action, Purposive Activity, and Communication," 171.
7. Gowland, *Worlds of Renaissance Melancholy*, 34.
8. Lund, *Melancholy, Medicine and Religion*, 93.
9. For studies of the relations between medical knowledge and rhetoric, see Pender and Struever, *Rhetoric and Medicine*.
10. Maclean, *Logic, Signs and Nature*, 236–51.
11. Siraisi, *History, Medicine, and the Traditions*, 4–8.
12. Eisenstein, *Printing Revolution*, 539–41.
13. Maclean, *Logic, Signs and Nature*, 49.
14. Siraisi, "Fielding H. Garrison Lecture," 15, 22.
15. Kiessling, *Library of Robert Burton*, 163.
16. Kiessling, *Legacy of Democritus Junior*, 26–30.
17. Bennett, "Early Modern Mathematical Instruments."
18. Vidal, *Sciences of the Soul*, 33.
19. Pomata, "Sharing Cases."
20. Pomata, "Medical Case Narrative"; Pomata and Siraisi, *Historia*; Siraisi, *Medieval and Early Renaissance Medicine*; Siraisi, "Anatomizing the Past."
21. Pomata, "Medical Case Narrative," 9.

22. O'Malley, *First Jesuits*, 136–51.

23. Kiessling, *Library of Robert Burton*, 376.

24. Cook, "Markets and Cultures."

25. Pomata and Siraisi, *Historia*, 221.

26. Daston, "On Scientific Observation."

27. Lund, *Melancholy, Medicine and Religion*, 77–111.

28. For an analogous process, see Latour and Woolgar, *Laboratory Life*, 69–72.

29. Wear, *Knowledge and Practice*; Dear, *Discipline and Experience*, 13.

30. Pender, "Examples and Experience."

31. Daston, "On Scientific Observation," is a convenient introduction to this body of research. For observation in the new sciences in the late seventeenth century, see also Shapin and Schaffer, *Leviathan and the Air-Pump*, and Shapin, *Social History of Truth*.

32. Aristotle, *Metaphysics* 6.2 (trans. Ross, 1027a).

33. Dear, "Narratives, Anecdotes, and Experiments," 139.

34. Shapin and Schaffer, *Leviathan and the Air-Pump*, 22–80.

35. There are exceptions, such as Burton's accounts of Mercurialis scolding a patient (1:245) and of Platter's version of the hardy perennial story of the swallowed frog (1:412).

36. Guainerius, *Practica et omnia opera*, 23.

37. Du Laurens, *Discourse*, facsimile; for Burton's use of this text, see Bamborough, introduction, 1:xxi.

38. Du Laurens, *Discourse*, 103.

39. Gunnoe and Shackelford, "Johannes Crato von Krafftheim"; Crato, *Consiliorum et Epistularum Medicinalium*.

40. "If your lordship will follow this regimen, you will be restored to pristine health. If the disease continues, the body is completely undermined and loses all its native heat," Crato, *Consiliorum et Epistularum Medicinalium*, 125.

41. Quintilian, *Institutio oratoria* 5.11.15 (trans. Butler, 3:245).

42. Quintilian, *Institutio oratoria* 8.3.61 (trans. Butler, 2:116).

43. Hippocrates, *On Regimen*; Hippocrates, *On Regimen in Acute Illness*. On editions and translations of Hippocrates, see Monfort, "First Printed Editions." For the importance of the Hippocratic corpus in medical education, see French, "Berengario da Carpi," 65. For more specialized sources, see Mattern, *Galen and the Rhetoric of Healing*; Ficino, *Three Books on Life*; Crato, *Consiliorum et Epistularum Medicinalium*; Pomata, "Uses of Historia," 135; Elyot, *Castel of Health*.

44. Richards, "Useful Books."

45. Ibid., 252.

46. Siraisi, *Communities of Learned Experience*, chapter 1.

47. Crato, *Consiliorum et Epistularum Medicinalium*, 5:120.

48. Ibid., 5:257.

49. Richards, "Useful Books."

50. Lund, *Melancholy, Medicine and Religion*, 24–50.

51. Burton was paradoxically following advanced neo-Galenic opinion on regimen. Andrew Wear has shown that the works of Luigi Cornaro (1463–1566) and his follower Leonhard Lessius (1554–1623) were reactions against contradictory regimens. Both Cornaro and Lessius, who are quoted sparsely in the *Anatomy*, held that each individual knew his own temperament through experience, and was the best judge of the food, drink, and exercise that agreed with it—although Lessius advised that everyone would do well on twelve ounces of solid food and fourteen of wine. See Wear, *Knowledge and Practice*, 175.

52. Maclean, *Logic, Signs and Nature*, 148–66.

53. "Quantum ut non contenti siti res alequis semel aut bis lecticassi et percepisse, sed eas animis saepius obversetis atque dum occasio datur, cum amicis atque praeceptoribus conferatis, examinetis, atque disputetis," in Durling, "Girolamo Mercuriale's *De modo studendi*," 194–95. The lecture was probably given in 1570.

54. Jones, "Medical Literacies and Medical Culture," 37–38.

55. Ibid.

56. Shapin and Schaffer, *Leviathan and the Air-Pump*, 336.

57. Siraisi, *Medieval and Early Renaissance Medicine*, 65–70.

58. Hippocrates, *On Regimen* 4.1.2.

59. Hippocrates, *Aphorisms* 2.24 (trans. Jones, 115).

60. Bos and Langerman, *Alexandrian Summaries of Galen's "On Critical Days"*. This volume collects and translates Hunayn ibn Ishāq and Shimeon ben Sholmo's summaries of Galen's treatise.

61. Bos and Langerman, *Alexandrian Summaries*, 100.

62. Hippocrates, *Aphorisms* 1.1.99.

63. Genette, *Narrative Discourse*.

64. Donovan, Hartley Herman, and Imbrie, *Sir Thomas Browne and Robert Burton*.

65. Hirai, *Medical Humanism and Natural Philosophy*, 57–60.

66. Siraisi, *Medieval and Early Renaissance Medicine*, 107–9; Bono, *Word of God*.

67. For general discussions of spirit in Early Modern medicine and philosophy, see Park, "Psychology"; Wear, *Knowledge and Practice*; and especially Bono, *Word of God*, chapter 2. For more specialized studies of the implications of spirit to the understanding of melancholy, see Caciola and Sluhovsky, "Spiritual Physiologies"; Pender, "Rhetoric, Grief, and the Imagination"; Suzuki, "Melancholy and the Material Unity of Man."

68. Bono, *Word of God*, chapter 2.

69. Bono, "Reform and the Languages," includes an account of various theories of spirit.

70. Paster, *Humoring the Body*, 1–25.

71. Schmidt, "Melancholy and the Therapeutic Language."

72. Melanchthon, "*De anima*," column 89. My translation.

73. See the discussion of spirits, sensation, and melancholy in Shirilan, *Robert Burton*, chapter 3.

74. Hankins, "Ficino, Avicenna, and the Occult Powers."

75. Ficino, *Three Books on Life*, 247.

76. Elyot, *Castel of Health*, fol. 1.

77. Harvey, "Anatomical Disquisition," 32. See Bono, *Word of God*, 103–22.

78. There are similar pairings of philosophy and medicine throughout the *Anatomy*. See the discussion of diseases of the head, which places melancholy both among "diseases of the brain" and among "diseases of the mind" (1:131), or the discussion of why not every melancholy mood would lead to the disease of melancholy: patients could escape the disease "as their temperature of Body, or Rationall soule is better able to make resistance" (1:138).

79. Du Laurens, *Discourse*, 72, 80.

Chapter 4

1. Mack, *Elizabethan Rhetoric*, 51–52. See also Baldwin, *William Shakespeare's "Small Latine and Lesse Greeke"*; Clark, *John Milton at St. Paul's School*; McConica, *History of the University of*

Oxford, vol. 3; Tyacke, *Seventeenth-Century Oxford*; Rainolds, *John Rainold's Oxford Lectures*; Ruys, Ward, and Hayworth, *Classics in the Medieval and Renaissance Classroom*.

2. Kiessling, *Library of Robert Burton*, 376.

3. Bede, *De schematibus et tropis*; Nascimbaenius, *In M. Tullii Ciceronis*; Erasmus, *De duplici copia rerum ac verborum*; Castilio, *De curiali sive aulico libri quatuoi*.

4. Agricola, *De inventione dialectica*; Horatius Flaccus, Quintus, and Marcus Tullius Cicero, *In epistolam A. Horatii Flacci*.

5. Bucoldianus, *De inventione, et amplificatione oratoria*.

6. Agricola, *De inventione dialectica* 3.423. In this chapter, I use a modern facsimile of the Cologne 1539 edition, *De inventione dialectica lucubratione* (1967), occasionally consulting Phrissemius's edition, *Rodolphi Agricolae Phrisii De inuentione dialectica* (1528). I have also consulted Burton's copy of *De inventione* (1542).

7. Vergile, *Abridgement*, title page.

8. Ibid., fol. xx.

9. Rainolds, *Oratio duodecim*.

10. Rainolds lectured on Aristotle's *Rhetoric* in the 1570s, some twenty years before Burton came to Oxford, but those lectures only survived in manuscript. The manuscript was bound with Rainold's working copies of Aristotle's *Rhetoric* and *Politics*, and so it is difficult to see how Burton might have had access to them. Late in the 1570s, Rainolds also wrote an extensive commentary on Aristotle's *Rhetoric*, bound with a Greek text of that book and held in the Bodleian, as discussed in Schmitt, *John Case and Aristotelianism*, 71. For the provenance of the lectures on Aristotle, see Green, introduction, 9–22.

11. Ramus, *Scholae in tres primas liberals artes*. Burton also owned two other books by Ramus, *Scholarum metaphysicarum* and *Scholarum physicarum*.

12. Paynell, *Frutefull Book of the Comon Places*.

13. Coote, *English schoole-master*.

14. Scaliger, *Oratio*; Agrippa, *Orationes X*.

15. Albertanus Causidicus Brixiensis, *Libellus de modo loquendi & tacendi*.

16. Aristotle, *On Rhetoric* 1.1.14 (trans. Kennedy, 35).

17. The 1665 Christ Church Library catalogue shows that the library owned a copy of the *Adages*, but it is impossible to tell whether Burton would have had access to this book during his time at the college. The Bodleian's earliest printed catalog (1605) records the 1540 and 1574 editions of Erasmus's *Opera omnia*, which would have included the *Adages* (personal communication, David Stumpp, Antiquarian Cataloguer, Christ Church Library, Oxford, September 27, 2017). The 1605 catalogue for St. John's college also lists a copy of the *Adages* (personal communication, Stuart Tiley, College Librarian, St. John's College, September 28, 2017). See also the Bodleian Library's *Oxford College Libraries in 1556*, 51–52, item 98, which shows that copies of the *Adages* were held at All Souls and Balliol; Magdalen may have also owned the *Adages* as part of Erasmus's collected works. On students' ownership of works by Erasmus, see Feingold, "Humanities," 260; see also McConica, *History of the University of Oxford*, 450 on the purchase of Erasmus's *Opera* by the Magdalen College library, and Mack, *Elizabethan Rhetoric*, 31 on the centrality of *De copia* to the grammar school curriculum.

18. Spranzi, *Art of Dialectic*, 76.

19. Ibid., 78.

20. Leff, "Commonplaces and Argumentation in Cicero and Quintilian."

21. Agricola, *De inventione dialectica* (1528), 1:1.

22. Agricola, *De inventione dialectica* (1539), 1:26–34.

23. "Neque enim melius rem noscere videtur, quam qui quid ea sit, brevitur et apte possit explicare," Agricola, *De inventione dialectica* (1539), 1:29.

24. "Utilissimum esse cogitam sibi naturam eius et diligenter perlustratam habere," Agricola, *De inventione dialectica* (1539), 1:27.

25. "Utilem autem esse hanc locorum rationem apparet, cum magnae parti humanorum studiorum (quandoquidem plaeraque in ambiguo haerent, et dissentientium certaminibus sunt exposita.... Certè plaeraque pro cuiusque ingenio, ut accōmodatissimè ad probandum quisque excogitare potuerit, aliò atque aliò trahuntur," Agricola, *De inventione dialectica* (1539), 1:2.

26. Mack, *Renaissance Argument*, 156.

27. Walker, *Of Education*, 110.

28. For Aristotle's definition of the soul, see Bolton, "Aristotle's Definitions of the Soul." Bolton summarizes Aristotle's definition: the soul is the substance of a natural body that has life potentially, and is the first actuality of such a body.

29. Shirilan, "Exhilarating the Spirits."

30. Agricola, *De inventione dialectica* (1539), 1:25; Mack, *History of Renaissance Rhetoric*, 62–65.

31. "Inest tamen omnibus (tametsi suis quaeque discreta sint notis) communis quaedam habitudo, et cuncta ad naturae tendunt similtudinem, ut quod est omnibus substantia quaedam sua, omnia ex aliquibus oriuntur causis, omnia aliquid efficiunt. Ingeniosissimi itaque virorum, ex effusa illa rerum varietate, communia ista capita, velut substantiam, causam, eventum.... Velut cum ad considerandam rem quampiam animum advertissemus, sequentes ista statim per omnem rei naturam et partes, perque omnia consentanea et dissidentia iremus, et duceremus inde argumentum propositis rebus accommodatum," Agricola, *De inventione dialectica* (1539), 1:2,9; translation and transcription in Mack, *Renaissance Argument*, 140.

32. "Minus hanc dialectices iacturam indigne ferendam, in tanta omnium studiorum colluuie: cum cuncta, uelut ferae caueis effractis, in proximorum ius & fines irruerint, nec quicque serme discatur hoc tempore suo loco," Agricola, *De inventione dialectica* (1539), 2:1,179.

33. Agricola, *De inventione dialectica* (1539), 3:5, 400; Mack, *Renaissance Argument*, 216.

34. Park and Daston, *Early Modern Science*, especially part 2, Personae and Sites of Natural Knowledge.

35. For late seventeenth-century scientific writing, see Preston, *Thomas Browne*.

36. Blair, *Too Much to Know*; for Burton's dismay at the flood of books, see *Anatomy of Melancholy*, 1:110.

37. Agricola, *De formando studio*, in *Lucbrationes*, 193–202, 197.

38. For a contrary view, see Breitenberg, *Anxious Masculinity*, 35–69.

39. Daston and Lunbeck, *Histories of Scientific Observation*; Pomata and Siraisi, *Historia*; Siraisi, *History, Medicine, and the Traditions*; Findlen, *Possessing Nature*.

40. Pomata, "Observation Rising," 50–51.

41. Barbara J. Shapiro has observed, "Natural history based on careful observation and experiment in the Baconian and Harvean modes ... became the dominant, albeit not the exclusive form of English scientific inquiry in the generations following Bacon's death," in *Culture of Fact*, 111.

42. Siraisi, *History, Medicine and the Traditions*, 23.

43. Pomata, "Observation Rising," 60–61.

44. Giuliano Mori finds that the copious lists of authorities in the *Anatomy* "spring from a compositional necessity that is utterly in keeping with the attempt to create a general unity

in which differences and contradictions among particular instances may dissolve," in "Democritus Junior as a Reader of Auctoritates," 396.

45. Daston, "Empire of Observation," 94.

46. Siraisi, *History, Medicine, and the Traditions*, 188.

47. Desiderius Erasmus, *Adages*, 31:102–3 (ed. Hoffmann). See Lisa Jardine's amusing and exhaustive treatment of the Agricola-Erasmus lineage, "Inventing Rudolph Agricola."

48. Melanchthon, *"Vita Agricolae."* Quoted by Jardine, "Inventing Rudolph Agricola," columns 79–80.

49. Colie, "Some Notes on Burton's Erasmus"; Kiessling, *Library of Robert Burton*, item 537.

50. Blair, *Too Much to Know.*

51. Erasmus, *Adages.* Subsequent references to the *Adages* will be given parenthetically by volume and page number.

52. Bodleian Library, *Oxford College Libraries in 1556*, item 98.

53. Mynors, "Annotator's Foreword."

54. Quintilian, *Institutio oratoria* 5.11.14; 5.11.41; 8.3.76.

55. Cummings, "Encyclopedic Erasmus"; Murphy, "Robert Burton."

56. Montagu, *Diatribe*, 1–2; quoted in Cummings, "Encyclopedic Erasmus," 203.

57. Quintilian, *Institutio oratoria* 8.31.24.

58. For a subtle account of the relationship between narrative and theory in seventeenth-century political theory, see Struever, *Theory as Practice*, 215, 222–24. "Useful knowledge is neither of events nor of results in propositional form, neither of events in their specificity nor of succeeding statements of results in their independence. Since all particulars are grasped attached to modalities, all results are inseparable from experience," ibid., 223.

59. I have used Kathy Eden's exemplary *Friends Hold All Things in Common* to guide my reading of the eagle and the dung beetle.

60. Pomata and Siraisi, *Historia.*

61. Drysdall, "Erasmus on Tyranny and Terrorism," 91–92.

62. Martin, "Intractable Dialectic of Tyranny and Terror."

63. For *De copia* and the importance of argument *ad utramque partem*, see Sloane, "Schoolbooks and Rhetoric."

64. Erasmus, *De copia*, 290–633, 300 (ed. Hoffmann).

65. Ibid., 632.

66. Erasmus, *"De conscribendis epistolis / On the Writing of Letters,"* 19 (ed. Hoffmann).

67. Erasmus, "Letter to Nicholas Kass, 1527," 13:157, letter 1833.

68. For a reading that places this proverb in the early modern controversy between rhetoric and philosophy, see Mack, "Rhetoric, Ethics, and Reading." For a penetrating analysis of the analogous use of the octopus in sophistic rhetoric, see Hawhee, *Bodily Arts*, chapter 2, "Sophistic Metis."

69. Erasmus, *De copia*, 642–46 (ed. Hoffmann).

70. Ibid., 644.

71. Ibid., 647.

72. Walker, *Rhetoric and Poetics in Antiquity*, 9–10.

73. Blair, *Too Much to Know*, 141.

74. Erasmus, *De copia*, 647 (ed. Hoffmann).

75. Ibid., 369–72.

76. Ibid., 554.

77. Boswell, *Boswell's Life of Johnson*, 2:50. Johnson tells Boswell that the *Anatomy* was "the only book that ever took him out of bed two hours earlier than he wished to rise."

78. Shirilan, *Robert Burton*, epilogue.
79. Gowland, "'As Hunters Find Their Game,'" 11–12.
80. Leushuis, "Mimesis of Marriage."
81. Latour, "Socrates and Callicles' Settlement."

Chapter 5

1. For code-meshed texts, see Canagarajah, *Translingual Practice*, 112.
2. For language brokers, see Buriel, "Language Brokers."
3. Pratt, "Aesthetics, Politics, and Sociolinguistic Analysis," 21.
4. Blommaert, *Sociolinguistics of Globalization*, 102. Blommaert's book is a very useful introduction to translingual theory.
5. Ibid., 25.
6. For current literary research on translingualism, see Kellman, *Translingual Imagination*. For a summary of pedagogical research in writing studies, see Lu and Horner, "Translingual Work in Composition." For examples of historical work, see Canagarajah, *Translingual Practice*, 35–55.
7. For critiques of translingualism as a pedagogical approach, see Williams and Condon, "Translingualism in Composition Studies"; Atkinson et al., "Clarifying the Relationship"; and especially Matsuda, "Lure of Translingual Writing."
8. Frame, introduction, viii.
9. De Montaigne, "Of the Education of Children," 128.
10. Frame, *Montaigne*.
11. Yates, *Astrea*, vol. 5.
12. Davies, *Welsh Language*, 43.
13. Helgerson, *Forms of Nationhood*, 1–18 and 25–40. See also Helgerson, "Language Lessons."
14. Mullaney, *Place of the Stage*, 82.
15. We know of Burton's ownership of John Gerard's *The Herball or General History of Plants* only from his will, and so it is unclear whether he owned the 1597, 1633, or 1636 edition. Kiessling, *Library of Robert Burton*, 125.
16. Leonhardt, *Latin*, 197.
17. Waquet, *Latin or the Empire of a Sign*.
18. Burke, "Translations into Latin," 65.
19. Castiglione (Castillio), *De curiali*. Clerke writes that he will forestall any judgment that "*Anglorum Aula Urbanitum vil in re interior fuerit*," and insure that "*tua serenitas omnibus Aemiliis et Gonsagis multis gradibus antecellat*" (4). "*Aemiliis*" was a reference to Lorenzo de Medici. For the connection between Aemillius Paulus and Lorenzo di Medici, see Trexler, *Public Life in Renaissance Florence*, 451.
20. Chaucer, *Amorum Troili et Creseidae*, sig. A3. "... si in rerum humanarum vicissitudine (quam quotidie nos cernimus) quicquam in codem statu sine variation fixum et immotum permaneret."
21. Money, "New Year Books."
22. Oxford University, *Panegyrica. In auspicatissimam pientissimi*, sig. 3.
23. Oxford University, *Justa Oxoniensium*, sig. A2.
24. Hamilton, "Egyptian Traveler."
25. Oxford University, *Academiae Oxoniensis funebris sacra*, sigs. B3v–B4r; Oxford University, *Academiae Oxoniensis pietas*, 155–56; Oxford University, *Carolus redux*, sig. B2v.

26. *New-Found Politike* translates Trajano Boccalini's *Ragguaglio di Paradiso* (1612–15). Frances Yates makes this attribution in *John Florio*, 308. For Florio as a disseminator of languages, see Pfister, "Inglese Italianato—Italiano Anglizzato."

27. See, for example, Calepino, *Dictionarium octo linguarum*.

28. Cummings, *Literary Culture of the Reformation*.

29. MacCulloch, *Reformation*, 89.

30. Erasmus, "Paraclesis," 101.

31. Jewel, *Apology or Answer*, 53–54.

32. Harding, *Confutation of the book*, 271.

33. Mazzio, *Inarticulate Renaissance*, 23.

34. "Demands of the Western Rebels."

35. "Decree Concerning the Canonical Scriptures, 4th Session (1546)," in Council of Trent, *Canons and Decrees*.

36. "Canon Nine (1563), Session 23," in ibid.

37. *First and Second Prayer-Books of Edward VI*, 1.

38. Cummings, *Literary Culture of the Reformation*.

39. Jeremy Allen, "Sermons preached by severall men vppon seuerall occasions in St. Maryes & other Places in Oxford," 1633, Bodleian Library shelfmark MS. Eng. th. f. 7; mention of Burton is at folio 123r; I have silently expanded Allen's abbreviations. See also Cranfield, "Must the Fire Either Go Out?"

40. For indexical language uses, see Blommaert, *Sociolinguistics of Globalization*, chapter 1.

41. Leonhardt, *Latin*.

42. Moss, *Renaissance Truth*.

43. Waquet, *Latin or the Empire of a Sign*, 161.

44. McConica, *History of the University of Oxford*, 34–35.

45. Oxford University, *Oxford University Statutes*, 63.

46. Bill, *Education at Christ Church Oxford*, 250.

47. Moss, *Renaissance Truth*.

48. Wear, *Knowledge and Practice*, 67–68.

49. Melanchthon, *Erotemata Dialectices*, 88. Thanks to Jeanne D. Fahnestock, who translated this passage and brought it to my attention in an exchange of emails, July 2016.

50. Blair, "Persistence du latin."

51. Binns, *Intellectual Culture*, 1–2.

52. Waquet, *Latin or the Empire of a Sign*, 82–83.

53. Jensen, "Printing at Oxford," 39.

54. McConica, *History of the University of Oxford*, 467, 477.

55. Leonhardt, *Latin*, 163–69.

56. Deneire, *Dynamics of Neo-Latin*, 2–3.

57. Anglin, "'The Glass, the School, the Book.'"

58. Hamilton, "Gregory, John."

59. Shirilan, *Robert Burton*, 27.

60. Kiessling, *Library of Robert Burton*, xxxi.

61. Holyband, *French Littleton*.

62. Cebes, *Familiarium colloquiroum formulae Gracae et Latine*.

63. Estienne, *De latinitate falso suspecta*.

64. Gyllius, *Lexicon Graeco-latinum*.

65. Burton, "Ad Eundem." Thanks to Daniel Tompkins for translation help.

66. Martial, *On the Spectacles* 3 (in *Epigrams*, ed. Kerr, 1:9).

67. Boas, *University Drama*, 16–19; Binns, *Intellectual Culture*, 122. My discussion on Latin university drama is heavily indebted to Binns.

68. Binns, *Intellectual Culture*, 124.

69. Young, "William Gager's Defence," 614.

70. Wright, "Gwinne, Matthew."

71. Elliott et al., *Records of Early English Drama*, 650.

72. Ibid., 645–46.

73. Nelson, "Emulating Royalty," 67–76.

74. Fletcher, "Faculty of Arts," 197.

75. Burton, *Philosophaster*. Subsequent references given in parentheses.

76. For a comparison of the contents of Latin and vernacular medical works, see Lund, *Melancholy, Medicine and Religion*, 77–92.

77. Primrose, *Popular Errours of the People*, 19; quoted in Whaley, *Women and the Practice of Medical Care*, 57.

78. Waquet, *Latin or the Empire of a Sign*, 244–45.

79. Crawford, "Sexual Knowledge in England," 87.

80. Moulton, *Before Pornography*, chapter 2.

81. Morales and Hanson, "Language Brokering."

82. Geertz, "Javanese *Kijaji*"; Hlavac, "Participation Roles of a Language Broker."

83. Goncalves and Schluter, "'Please Do Not Leave Any Notes.'"

84. For examples, see Reyes and Bonnin, "Negotiating Use, Norm and Authority"; Krieger and Gallois, "Translating Science."

85. Buriel, "Language Brokers."

86. Ovid, *Metamorphoses* 2.748–50 (trans. Raeburn). The Latin reads: "adspicit hunc oculis isdem, quibus abdita nuper / viderat Aglauros flavae secreta Minervae" (Ovid, *Metamorphoses*, ed. Magnus).

87. Bolden, "Across Languages and Cultures."

88. Fuller, "Rev. Robert Burton," in *History of the Worthies of England*, 2:134.

89. Wood, *Athenae Oxonienses*, 1:626–28.

90. Fuller, *History of the Worthies of England*, 1:26.

91. Martianus Capella, a fifth-century writer, presented an allegory of the union between literature and science in his *De nuptiis Philologae et Mercurii*. Lady Philology was attended by seven bridesmaids representing the liberal arts. See Stahl, Johnson, and Burge, *Martianus Capella and the Seven Liberal Arts*.

92. I arrived at this rough estimate by sampling three ten-page sections of the *Anatomy*, and counting the lines that included Latin words. The sections were Partition 1, 49–59 (Democritus to the Reader); Partition 2, 114–24 (Music a Remedy; Mirth and Merry Company a Remedy) and Partition 3, 266–76 (Cure of Love Melancholy, Jealousy). For all samples, I counted all numbered lines of text, including blanks, but not the glosses. I counted a line as containing Latin if it included a word of Latin, excluding citations or proper names. Within each sample, the amount of Latin varied from page to page: in the whole sample of thirty pages, there were eleven pages that had more than ten lines in Latin, or about a third of the text. There were only two pages without any Latin. But the overall percentage of Latin in Burton's text was consistent across the partitions: 20 percent in Partition 1, 17 percent in Partition 2, and 22 percent in Partition 3, for an overall range of 20 percent.

93. Canagarajah, *Translingual Practice*, 35–55.

94. Ibid., 43.

95. Baca, "Rethinking Composition"; Gunesekera, *Postcolonial Identity of Sri Lankan English*.

96. Burke, *Languages and Communities*, 131–35.

97. Anzaldúa, *Borderlands / La Frontera*; an excerpt from Minae Mizumura's *Shishosetsu from Left to Right* appeared in *The White Review* in January 2015.

98. Mizumura, *Fall of Language*, 64–65.

99. Taylor, *Of the Sacred Order*, 11.

100. de Montaigne, *Essays of Montaigne*, 3:30. For the ever-changing nature of French, see 3:229; for the use of unattributed quotations, see the essay "Of Books," vol. 2, essay 10.

101. Donato, "Boethius' *Consolation of Philosophy*"; Ochs, *Consolatory Rhetoric*, 104–18.

102. Gowland, "Consolations for Melancholy."

103. Blommaert, *Sociolinguistics of Globalization*, 102. The quotations reference Blommaert's belief that, since languages display enormous variation and are constantly changing, the sense of any one language as a stable entity is always a construction.

Chapter 6

1. Browne, *Religio Medici and Urne-Buriall*; Browne, *Pseudodoxia Epidemica*; Barbour, *Sir Thomas Browne*; Preston, *Thomas Browne*; Murphy and Todd, *"Man Very Well Studyed"*; Killeen, *Biblical Scholarship, Science and Politics*.

2. Browne, *Pseudodoxia Epidemica*, 144.

3. Ibid.

4. Ibid., 145.

5. Ibid., 264–71.

6. Ibid., 270.

7. Burke, *Permanence and Change*, chapter 1.

8. Ibid., 40.

9. Ibid., 36.

10. Habermas, *Theory of Communicative Action*, 1:159–68.

11. Ibid., 397. For applications and developments of Habermas's theory of differentiation, see Carter, "Dialectic of War and Utopia"; Hohendahl, "*Dialectic of Enlightenment* Revisited"; Poster, "Postmodernity and the Politics of Multiculturalism"; Potolsky, "Whither Secrecy?" For a critique of the concept, see Durant, "Public Participation."

12. Habermas, *Theory of Communicative Action*, 1:287.

13. Burke, *Permanence and Change*, 80–96.

14. Lund, *Melancholy, Medicine and Religion*; Shirilan, *Robert Burton*; Sullivan, *Beyond Melancholy*.

15. Burke, *Permanence and Change*, 76.

16. Walker, *Rhetoric and Poetics in Antiquity*, x.

17. Hippocrates, *Airs, Waters, Places*.

18. Gowland, *Worlds of Renaissance Melancholy*. For a more explicit account of Gowland's rejection of materialist understandings of melancholy, see his "Melancholy, Passions, and Identity."

19. Radden, *Melancholic Habits*.

20. Burton, *Anatomy of Melancholy*, 1:249, quoted in Radden, *Melancholic Habits*, 51. Radden has silently translated Burton's *laesa Imaginatio* to "disordered imagination." Generally, in quoting Burton, Radden modernizes spelling, translates foreign languages, and elides the names of his authorities.

21. Burton, *Anatomy of Melancholy*, 1:393, quoted in Radden, *Melancholic Habits*, 166.
22. Daniel, *Melancholy Assemblage.*
23. Ibid., 163.
24. Plato, *Gorgias* 455 (trans. Lewis, 287–89).
25. Aristotle, *On Rhetoric* 1.2.14 (trans. Kennedy, 42–43).

Bibliography

Agricola, Rudolph. *De inventione dialectica*. Cologne: Iohann Gymnich, 1539.
———. *De inventione dialectica, Lucubrationes* [facsimile of Cologne: Gymnich, 1539]. Monu-
menta Humanistica Belgica. Nieuwkoop: B. de Graaf, 1967.
———. *De inventione dialectica omnes*. Cologne: J. Kempensis, 1542.
———. *Lucubrationes* [...] Cologne: apud Ioannem Gymnicum, 1539.
Agrippa, Henricus Cornelius. *Orationes X* [...]. Cologne: J. Soter, 1535.
Albertanus Causidicus Brixiensis. *Libellus de modo loquendi & tacendi*. Antwerp: Gher. Leeu,
1487.
Allen, Jeremy. "Sermons preached by severall men vppon seuerall occasions in St. Maryes &
other Places in Oxford." Manuscript notebook, 1633. Bodleian Library.
Anglin, Emily. "'The Glass, the School, the Book': *The Anatomy of Melancholy* and the Early
Stuart University of Oxford." *English Studies in Canada* 35, no. 22 (June–September
2009): 55–76.
Anzaldúa, Gloria. *Borderlands / La Frontera: The New Mestiza*. San Francisco: Aunt Lute
Books, 2012.
Aristotle. *Metaphysics*. Translated by W. D. Ross. Oxford: Clarendon Press, 1908. Available
online at the Internet Classics Archive, http://classics.mit.edu/Aristotle/metaphysics
.html.
———. *On Rhetoric: A Theory of Civic Discourse*. Translated by George A. Kennedy. New
York: Oxford University Press, 1991.
———. *Poetics*. Translated by George Whalley. Montreal: McGill-Queen's University Press,
1997.
———. *Problemata physica*. Edited by Helmut Flashar. Berlin: Akademie Verlag, 1962.
Ashbery, John. "The Dong with the Luminous Nose." In *Wakefulness*, 75–76. New York: Far-
rar, Straus and Giroux, 1998.
Atkinson, Dwight, Deborah Crusan, Paul Kei Matsuda, Christina Ortmeier-Hooper, Todd
Ruecker, Steve Simpson, and Christine Tardy. "Clarifying the Relationship Between
L2 Writing and Translingual Writing: An Open Letter to Writing Studies Editors
and Organization Leaders." *College English* 77, no. 4 (2015): 383–86.
Ausonius, Decimus Magnus. *Works*, vol. 1. Translated by Hugh Evelyn White. Loeb Classical
Library. London: Heinemann, 1919.
Baca, Damián. "Rethinking Composition, Five Hundred Years Later." *Journal of Advanced
Composition* 29, nos. 1–2 (2009): 229–42.
Bacci, Andrea. *De natura vinorum historia de vinis italiae*. Rome: Niccolo Musi, 1601.
Bakhtin, Mikhail. *Rabelais and His World*. Translated by Hélène Iswolsky. Cambridge: MIT
Press, 1968.
Baldwin, T. W. *William Shakespeare's "Small Latine and Lesse Greeke."* Urbana: University of
Illinois Press, 1944.
Bamborough, J. M. Introduction to *The Anatomy of Melancholy*, by Robert Burton, 1:xiii–
xxxvi. Oxford: Oxford University Press, 1989.

————. "Robert Burton (1577–1640): Writer." In *Oxford Dictionary of National Biography*, 2009. Available online at http://www.oxforddnb.com/abstract/10.1093/ref:odnb/978 0198614128.001.0001/odnb-9780198614128-e-4137.

Bamborough, J. B., and J. C. Eade. "Robert Burton's Astrological Notebook." *Review of English Studies*, n.s., 32, no. 127 (1981): 267–85.

Barbour, Reid. *Sir Thomas Browne: A Life*. Oxford: Oxford University Press, 2013.

Bawarshi, Anis S., and Mary Jo Reiff. *Genre: An Introduction to History, Theory, Research, and Pedagogy*. West Lafayette, IN: Parlor, 2010. The WAC Clearinghouse. Available online at https://wac.colostate.edu/books/referenceguides/bawarshi-reiff.

Bazerman, Charles. *Shaping Written Knowledge: The Genre and Activity of the Experimental Article in Science*. Madison: University of Wisconsin Press, 1988.

Bede. *De schematibus et tropis*. Basel: A. Petrum, 1527.

Benefactor's Register. Library records. Bodleian Library, Oxford University.

Bennett, Jim. "Early Modern Mathematical Instruments." *Isis* 102, no. 4 (2011): 697–705.

Bill, Edward G. *Education at Christ Church Oxford, 1660–1800*. Oxford: Clarendon, 1988.

Binns, J. W. *Intellectual Culture in Elizabethan and Jacobean England: The Latin Writings of the Age*. Leeds: Francis Cairns, 1990.

Blair, Ann. "La persistence du latin comme langue de science à la fin de la Renaissance." In *Sciences et langues en Europe*, edited by Pietro Corsi and Roger Chartier, 21–43. Paris: Ecole des Hautes Études des Sciences Sociales, 1996.

————. *Too Much to Know: Managing Scholarly Information Before the Modern Age*. New Haven: Yale University Press, 2010.

Blanchard, W. Scott. *Scholars' Bedlam: Menippean Satire in the Renaissance*. Lewisburg: Bucknell University Press, 1995.

Blommaert, Jan. *The Sociolinguistics of Globalization*. Cambridge Approaches to Language. Cambridge: Cambridge University Press, 2010.

Boas, Fredrick. *University Drama in the Tudor Age*. Oxford: Clarendon, 1914.

Boccalini, Trajano. *The New-Found Politike* [. . .]. London: Eliot's Court, 1624.

Bodleian Library. *Oxford College Libraries in 1556: A Guide to an Exhibition Held in 1956*. Oxford: Bodleian, 1956.

Bolden, Galina. "Across Languages and Cultures: Brokering Problems of Understanding in Conversational Repair." *Language in Society* 41, no. 1 (2012): 97–121.

Bolton, Robert. "Aristotle's Definitions of the Soul: *De Anima* II, 1–3." *Phronesis* 23, no. 3 (1978): 258–78.

Bono, James J. "Reform and the Languages of Renaissance Theoretical Medicine: Harvey Versus Fernel." *Journal of the History of Biology* 23, no. 3 (1990): 341–87.

————. *The Word of God and the Languages of Man: Interpreting Nature in Early Modern Science and Medicine, Ficino to Descartes*. Madison: University of Wisconsin Press, 1998.

Bos, Gerrit, and V. Tzvi Langerman, ed. and trans. *The Alexandrian Summaries of Galen's "On Critical Days."* Boston: Brill, 2014.

Boswell, James. *Boswell's Life of Johnson*. Albany: James Lyon, 1889.

Breitenberg, Mark. *Anxious Masculinity in Early Modern England*. Cambridge Studies in Renaissance Literature and Culture. Cambridge: Cambridge University Press, 1996.

Browne, Thomas. *Pseudodoxia Epidemica*. Edited by Robin Robbins. Oxford: Clarendon, 1981.

————. *Religio Medici and Urne-Buriall*. Edited by Stephen Greenblatt and Ramie Targoff. New York: New York Review of Books, 2011.

Bucoldianus, Gerardus. *De inventione, et amplificatione oratoria* [. . .]. Strasburg: J. Albertus, 1534.

Buriel, Raymond. "Language Brokers." In *Multicultural America: A Multimedia Encyclopedia*, edited by Carlos E. Cortes. Thousand Oaks, CA: Sage, 2013. Available online at http://sk.sagepub.com/reference/multicultural-america.

Burke, Kenneth. *Permanence and Change: An Anatomy of Purpose.* 3rd ed. Berkeley: University of California Press, 1984.

Burke, Peter. *Languages and Communities in Early Modern Europe.* Cambridge: Cambridge University Press, 2004.

———. "Translations into Latin in Early Modern Europe." In *Cultural Translation in Early Modern Europe*, edited by Peter Burke and R. Po-chia Hsia, 65–80. Cambridge: Cambridge University Press, 2007.

Burton, Robert. "Ad Eundem." In Oxford University, *Iusta funebria Ptolomaei Oxoniensis Thomae Bodleii* [. . .], 43–44. Oxford: Joseph Barnes, 1613.

———. *The Anatomy of Melancholy.* Edited by Thomas C. Faulkner, Nicolas Kiessling, and Rhonda Blair. Commentary by J. B. Bamborough and Martin Dodsworth. 6 vols. Oxford: Clarendon, 1989–2000.

———. *The Anatomy of Melancholy.* Edited by Holbrook Johnson. London: Dent, 1961–64.

———. *The Anatomy of Melancholy.* Edited by Holbrook Johnson. New York: New York Review of Books, 2001.

———. *Philosophaster.* Edited and translated by Connie McQuillen. Binghamton, NY: Medieval and Renaissance Texts and Studies, 1993.

Burton, William. *The Description of Leicester Shire* [. . .]. London: John Welsh, 1622.

Caciola, Nancy, and Moshe Sluhovsky. "Spiritual Physiologies: The Discernment of Spirits in Medieval and Early Modern Europe." *Preternature* 1, no. 1 (2012): 1–48.

Calanius, Prosperus. *Paraphrasis in librum Galeni de inaequali intemperie.* London: S. Gryphium, 1538.

Calepino, Ambrosio. *Dictionarium octo linguarum: in quo primis et praecipuis dictionibus Latinis, Hebraeas, Graecas, Gallicas, Italicas, Germanicas, Hispanicas, nunc Anglicas dictiones propriis iisque, dissimillimis characteribus* [. . .]. Paris: Apud Nicolaum Niuellium, 1588.

Canagarajah, Suresh. *Translingual Practice: Global Englishes and Cosmopolitan Relations.* London: Routledge, 2013.

Carter, Stephen D. "The Dialectic of War and Utopia: Systemic Closure and Embattled Social Life in the Work of Fredric Jameson." *Criticism* 58, no. 2 (2016): 177–204.

Castiglione, Baldassare (Balthasar Castilio). *De curiali sive aulico libri quatuor* [. . .]. Translated by Bartholomew Clerke. London: Eliot's Court, 1593.

Cave, Terence. *The Cornucopian Text: Problems of Writing in the French Renaissance.* Oxford: Oxford University Press, 1979.

Cebes. *Familiarium colloquiorum formulae Gracae et Latine* [. . .]. Antwerp: In aed. J. Steelaii, 1547.

Chaucer, Geoffrey. *Amorum Troili et Creseidae.* Translated by Francis Kinaston. Oxford: J. Lichfield, 1635.

Cicero. *De oratore, Book II, De fato, Paradoxa Stoicorum, De partitione oratoria.* Translated by H. Rackham. Loeb Classical Library. Cambridge: Harvard University Press, 1942.

Clark, Donald L. *John Milton at St. Paul's School: A Study of Ancient Rhetoric in English Renaissance Education.* New York: Columbia University Press, 1948.

Clement, Jennifer. "The Art of Feeling in Seventeenth-Century English Sermons." *English Studies* 98, no. 7 (2017): 675–88.

Cohen, Margaret. "Travelling Genres." *New Literary History* 34, no. 3 (2003): 481–99.

Colclough, David. "Verse Libels and the Epideictic Tradition in Early Stuart England." *Huntington Library Quarterly* 69, no. 1 (2006): 15–30.

Colie, Rosalie L. *Paradoxia Epidemica: The Renaissance Tradition of Paradox.* Princeton: Princeton University Press, 1966.

———. *The Resources of Kind: Genre-Theory in the Renaissance.* Berkeley: University of California Press, 1973.

———. "Some Notes on Burton's Erasmus." *Renaissance Quarterly* 20, no. 3 (Autumn 1967): 335–41.

Conley, Thomas. "Vituperation in Seventeenth Century Historical Studies." *Rhetorica* 22, no. 2 (2004): 169–82.

Cook, Harold. "Markets and Cultures: Medical Specifics and the Reconfiguration of the Body in Early Modern Europe." *Transactions of the RHS* 21 (2011): 123–45.

Coote, Edward. *The English schoole-master: teaching all his schollers [. . .] reading, and true writing our English tongue.* London: G. Purslowe, 1627.

Council of Trent. *The Canons and Decrees of the Council of Trent.* Edited and translated by J. Waterworth. London: Dolman, 1848. Available online at https://history.hanover .edu/texts/trent/ct04.html.

Cranfield, Nicholas W. S. "Must the Fire Either Go Out, Or Become All Wildfire?" *Bodleian Library Record* 13 (April 1989): 122–32.

Crato, Joannes, of Krafftheim. *Consiliorum et Epistularum Medicinalium.* Vol. 5. Hanover: Wechel, 1611.

Crawford, Patricia. "Sexual Knowledge in England, 1500–1750." In *Sexual Knowledge, Sexual Science: The History of Attitudes to Sexuality,* edited by Roy Porter and Mikulás Teich, 82–107. Cambridge: Cambridge University Press, 1994.

Cummings, Brian. "Encyclopedic Erasmus." *Renaissance Studies* 28, no. 2 (2014): 183–204.

———. *Literary Culture of the Reformation: Grammar and Grace.* Oxford: Oxford University Press, 2003.

Daniel, Drew. *The Melancholy Assemblage: Affect and Epistemology in the English Renaissance.* New York: Fordham University Press, 2012.

Daston, Lorraine. "The Empire of Observation." In Daston and Lunbeck, *Histories of Scientific Observation,* 81–155.

———. "The Ideal and Reality of the Republic of Letters in the Enlightenment." *Science in Context* 4, no. 2 (1991): 367–86.

———. "On Scientific Observation." *Isis* 99, no. 1 (2008): 97–110.

Daston, Lorraine, and Peter Galison. *Objectivity.* Boston: Zone, 2007.

Daston, Lorraine, and Elizabeth Lunbeck, eds. *Histories of Scientific Observation.* Chicago: University of Chicago Press, 2011.

Davies, Janet. *The Welsh Language: A History.* Cardiff: University of Wales Press, 2014.

Dear, Peter. *Discipline and Experience: The Mathematical Way in the Scientific Revolution.* Chicago: University of Chicago Press, 1995.

———. "Narratives, Anecdotes, and Experiments: Turning Experience into Science in the Seventeenth Century." In *The Literary Structure of Scientific Argument: Historical Studies,* edited by Peter Dear, 135–63. Philadelphia: University of Pennsylvania Press, 1991.

"The Demands of the Western Rebels, 1549." In *Tudor Rebellions,* edited by Anthony Fletcher and Diarmaid MacCulloch, 151–53. 5th ed. Harlow: Pearson Longman, 2004.

Deneire, Tom B., ed. *Dynamics of Neo-Latin and the Vernacular: Language and Poetics, Translation, and Transfer.* London: Brill, 2014.

Derrida, Jacques. "The Law of Genre." *Glyph* 7 (1980): 202–13. In *Modern Genre Theory*, edited by David Duff, 219–31. London: Longmans, 2000.

Dingo, Rebecca. *Networking Arguments: Rhetoric, Transnational Feminism, and Public Policy Writing.* Pittsburgh: University of Pittsburgh Press, 2012.

Donato, Antonio. "Boethius' *Consolation of Philosophy* and the Greco-Roman Consolatory Tradition." *Traditio* 67 (2012): 1–42.

Donovan, Dennis G., Margaretha G. Hartley Herman, and Ann E. Imbrie. *Sir Thomas Browne and Robert Burton: A Reference Guide.* Boston: G. K. Hall, 1981.

Drysdall, Denis L. "Erasmus on Tyranny and Terrorism: *Scarabaeus aquilam quaerit* and the *Institutio principis christiani.*" *Erasmus of Rotterdam Society Yearbook* 29 (2009): 89–102.

Du Laurens, André. *A Discourse of the Preservation of the Sight: Of Melancholike Diseases; of Rheumes, and of Old Age.* Translated by Richard Surphlet. London: Oxford University Press for The Shakespeare Association, 1938.

Durant, Darrin. "Public Participation in the Making of Science Policy." *Perspectives in Science* 18, no. 2 (2010): 189–225.

Durling, Richard. "Girolamo Mercuriale's *De modo studendi.*" *Osiris*, 2nd ser. (1990): 181–95.

Du Terme, Laurence. *The flovver de luce planted in England* [. . .]. London: Nicholas Okes, 1619.

Eden, Kathy. *Friends Hold All Things in Common: Tradition, Intellectual Property, and the Adages of Erasmus.* New Haven: Yale University Press, 2001.

Eisenstein, Elizabeth. *The Printing Revolution in Early Modern Europe.* 2nd ed. Cambridge: Cambridge University Press, 2005.

Elliott, John R., and Alan Nelson, Alexandra Johnston, and Diana Wyatt. *Records of Early English Drama: Oxford.* London: British Library, 2004.

Elyot, Thomas, Sir. *The Castel of Health* [. . .]. London: Bertheleti, 1534. EEBO.

Erasmus, Desiderius. *Adages.* Edited and annotated by Margaret Mann Phillips, R. A. B. Mynors, Denis Drysdale, John Grant, and Betty Knott. Vols. 31–36 of *The Collected Works of Erasmus*, edited by Manfred Hoffmann. 6 vols. Toronto: University of Toronto Press, 1982–2006.

———. *De conscribendis epistolis / On the Writing of Letters.* Edited by J. Kelley Sowkunda, 3:1–255. In *The Collected Works of Erasmus: Literary and Educational Writings*, edited by Manfred Hoffmann. Toronto: University of Toronto Press, 1985.

———. *De copia.* Edited by Craig Thompson, 24:279–660. In *The Collected Works of Erasmus, Literary and Educational Writings*, edited by Manfred Hoffmann. Toronto: University of Toronto Press, 1978.

———. *De duplici copia rerum ac verborum.* Paris: Jod. Badius, 1512.

———. "Letter to Nicholas Kass, 1527." In *Correspondence of Erasmus, Letters 1802 to 1925, March–December 1527*. Edited by James K. Farge and Charles Fantazzi, 13:155–57. In *Collected Works of Erasmus*, edited by Manfred Hoffmann. Toronto: University of Toronto Press, 2011.

———. "Paraclesis." In *Christian Humanism and the Reformation: Selected Writings of Erasmus*, edited by Jon Olin, 97–131. New York: Fordham University Press, 1987.

Estienne, Henri [Henricus Stephanus]. *De latinitate falso suspecta* [. . .]. Geneva: H. Stephanus, 1576.

Fahnestock, Jeanne. "The Stylistic Core of Rhetoric and Dialectic." Paper presented at the International Society for the History of Rhetoric Conference, Los Angeles, CA, July 2005.

Farrell, Joseph. "Classical Genre in Theory and Practice." *New Literary History* 34, no. 3 (2003): 383–408.

———. "Roman Homer." In *The Cambridge Companion to Homer*, edited by Robert Fowler, 254–71. Cambridge: Cambridge University Press, 2004.

Feingold, Mordechai. "The Humanities." In *Seventeenth-Century Oxford*, edited by Nicholas Tyacke, 211–359. Vol. 4 of *The History of the University of Oxford*, edited by T. H. Ashton. Oxford: Clarendon, 1997.

Ficino, Marsilio. *Three Books on Life*. Edited and translated by Carol Kaske and John Clark. Binghamton: Center for Medieval and Early Renaissance Studies, State University of New York Press, 1989.

Findlen, Paula. *Possessing Nature: Museums, Collecting, and Scientific Culture in Early Modern Italy*. Studies in the History of Society and Culture. Berkeley: University of California Press, 1994.

The First and Second Prayer-Books of Edward VI. London: Dent, 1910.

Fish, Stanley. *Self-Consuming Artifacts: The Experience of Seventeenth-Century Literature*. Medieval and Renaissance Literary Studies. Berkeley: University of California Press, 1972.

Flannery, Kathryn. *The Emperor's New Clothes: Literature, Literacy, and the Ideology of Style*. Composition, Literacy, and Culture. Pittsburgh: University of Pittsburgh Press, 1995.

Fletcher, J. M. "The Faculty of Arts." In *The Collegiate University*, edited by James McConica, 157–200. Vol. 4 of *The History of the University of Oxford*, edited by T. H. Ashton. Oxford: Clarendon, 1986.

Fowler, Alastair. "The Formation of Genres in the Renaissance and After." *New Literary History* 34, no. 2 (2003): 185–200.

———. *Kinds of Literature: An Introduction to the Theory of Genres and Modes*. Cambridge: Harvard University Press, 1987.

Fox, Ruth. *The Tangled Chain: The Structure of Disorder in "The Anatomy of Melancholy."* Berkeley: University of California Press, 1976.

Frame, Donald. Introduction to *The Complete Essays of Montaigne*, i–xiv. Stanford: Stanford University Press, 1965.

———. *Montaigne: A Biography*. New York: Harcourt Brace, 1965.

French, R. K. "Berengario da Carpi and the Use of Commentary in Anatomical Teaching." In *The Medical Renaissance of the Sixteenth Century*, edited by Andrew Wear, R. K. French and I. M. Lonie, 42–74. Cambridge: Cambridge University Press, 1985.

Frye, Northrop. *Anatomy of Criticism: Four Essays*. New York: Athenaeum, 1957.

Fuller, Thomas. *The History of the Worthies of England* [. . .], 3 vols. London: Thomas Williams, 1662.

Furdell, Elizabeth. *Publishing and Medicine in Early Modern England*. Rochester: University of Rochester Press, 2002.

Garver, Eugene. "Aristotle on the Kinds of Rhetoric." *Rhetorica* 27, no. 1 (2009): 1–18.

Geertz, J. Clifford. "The Javanese *Kijaji*: The Changing Role of a Cultural Broker." *Comparative Studies in Society and History* 2, no. 2 (1960): 228–49.

Genette, Gérard. *The Architext: An Introduction*. Translated by Jane E. Lewin. Berkeley: University of California Press, 1992.

———. *Narrative Discourse: An Essay in Method*. Ithaca: Cornell University Press, 1983.

Goldgar, Anne. *Impolite Learning: Conduct and Community in the Republic of Letters, 1680–1750*. New Haven: Yale University Press, 1995.

Gonçalves, Kellie, and Anne Schluter. "'Please Do Not Leave Any Notes for the Cleaning Lady, as Many Do Not Speak English Fluently': Policy, Power, and Language Brokering in a Multilingual Workplace." *Language Policy* 16, no. 3 (2016): 241–65.

Gowland, Agnus. "'As Hunters Find Their Game by the Trace': Reading to Discover in *The Anatomy of Melancholy*." *Review of English Studies* 70, no. 292 (December 2018): 1–30.

———. "Consolations for Melancholy in Renaissance Humanism." *Society and Politics* 6, no. 1 (2012): 10–38.

———. "Melancholy, Passions, and Identity in the Renaissance." In *Passions and Subjectivity in Early Modern Culture*, edited by Brian Cummings and Freya Sierhuis, 59–70. Burlington: Routledge, 2013.

———. "Rhetorical Structure and Function in *The Anatomy of Melancholy*." *Rhetorica* 19, no. 1 (2001): 1–48.

———. *The Worlds of Renaissance Melancholy: Robert Burton in Context*. Ideas in Context. Cambridge: Cambridge University Press, 2006.

Green, Lawrence. Introduction to *John Rainolds' Oxford Lectures on Aristotle's Rhetoric*, 9–90. Edited and translated by Lawrence Green. Chicago: University of Chicago Press, 1986.

Gross, Alan, Joseph Harmon, and Michael Reidy. *Communicating Science: The Scientific Article from the 17th Century to the Present*. West Lafayette: Parlor, 2002.

Gross, Daniel M. "Melanchthon's Rhetoric and the Practical Origins of Reformation Human Science." *History of the Human Sciences* 13, no. 5 (2000): 5–22.

Guainerius, Antonius. *Practica et omnia opera*. Venice: Antonio de Giunta, 1517.

Guillén, Claudio. *Literature as System: Essays Toward the Theory of Literary History*. Princeton: Princeton University Press, 1971.

Gunesekera, Manique. *The Postcolonial Identity of Sri Lankan English*. Colombo, Sri Lanka: Katha Publishers, n.d.

Gunnoe, Charles D., Jr., and Joel Shackelford. "Johannes Crato von Krafftheim (1519–1585): Imperial Physician, Irenicist, and Anti-Paracelsan." In *Ideas and Cultural Margins in Early Modern Germany: Essays in Honor of H. C. Erik Midelfort*, edited by Marjorie Elizabeth Plummer and Robin Barnes, 201–17. London: Ashgate, 2009.

Gyllius, Petrus. *Lexicon Graeco-latinum* [. . .]. Basel: ex off. V. Curionis, 1532.

Habermas, Jürgen. "Social Action, Purposive Activity, and Communication." In *On the Pragmatics of Communication*, edited by Maeve Cooke, 105–82. Cambridge: MIT, 1998.

———. *The Theory of Communicative Action*. Vol. 1, *Reason and the Rationalization of Society*. Translated by Thomas McCarthy. Boston: Beacon, 1981.

Hamilton, Alastair. "An Egyptian Traveler in the Republic of Letters: Josephus Barbatus or Abudacnus the Copt." *Journal of the Warburg and Courtauld Institutes* 57 (1994): 123–50.

———. "Gregory, John (1607–1646)." *Oxford Dictionary of National Biography*. Oxford: Oxford University Press, 2004. Available online at http://www.oxforddnb.com/view/10.1093/ref:odnb/9780198614128.001.0001/odnb-9780198614128-e-11467.

Hankins, J. "Ficino, Avicenna, and the Occult Powers of the Rational Soul." In *Tra antica sapienza e filosofia naturale: La magia nell'Europa moderna*, edited by F. Meroi with E. Scapparone, 1:35–52. Atti del convegno Florence, October 2003, Istituto Nazionale di Studi sul Rinascimento. Florence: Leo S. Olschki, 2007.

Harding, Thomas. *A Confutation of the book, intituled An Apologie of the Church of England*. Antwerp: Jhon Laet, 1565.

Harvey, William. "An Anatomical Disquisition on the Motion of the Heart and Blood in Animals." In *The Circulation of the Blood*, 1–131. New York: Cosimo, 2006.

Hawhee, Debra. *Bodily Arts: Rhetoric and Athletics in Ancient Greece*. Austin: University of Texas, 2004.

Helgerson, Richard. *Forms of Nationhood: The Elizabethan Writing of England*. Chicago: University of Chicago Press, 1992.

———. "Language Lessons: Linguistic Colonialism, Linguistic Postcolonialism, and the Early Modern English Nation." *Yale Journal of Criticism* 11, no. 1 (1998): 289–99.

Hippocrates. *Airs, Waters, Places*. In *Hippocrates*, vol. 4. Translated by W. H. S. Jones. Loeb Classical Library. Cambridge: Harvard University Press, 1929.

———. *Aphorisms*. In *Hippocrates*, vol. 4. Translated by W. H. S. Jones. Loeb Classical Library. Cambridge: Harvard University Press, 1929.

———. *On Regimen*. In *Hippocrates*, vol. 4. Translated by W. H. S. Jones. Loeb Classical Library. Cambridge: Harvard University Press, 1929.

———. *On Regimen in Acute Illness*. In *Hippocrates*, Vol. 6. Translated by Francis Adams. Loeb Classical Library. Cambridge: Harvard University Press, 1923.

Hirai, Hiro. *Medical Humanism and Natural Philosophy: Renaissance Debates on Matter, Life, and the Soul*. Medieval and Early Modern Debates on Philosophy and Science. Leiden: Brill, 2011.

Hlavac, Jim. "Participation Roles of a Language Broker and the Discourse of Brokering: An Analysis of English-Macedonian Interactions." *Journal of Pragmatics* 70 (2014): 52–67.

Hohendahl, Peter Uwe. "*Dialectic of Enlightenment* Revisited: Habermas' Critique of the Frankfurt School." In *Reappraisals: Shifting Alignments in Postwar Critical Theory*, 99–130. Ithaca: Cornell University Press, 1991.

Holyband, Claudius. *The French Littleton: The Most Easy Perfect, and Absolute Way to Learne the French Language*. London: Richard Field, 1601.

Horatius Flaccus, Quintus, and Marcus Tullius Cicero. *In epistolam Q. Horatii Flacci de arte poetica* [. . .] *ejusdem brevis, et distincta summa praeceptorum de arte dicendi ex tribus Ciceronis libris de oratore collecta*. Venice: Aldi Filios, 1553.

Hume, Christine. "Some Capacities and Fallacies of Literary Hybridity: A Card Game." *American Poets* 39 (2010): 51–55.

Jacobus, Mary. "The Law of/and Gender: Genre Theory and 'The Prelude.'" [Review of Fowler, *Kinds of Literature*] *Diacritics* 14, no. 4 (Winter 1984): 47–57.

Jameson, Fredric. *The Political Unconscious: Narrative as a Socially Symbolic Act*. London: Routledge, 1981.

Jardine, Lisa. "Inventing Rudolph Agricola: Cultural Transmission, Renaissance Dialectic, and the Emerging Humanities," In *The Transmission of Culture in Early Modern Europe*, edited by Anthony Grafton and Ann Blair, 39–85. Philadelphia: University of Pennsylvania Press, 1990.

Jensen, Kristian. "Printing at Oxford in Its European Context, 1478–1584." In *The Beginnings to 1780*, edited by Ian Gadd, 1:31–51. *History of Oxford University Press*. Oxford: Oxford University Press, 2013.

Jewel, John. *Apology or Answer in Defence of the Church of England* [. . .]. London: Reginald Wolf, 1562.

Jones, Kathleen. "Hannah Arendt's Female Friends." *Los Angeles Review of Books* (November 12, 2013). Available online at https://lareviewofbooks.org/article/hannah-arendts-female-friends.

Jones, Peter Murray. "Medical Literacies and Medical Culture in Early Modern England." In *Medical Writing in Early Modern English*, edited by Irma Taavitainen and Palvi Phata, 30–43. Studies in English Language. Cambridge: Cambridge University Press, 2011.

Joy, Lynn S. "Scientific Explanation from Formal Causes to Laws of Nature." In Park and Daston, *Early Modern Science*, 70–105.

Kellman, Steven. *The Translingual Imagination*. Lincoln: University of Nebraska Press, 2014.

Kiessling, Nicolas. *The Legacy of Democritus Junior: An Exhibition to Commemorate the 350th Anniversary of the Death of Robert Burton*. Oxford: Bodleian Library, 1990. Exhibition catalog.

——. *The Library of Robert Burton*. Oxford: The Oxford Bibliographical Society, 1988.

Killeen, Kevin. *Biblical Scholarship, Science and Politics in Early Modern England: Thomas Browne and the Thorny Place of Knowledge*. Literary and Scientific Cultures of Early Modernity. Burlington: Ashgate, 2009.

Krieger, Janice, and Cindy Gallois. "Translating Science: Using the Science of Language to Explicate the Language of Science." *Journal of Language and Social Psychology* 36, no. 1 (2017): 3–13.

Kusukawa, Sachiko. *The Transformation of Natural Philosophy: The Case of Philip Melanchthon*. Cambridge: Cambridge University Press, 1995.

Latour, Bruno. "Socrates and Callicles' Settlement—or, The Invention of the Impossible Body Politic." *Configurations* 5, no. 2 (1997): 189–240.

Latour, Bruno, and Stephen Woolgar. *Laboratory Life: The Construction of Scientific Facts*. Beverly Hills: Sage, 1979.

Leff, Michael. "Commonplaces and Argumentation in Cicero and Quintilian." *Argumentation* 10, no. 4 (1996): 445–52.

Leonhardt, Jürgen. *Latin: Story of a World Language*. Translated by Kenneth Kronenberg. Cambridge: Harvard University Press, 2013.

Leushuis, Reinier. "The Mimesis of Marriage: Dialogue and Intimacy in Erasmus's Matrimonial Writings." *Renaissance Quarterly* 57, no. 4 (2004): 1278–307.

Lipsius, Justus. *Politica [Politicorum sive civilis doctrinae libri sex]*. Edited by Jan Waszink. Assen: Biblioteca Latinitatis Novae, 2004.

Lu, Min-Zhan, and Bruce Horner, eds. "Translingual Work in Composition." Special issue, *College English* 78, no. 3 (January 2016).

Lund, Mary Ann. *Melancholy, Medicine and Religion in Early Modern England: Reading "The Anatomy of Melancholy."* New York: Cambridge University Press, 2010.

MacCulloch, Diamaid, *The Reformation: A History*. New York: Viking, 2004.

Mack, Peter. *Elizabethan Rhetoric: Theory and Practice*. Cambridge: Cambridge University Press, 2002.

——. *A History of Renaissance Rhetoric, 1380–1620*. Oxford Warburg Studies. Oxford: Oxford University Press, 2011.

——. *Renaissance Argument: Valla and Agricola in the Traditions of Rhetoric and Dialectic*. Leiden: Brill, 1993.

——. "Rhetoric, Ethics, and Reading in the Renaissance." *Renaissance Studies* 19, no. 1 (2003): 1–21.

Maclean, Ian. *Logic, Signs and Nature in the Renaissance: The Case of Learned Medicine*. Cambridge: Cambridge University Press, 2002.

MacCulloch, Diarmaid. *The Reformation: A History*. New York: Viking, 2004.

Martial. *Epigrams*. Edited and translated by Walter Kerr. Loeb Classical Library. New York: Heinemann, 1919.

Martin, Terence J. "The Intractable Dialectic of Tyranny and Terror: A Reading of an Erasmian Adage." *Soundings* 98, no. 2 (2015): 163–91.

Matsuda, Paul Kei. "The Lure of Translingual Writing." *Publications of the Modern Language Association* 129, no. 3 (2014): 478–83.

Mattern, Susan. *Galen and the Rhetoric of Healing*. Baltimore: Johns Hopkins University Press, 2008.

Mayhew, Robert. "British Geography's Republic of Letters: Mapping an Imagined Community, 1600–1800." *Journal of the History of Ideas* 65, no. 2 (2004): 251–76.

Mazzio, Carla. *The Inarticulate Renaissance: Language Trouble in an Age of Eloquence*. Philadelphia: University of Pennsylvania Press, 2008.

McConica, James, ed. "Elizabethan Oxford: The Collegiate Society." In *The Collegiate University*, edited by James McConica, 645–732. Vol. 3 of *The History of the University of Oxford*. Oxford: Clarendon, 1986.

———. *The History of the University of Oxford*. Vol. 3 of *The Collegiate University*. Oxford: Clarendon, 1986.

McGill, Scott. *Virgil Recomposed: The Mythological and Secular Centos in Antiquity*. Oxford: Oxford University Press, 2005.

Meek, Richard, and Erin Sullivan. Introduction to *The Renaissance of Emotion: Understanding Affect in Shakespeare and His Contemporaries*, edited by Richard Meek and Erin Sullivan, 1–22. Manchester: University of Manchester Press, 2015.

Melanchthon, Phillipp. *Corpus reformatorium: Phillippi Melanthonis opera quae supersunt omnia*. 28 vols. Edited by C.G. Breschneider. Brunswick: Halle, 1834–60. Reprinted New York: Johnson Reprint Corporation, 1963.

———. "De anima." In *Corpus reformatorum Philippi Melanthonis opera quae supersunt omnia*, edited by C. G. Breschneider, 13: columns 5–178, Brunswick: Halle, 1846.

———. *De rhetorica libri tres*. Cologne: E. Cervicorni. 1525. Bibliothèque nationale de France. Available online at http://gallica.bnf.fr/ark:/12148/bpt6k1093811q.

———. *Elementorum rhetorices libri duo* [1529]. In *Corpus reformatorum Philippi Melanthonis opera quae supersunt omnia*, edited by C. G. Breschneider, 13, columns 412–506. Brunswick: Halle, 1846.

———. *Erotemata Dialectices*. Wittenburg: Crato, 1555.

———. *Initia doctrinae physica*. In *Corpus reformatorum Philippi Melanthonis opera quae supersunt omnia*, edited by C. G. Breschneider, 13: columns 178–412. Brunswick: Halle, 1846.

———. *Philip Melanchthon: Orations on Philosophy and Education*. Edited by Sashiko Kusakawa. Cambridge: Cambridge University Press, 1999.

———. "Vita Agricolae." In *Corpus reformatorum Philippi Melanthonis opera que suspersunt omnia*, edited by C. G. Breschneider, 11, columns 438–46. Brunswick: Halle, 1843.

Menander Rhetor. *De genere demonstrativo libri duo*. Translated into Latin by Natale Conti. Venice: Peter Bosellum, 1588.

———. *Menander Rhetor*. Edited by D. A. Russell. Oxford: Clarendon, 1981.

———. *Rhetores graeci*. Edited by Manutius Aldus. Venice: Aldine, 1508.

Miller, Carolyn. "Genre as Social Action." *Quarterly Journal of Speech* 70 (1984): 151–67.

Milowicki, Edward J., and R. Rawdon Wilson. "A Measure of Menippean Discourse: The Example of Shakespeare." *Poetics Today* 23, no. 2 (2002): 291–326.

Mizumura, Minae. *The Fall of Language in the Age of English*. Translated by Mari Yoshihara and Juliet Winters Carpenter. New York: Columbia University Press, 2015.

———. *Shishosetsu from Left to Right* [excerpt]. Translated by Juliet Winters Carpenter. *White Review* (January 2015). Available online at http://www.thewhitereview.org/fiction/an-i-novel-from-left-to-right.

Money, David. "The Learned Press: Classics and Related Works: New Year Books, University Verses, and Neo-Latin Works." In *Beginnings to 1780*, edited by Ian Gadd, 1:385–98. *The History of Oxford University Press*, edited by Ian Gadd, Simon Eliot, and William Roger. Oxford: Oxford University Press, 2013.

Monfort, Marie-Laure. "First Printed Editions of the Hippocratic Collection at the Bibliothèque Interuniversitaire de Médecine of Paris (BIU Santé)." *Bibliothèque Numerique Medic@*. Available online at http://www.bium.univ-paris5.fr/histmed/medica/hipp _va.htm.

Montagu, Richard. *Diatribe upon the First Part of the Late History of Tithes*. London, 1621.

Montaigne, Michel de. *The Essays of Montaigne, Done into English by John Florio*. 3 vols. New York: AMS, 1967.

———. "Of the Education of Children." In *The Complete Essays of Montaigne*. Translated by Donald Frame, 106–31. Stanford: Stanford University Press, 1965.

Morales, Alejandro, and William E. Hanson. "Language Brokering: An Integrative Review of the Literature." *Hispanic Journal of the Behavioral Sciences* 27, no. 4 (2005): 471–503.

Moretti, Franco. "Graphs, Maps, Trees 3." *New Left Review* 28 (July–August 2004): 1–28.

Mori, Giuliano. "Democritus Junior as a Reader of Auctoritates: Robert Burton's Method and *The Anatomy of Melancholy*." *Journal of the History of Ideas* 77, no. 3 (July 2016): 379–99.

Moss, Ann. *Renaissance Truth and the Latin Language Turn*. Oxford: Oxford University Press, 2003.

Moulton, Ian Frederick. *Before Pornography: Erotic Writing in Early Modern England*. New York: Oxford University Press, 2004.

Mullaney, Steven. *The Place of the Stage: License, Play, and Power in the English Renaissance*. Ann Arbor: University of Michigan Press, 1995.

Murphy, Kathryn. "Robert Burton and the Problems of Polymathy." *Renaissance Studies* 28, no. 2 (2014): 279–97.

Murphy, Kathryn, and Richard Todd, eds. *"A Man Very Well Studyed": New Contexts for Thomas Browne*. Leiden: Brill, 2008.

Murphy, Timothy. "Welcome to Our Readers." *Genre* 44, no. 1 (2011): 1–4.

Mynors, R. A. B. "Annotator's Foreword." In *Adages I i 1 to iv 100*. Vol. 31 of *Collected Works of Erasmus*, translated by Margaret Mann Phillips, xiii. Toronto: University of Toronto Press, 1982.

Nascimbaenius, Nascimbaenus. *In M. Tullii Ciceronis de inventione libros commentarius*. Venice: B. Zalterium, 1564.

Nelson, Alan. "Emulating Royalty: Cambridge, Oxford, and the Inns of Court." *Shakespeare Studies* 37 (2009): 67–76.

Newman, William R. "From Alchemy to 'Chymistry.'" In Park and Daston, *Early Modern Science*, 497–517.

Newton, Isaac. *The Mathematical Principles of Natural Philosophy*. Translated by Andrew Motte. London, 1729. ECCO.

Ochs, Donovan J. *Consolatory Rhetoric: Grief, Symbol, and Ritual in the Greco-Roman Era*. Studies in Rhetoric/Communication. Columbia: University of South Carolina Press, 1993.

Okáčová, Marie. "Centones: Recycled Art or the Embodiment of Absolute Intertextuality?" *Kakanien Revisited* (2009): 1–7. Available online at http://www.kakanien.ac.at/beitr/ graeca_latina/MOkacova1.pdf.

Olmsted, Wendy. *The Imperfect Friend: Emotion and Rhetoric in Sidney, Milton, and Their Contexts*. Toronto: University of Toronto Press, 2008.

Olson, Christa J. *Constitutive Visions: Indigeneity and Commonplaces of National Identity in Republican Ecuador*. University Park: Pennsylvania State University Press, 2013.

———. "'Raíces Americanas': Indigenist Art, América, and Arguments for Ecuadorian Nationalism." *Rhetoric Society Quarterly* 42, no. 3 (2012): 233–50.

O'Malley, John W. *The First Jesuits*. Cambridge: Harvard University Press, 1993.

Ovid. *Heroides and Amores*. Edited by James Henderson. Translated by Grant Showerman. Cambridge: Harvard University Press, [1914] 1977.

————. *Metamorphoses*. Edited by Hugo Magnus. Gotha, 1892. Available online at Perseus Project, http://www.perseus.tufts.edu/hopper/text?doc=Perseus:text:1999.02.0029.

————. *Metamorphoses*. Translated by David Raeburn. London: Penguin, 2004.

Oxford University. *Academiae Oxoniensis funebris sacra*. Oxford: Lichfield and Short, 1619.

————. *Academiae Oxoniensis pietas erga serenissimum et potentissimum Jacobum Angliae Scotiae Franciae et Hiberinae regem*. Oxford, Joseph Barney, 1603.

————. *Carolus redux*. Oxford: Lichfield and Short, 1623.

————. *Justa Oxoniensium*. London: [Eliot's Court], 1612.

————. *Oxford University Statutes*, vol. 1. Translated by G. R. M. Ward. London: William Pickering, 1845.

————. *Panegyrica. In auspicatissimam pientissimi ac potentiss. Regis Iacobi Inthronizationem: Carmen Seculare*. London: Stansby, 1613.

Park, Katharine. "Psychology: The Organic Soul." In *The Cambridge History of Renaissance Philosophy*, edited by C. B. Schmitt, Quentin Skinner, Eckhard Kessler, and Jill Craye, 464–84. Cambridge: Cambridge University Press, 1987.

Park, Katharine, and Lorraine Daston, eds. *Early Modern Science*. Vol. 3 of *Cambridge History of Science*, edited by David C. Lindberg and Ronald L. Numbers. Cambridge: Cambridge University Press, 2006.

Paster, Gail Kern. *Humoring the Body: Emotions and the Shakespearean Stage*. Chicago: University of Chicago Press, 2004.

Paynell, Thomas. *A Frutefull Book of the Comon Places of all S. Pauls Epistles [. . .]*. London: J. Tisdale, 1562.

Pender, Stephen. "Examples and Experience: On the Uncertainty of Medicine." *British Journal for the History of Science* 39, no. 1 (2006): 1–28.

————. "Rhetoric, Grief, and the Imagination in Early Modern England." *Philosophy and Rhetoric* 43, no. 1 (2010): 54–85.

Pender, Stephen, and Nancy S. Struever, eds. *Rhetoric and Medicine in Early Modern Europe*, Literary and Scientific Cultures of Early Modernity. Burlington: Ashgate, 2012.

Pethes, Nicolas. "Telling Cases: Writing Against Genre in Medicine and Literature." *Literature and Medicine* 32, no. 1 (2014): 24–45.

Pfister, Manfred "Inglese Italianato—Italiano Anglizzato: John Florio." In *Renaissance Go-Betweens: Cultural Exchange in Early Modern Europe*, edited by Andreas Höfele and Werner von Koppenfels, 32–54. Berlin: De Gruyter, 2005.

Phrissemius, Joannes Matthaeus, ed. *Rodolphi Agricolae Phrisii De inuentione dialectica*. Cologne: Alopecius, 1528. Available online at Bayerische StaatsBibliothek, http://bildsuche.digitale-sammlungen.de/index.html?c=viewer&lv=1&bandnummer=bsb00022892.

Plato. *Gorgias*. In *Lysis, Symposium, Gorgias*, translated by W. R. M. Lewis, 247–533. Loeb Classical Library. Cambridge: Harvard University Press, 1923.

Plett, Heinrich F. *Rhetoric and Renaissance Culture*. Berlin: De Gruyter, 2004.

Pomata, Gianna. "The Medical Case Narrative: Distant Reading of an Epistemic Genre." *Literature and Medicine* 32, no. 1 (2014): 1–23.

————. "Observation Rising: Birth of an Epistemic Genre, 1500–1650." In Daston and Lunbeck, *Histories of Scientific Observation*, 45–80.

————. "Sharing Cases: The *Observationes* in Early Modern Medicine." *Early Science and Medicine* 15, no. 3 (2010): 193–236.

————. "The Uses of Historia in Early Modern Medicine." In *Historia*, edited by Pomata and Siraisi, 105–46.

Pomata, Gianna, and Nancy Siraisi, eds. *Historia: Empiricism and Erudition in Early Modern Europe.* Transformations: Studies in the History of Science and Technology. Cambridge: MIT Press, 2005.

Poster, Mark. "Postmodernity and the Politics of Multiculturalism: The Lyotard-Habermas Debate over Social Theory." *MFS Modern Fiction Studies* 38, no. 3 (1992): 567–80.

Potolsky, Matthew. "Whither Secrecy? *American Literary History* 28, no. 4 (2016): 787–99.

Pratt, Mary Louise. "Aesthetics, Politics, and Sociolinguistic Analysis." *Language Sciences* 65 (2018): 18–25.

Preston, Claire. *Thomas Browne and the Writing of Early Modern Science.* Cambridge: Cambridge University Press, 2005.

Primrose, James. *Popular Errours of the People in the Matter of Physick.* London: Willson, 1651.

Puttenham, George. *The Arte of English Poesie.* 2 vols. London: Richard Field, 1589. Reprinted Aldershot, England: Scolar Press, 1968.

Quintilian. *Institutio oratoria.* Edited and translated by H. E. Butler. Loeb Classical Library. Cambridge: Harvard University Press, 1979.

Radden, Jennifer. *Melancholic Habits: Burton's "Anatomy" and the Mind Sciences.* New York: Oxford, 2017.

Rainolds, John. *John Rainold's Oxford Lectures on Aristotle's Rhetoric.* Edited and translated by Lawrence Green. Chicago: University of Chicago Press, 1986.

————. *Oratio duodecim; cum aliis quibusdam opusculis* [. . .]. London: Guil. Stanseibus pro H. Fetherstone, 1619.

Ramus, Peter. *Scholae in tres primas liberales artes* [. . .]. Frankfurt: A. Wecheli her., C. Marnium, and J. Aubrium, 1593–95.

————. *Scholarum metaphysicarum* [. . .]. Hanover: Typ. Wechelianis, ap. haer. J. Aubrii, 1610,

————. *Scholarum physicarum* [. . .]. Frankfurt: Typ. Wechelianis, ap. C. Marnium & J. Aubrii, 1610.

Rebhorn, Wayne A. *The Emperor of Men's Minds: Literature and the Renaissance Discourse of Rhetoric.* Ithaca: Cornell University Press, 1995.

Reyes, Antonio, and Juan Eduardo Bonnin. "Negotiating Use, Norm and Authority in Online Language Forums." *Current Issues in Language Planning* (August 2016): 1–25.

Rhetorica ad Herennium. Translated by Henry Caplan. Loeb Classical Library. Cambridge: Harvard University Press, 1954.

Rhetorica ad Herennium. Edited by Friedrich Marx. Leipzig: Tuebner, 1923. Online at Brepolis Latin Library of Latin Texts, 2010.

Richards, Jennifer. "Useful Books: Vernacular Regimens in Sixteenth-Century England." *Journal of the History of Ideas* 73, no. 2 (2012): 247–71.

Roberts, W. Rhys. *The Rhetoric and Poetics of Aristotle.* New York: Modern Library, 1954.

Roe, John. "Rhetoric, Style, and Poetic Form." In *The Cambridge Companion to Shakespeare's Poetry,* edited by Patrick Cheney, 33–53. Cambridge: Cambridge University Press, 2007.

Rubinstein, Raphael. "Gathered, Not Made: A Brief History of Appropriative Writing." U B U W E B papers (1999). Available online at http://www.ubu.com/papers/rubinstein .html.

Rutkin, H. Darrell. "Astrology." In Park and Daston, *Early Modern Science,* 541–61.

Ruys, Juanita Feros, John Ward, and Melanie Hayworth, eds. *The Classics in the Medieval and Renaissance Classroom: The Role of Ancient Texts in the Arts Curriculum as Revealed by Surviving Manuscripts and Early Printed Books.* Turnhout: Brepols, 2013.

Sawday, Jonathan. *The Body Emblazoned: Dissection and the Human Body in Renaissance Culture.* New York: Routledge, 1995.

Scaliger, Julius Caesar. *Oratio, pro M. Tullio Cicerone contra Ciceronianum Erasmi* [. . .]. Cologne: B. Gualtherium, 1600.

Scaligero, Giulio Cesare [Scaliger]. *Poetices libri septem* [. . .] *editio quinta* [1561]. Heidelberg. 1617.

Schäufelin, Hans. *The Choleric Temperament.* 1511. Oil on limewood. Metropolitan Museum of Art, New York. Available online at http://www.metmuseum.org/art/collection/search/693948.

———. *Melancholiker.* 1511. Oil on limewood. Kunsthistorisches Museum, Vienna.

Schmelzer, Mary. *'Tis All One: "The Anatomy of Melancholy" as Belated Copious Discourse.* New York: Peter Lang, 1999.

Schmidt, Jeremy. "Melancholy and the Therapeutic Language of Moral Philosophy in Seventeenth-Century Thought." *Journal of the History of Ideas* 65, no. 4 (2004): 583–601.

Schmitt, Charles B. *John Case and Aristotelianism in Renaissance England.* McGill-Queen's Studies in the History of Ideas. Toronto: McGill-Queen's Press, 1983.

Shapin, Steven. *A Social History of Truth: Civility and Science in Seventeenth-Century England.* Science and Its Conceptual Foundations. Chicago: University of Chicago Press, 1994.

Shapin, Steven, and Simon Schaffer. *Leviathan and the Air-Pump: Hobbes, Boyle, and the Experimental Life.* Princeton: Princeton University Press, 1985.

Shapiro, Barbara J. *A Culture of Fact: England, 1550–1720.* Ithaca: Cornell University Press, 2003.

Shepherd, Michael, and Carolyn Watters. "The Evolution of Cybergenres." *Proceedings of the Thirtieth-First Annual Hawaii International Conference on System Sciences,* Maui, Hawaii, 1998. Available online at http://web.cs.dal.ca/~shepherd/pubs/evolution.pdf.

Sherbert, Garry. *Menippean Satire and the Poetics of Wit: Ideologies of Self-Consciousness in Dunton, D'Urfey, and Sterne.* New York: Peter Lang, 1996.

Shirilan, Stephanie. "Exhilarating the Spirits: Burtonian Study as a Cure for Scholarly Melancholy." *Studies in Philology* 111, no. 3 (2014): 486–520.

———. *Robert Burton and the Transformative Powers of Melancholy.* Literary and Scientific Cultures of Early Modernity. Ashgate: Farnham, 2015.

Sidney, Philip. *A Defence of Poetry.* In *Miscellaneous Prose of Sir Philip Sidney,* edited by Katherine Duncan-Jones and Jan van Dosten, 99–110. Oxford: Clarendon, 1973.

Siraisi, Nancy G. "Anatomizing the Past: Physicians and History in Renaissance Culture." *Renaissance Quarterly* 53, no. 1 (2000): 1–30.

———. *Communities of Learned Experience: Epistolary Medicine in the Renaissance.* Baltimore: Johns Hopkins University Press, 2013.

———. "The Fielding H. Garrison Lecture: Medicine and the Renaissance World of Learning." *Bulletin of the History of Medicine* 78, no. 1 (Spring 2004): 1–36.

———. *History, Medicine, and the Traditions of Renaissance Learning.* Cultures of Knowledge in the Early Modern World. Ann Arbor: University of Michigan Press, 2010.

———. *Medieval and Early Renaissance Medicine: An Introduction to Knowledge and Practice.* Chicago: University of Chicago Press, 1990.

———. "Oratory and Rhetoric in Renaissance Medicine." *Journal of the History of Ideas* 65, no. 2 (2004): 191–211.

Sloane, Thomas O. "Schoolbooks and Rhetoric: Erasmus' *Copia*." *Rhetorica* 9, no. 2 (1991): 113–29.

Smith, Thomas. *The Common-wealth of England and Manner of Government Thereof* [. . .] *Also, a Table Added Thereto, of All The Principall Matters Contained in This Treatise.* London: James Roberts, 1601.

Spies, Marijke. "Scaliger in Holland." In *Rhetoric, Rhetoricians and Poets: Studies in Renaissance Poetry and Poetics*, edited by Henk Duits and Ton van Strein, 21–37. Amsterdam: Amsterdam University Press, 1999.

Spranzi, Marta. *The Art of Dialectic Between Dialogue and Rhetoric: The Aristotelian Tradition.* Amsterdam: John Benjamins, 2011.

Stahl, William, Richard Johnson, and Evan Laurie Burge. *Martianus Capella and the Seven Liberal Arts.* Records of Civilization: Sources and Studies. New York: Columbia University Press, 1971.

Stohr-Hunt, Patricia. "Monday Poetry Stretch: Cento." Miss Rumphius Effect (blog), August 13, 2007. Available online at http://missrumphiuseffect.blogspot.com.

Struever, Nancy S. "Petrarch's *Invective contra medicum*: An Early Confrontation of Rhetoric and Medicine." *Modern Language Notes* 108, no. 4 (1999): 659–79.

———. "Rhetoric and Medicine in Descartes' Passions de l'Âme: The Issue of Intervention." In *Renaissance-Rhetorik / Renaissance Rhetoric*, edited by Heinrich F. Plett, 196–212. Berlin: De Gruyter, 1993.

———. *Theory as Practice: Ethical Inquiry in the Renaissance.* Chicago: University of Chicago Press, 1992.

Stuckey, Mary, ed. "Forum on Rhetorical Circulation." *Rhetoric and Public Affairs* 15, no. 4 (2012): 609–94.

———. "On Rhetorical Circulation." *Rhetoric and Public Affairs* 15, no. 4 (2012): 609–12.

Sullivan, Erin. *Beyond Melancholy: Sadness and Selfhood in Renaissance England.* Oxford: Oxford University Press, 2016.

Suzuki, Akihito. "Melancholy and the Material Unity of Man, 17th–18th Centuries" [review essay]. *Bulletin of the History of Medicine* 82, no. 1 (Spring 2008): 192–94.

Taylor, Jeremy. *Of the Sacred Order and Offices of Episcopacy* [. . .]. Oxford: Printed by Leonard Lichfield, 1642.

Traister, Barbara. "New Evidence About Burton's Melancholy?" *Renaissance Quarterly* 29, no. 1 (1976): 66–70.

———. *The Notorious Astrological Physician of London: Works and Days of Simon Forman.* Chicago: University of Chicago Press, 2001.

Trevor, Douglas. *The Poetics of Melancholy in Early Modern England.* Cambridge Studies in Literature and Culture. Cambridge: Cambridge University Press, 2004.

Trexler, Richard. *Public Life in Renaissance Florence.* Ithaca: Cornell University Press, 1991.

Tucker, Hugo C. "Justus Lipsius and the Cento Form." In *(Un)Masking the Realities of Power: Justus Lipsius and the Dynamics of Political Writing in Early Modern Europe*, edited by Eric De Bom, Markjike Janssens, Toon Van Houdt, and Jan Papy, 163–94. Leiden: Brill, 2011.

Tyacke, N., ed. *Seventeenth-Century Oxford.* Vol. 4 of *The History of the University of Oxford*, edited by T. H. Ashton. Oxford: Oxford University Press, 1997.

Vergile, Polydore. *An Abridgement* [. . .] *conteygnyng the devisers and first finders out aswell of artes* [. . .]. London: R. Grafton, 1546.

Vicari, E. Patricia. *The View from Minerva's Tower: Learning and Imagination in "The Anatomy of Melancholy."* Toronto: University of Toronto Press, 1989.

Vickers, Brian. *In Defence of Rhetoric.* Oxford: Clarendon, 1989.

Vidal, Fernando. *The Sciences of the Soul: The Early Modern Origins of Psychology.* Translated by Saskia Brown. Chicago: University of Chicago Press, 2011.

Walker, Jeffrey. *Rhetoric and Poetics in Antiquity*. Oxford: Oxford University Press, 2000.

Walker, Obadiah. *Of Education, especially of young gentlemen*. Oxford: Printed at the Theater for Amos Curteyne, 1673.

Waquet, Françoise. *Latin or the Empire of a Sign: From the Sixteenth to the Twentieth Centuries*. London: Verso, 2001.

Wawrzyniak, Natalia. "Pity as a Political Emotion in Early Modern Europe." In *Affective and Emotional Economies in Medieval and Early Modern Europe*, edited by Andreea Marculescu and Charles-Louis Morand Métivier, 51–57. Cham, Switzerland: Springer, 2016.

Wear, Andrew. *Knowledge and Practice in English Medicine, 1550–1680*. Cambridge: Cambridge University Press, 2000.

Whaley, Leigh. *Women and the Practice of Medical Care in Early Modern Europe, 1400–1800*. London: Palgrave Macmillan, 2011.

Williams, Deanne. "Medievalism in English Renaissance Literature." In *A Companion to Tudor Literature*, edited by Ken Cartwright, 211–27. London: Blackwell, 2010.

Williams, Julia, and Frankie Condon. "Translingualism in Composition Studies and Second Language Writing: An Uneasy Alliance." *TESL Canada Journal* 33, no. 2 (2016): 1–18, Academic OneFile.

Williams, R. Grant. "Disfiguring the Body of Knowledge: Anatomical Discourse and Robert Burton's *The Anatomy of Melancholy*." *English Literary History* 68, no. 3 (2001): 593–613.

Wilson, Thomas. *The Arte of Rhetorique*. London: George Robinson, 1585. ProQuest.

Wood, Anthony. *Athenae Oxonienses* [. . .] 2 vols. London: Printed for Tho. Bennet, 1691–92.

Wright, Iain. "Gwinne, Matthew (1558–1627)." *Oxford Dictionary of National Biography*. Oxford: Oxford University Press, 2004. Available online at http://www.oxforddnb .com/view/10.1093/ref:odnb/9780198614128.001.0001/odnb-9780198614128-e-11813.

Yates, Frances. *Astrea: The Imperial Theme in the Sixteenth Century: Frances Yates, Selected Works*, vol. 5. London: Routledge, 1999.

———. *John Florio: The Life of an Italian in Shakespeare's England*. Cambridge: Cambridge University Press, 2011.

Yoran, Hanan. *Between Utopia and Dystopia: Erasmus, Thomas More, and the Humanist Republic of Letters*. Lanham: Lexington, 2010.

Young, Karl. "William Gager's Defence of the Academic Stage." *Transactions of the Wisconsin Academy of Sciences, Arts, and Letters* 18, no. 2 (1916): 593–638.

Index

References to illustrations are in italics.